MEGA-PROJECTS
AS A REFLECTION OF CHANGE IN ISRAELI SOCIETY

The Huleh Drainage & Road #6

ANDA ROSENBERG and IZHAK SCHNELL

©2014

MEGA-PROJECTS
AS A REFLECTION OF CHANGE IN ISRAELI SOCIETY
■I■ The Huleh Drainage & Road #6 ■I■

by Anda Rosenberg and Izhak Schnell

Published by **ISRAEL ACADEMIC PRESS**

(A subsidiary of MultiEducator, Inc.)

553 North Avenue • New Rochelle, NY 10801

Email: nhkobrin@Israelacademicpress.com

ISBN # 978-1-885881-29-8

Table of Contents

Preface

This book examines mega-engineering projects, and explains the connection between the project and the society that initiates them. It shows how changes in society impact the type and nature of mega projects.

The term "mega-engineering projects" refers to large scale projects that use advanced technologies for their times, make significant changes in the appearance of their surroundings, affect broad regions as well as large parts of the population and cause vast impacts on the environment.

Mega-engineering projects were built from ancient times, long before the term "technology" existed and was in use, e.g. the pyramids, the Roman aqueducts and other major physical accomplishments.

There is a strong link between the culture of a certain community at a given time and the mega-project it initiates. Large-scale national projects represent the institutions that created them – their power and their worldviews.

The research that underlies this book was performed on the assumption that there exists a strong link between mega-projects and the culture of the community. The society influences the project and the project impacts the society. Each culture creates a certain kind of large-scale and impressive projects that fit the worldviews, the norms and practices of that culture. The structures of that community mirror its values and norms. In many cases, they become symbols of the power and control of the elite that has built them. In turn, mega-projects, once created, have a great impact on the cultural landscape of the community. They influence and even change that culture.

As symbols of their times and the society that created them, mega-projects will evolve reflecting the ideological and socio-cultural changes their society underwent.

The wide impact of mega-projects on their environment and on the cultural landscape of their surroundings informs us about the community's culture. By studying the landscapes that a civilization builds, we can understand the values the institutions that built the projects that created the landscapes wished to convey.

Cultural landscapes created by mega projects represent ideologies, worldviews and socio-political attitudes of the community and its institutions. They represent values, aspirations and beliefs of their community. Furthermore, decision-making process that surrounds their creation and resulting responses by those who are affected by them bring to light basic social and cultural norms that are otherwise taken for granted and are therefore unrecognized.

Mega-projects can be considered monuments that enforce and represent the power of the community's elites.

Many times the economic benefit of a mega-project does not justify the material cost or effort it required in order to create it. It is built despite this fact since the main reason to undertake the project is the message it conveys and its symbolic importance. Its practical contribution to a civilization is often secondary at most.

Mega-engineering projects contribute to the comfort and quality of life of the community. At the same time, they often have a negative influence on the environment and damage people living in the surroundings.

In most cases, large parts of the population will enjoy the benefits of a large scale, national project, but another small group will suffer the consequences, thus creating a circumstance of social injustice.

This book focuses on the connection between mega engineering projects and the culture and social structure of a community, namely the Israeli society, at two different periods of time: the 1950s and the 2000s. The goal of this work was to find out what we can learn about a society by what mega-projects it initiates and how it goes about implementing them. In addition, this book compares the two periods, and thus highlights the magnitude of socio-cultural changes in the Israeli society as these changes are reflected in a mega-project typical of each period.

For that purpose, two large scale, national projects were investigated: the Huleh drainage and the Trans-Israel Highway. The first one is a representative mega-project of Israel of the 1950s – the first years of the new Israeli State; the second one, of the 2000s, represents the well-established and modern State of Israel.

The research focused on certain domains of everyday life, such as: national ideology, attitude toward nature and environment, social justice, the public discourse and the process of decision-making.

The study of the two mega-projects shows how deep is the connection and the mutual influence between each project and the cultural landscape, the social structure and the essence of the Israeli society, at each period of time.

Introduction

In the 20th century, a prevailing perception was that progress and technology can spur economic growth through the implementation of mega-engineering projects aimed at improving the human condition as well as the environment.

In his book "Future Shock," Alvin Toffler discussed the same phenomenon dubbing it 'future shock' and relating it to the vertiginous pace of technological changes. Following a Marxist approach, his contention was that these changes also influence the social and political shape of the society. Similarly, Heidegger referred to the issue and wrote that technological progress encompasses not only mechanical improvement of practical means, but also the profound impact of changing norms and every-day practices of the community.[1]

Large national engineering projects usually impact on a very significant proportion of the population, if not all of it. Such projects include bridges, dams, seaports and airports. The impacts of these projects are direct and external. They are meant to improve life for the population in general, but some population groups usually enjoy the benefits of a specific project more than others do and there are some who suffer negative consequences. For instance, the building of a large dam in order to produce clean and relatively cheap electrical energy will benefit all but the people dislocated from their homes in order to make room for the lake at the foot of the dam. Those dislocated individuals will be the only ones to suffer the damages and pay the high price for the project's benefits.

That scenario is common to almost all mega-projects, and for that reason it gives rise to questions regarding the social justice/injustice inherent in such projects; questions regarding environmental impacts, and in what way we analyze and weigh those impacts; the process of decision-making, and to what extent the public at large is involved in that process; and, generally speaking, the public reaction to mega-engineering projects.

Public reactions to these projects differ in different communities, depending on their social structure: in a mobilized society, the hegemonic elite makes decisions for the whole population, and the public accepts them almost without any remarks; while in a liberal society, many sectors of the community participate in the public debate, and try to influence the decisions in their interest and according to their point of view.

In order to understand and facilitate the answer to the above questions, we will address below the concept of mega-engineering projects, their place in Israeli society and the impact of each one on the other.

Mega-Engineering National Projects

Mega-projects use complex technologies to create impressive constructions that significantly change the human landscape around them. Meaningful change usually results, impacting both the population and geographic areas. Thus, they have a substantial effect on almost all aspects of life: economy, politics, environment, society and culture, etc.

The engineering projects referred to in this book are named mega-projects because most often they imply a large-scale construction, requiring vast financial investments and a significant number of workers. Such projects generally involve the work of various specialists, such as engineers, architects, workers, administrators, as well as politicians and "dreamers" or idealists.

In studying and discussing mega-engineering projects and their influence on their surroundings, we are of the opinion that human society and the general environment are inextricably linked and cannot be regarded and treated separately. They have a mutual influence on each other and, in fact, they form one interacting entity.[2]

Mega-engineering projects can be looked upon as significant artifacts that have a considerable imprint in their surroundings and landscapes. Hence, cultural landscapes are the result, at least partially, of mega-engineering projects, and they represent messages about status, norms, values and practices, messages that the creators of those landscapes strive to transmit and spread. Each message system has its own language, understood by the initiators of the mega-projects and by the members of the community. That system is specific to each community and to a specific period of time. In any cultural surrounding and at a certain time, there are predictable types of messages; they can appeal to power, esthetics, patriotism, etc. In accordance, mega-engineering projects may be viewed as monuments that institutionalize the power of the political elites.

In a given society and in a specific discourse, a certain kind of message will repeat itself through different landscapes. But societies change, develop and undergo transformations. With the development of a community, new forms of thought are born, new conceptions and ideals become popular and different communities have different ways of seeing life. These changes require new forms of cultural landscape and, as a result, different types of mega-projects will be created by different communities or in different periods of time.[3]

National, mega-engineering projects require vast financial investments and considerable political efforts; they are, in fact, among the most significant products of the powers that created them. They usually have a practical, functional role, but beyond that, large-scale national projects communicate to the public strong definite messages that justify the existence and the importance of the institutions that initiated them. Their messages become the symbol of the powers that created them and of the ideologies those powers propagate. In the words of Alan Baker:

> Ideologies exert their authority not only in language but also
> in landscape. Non-verbal "documents" in the landscape can
> be powerful visual symbols, conveying messages forcefully

> Ideologies create, unintentionally as well as deliberately, a landscape as a symbol of signification, expressive of authority.[4]

It seems that mega-engineering projects' symbolic value as representing national power in some cases accedes their functional values.[5]

> Mega-engineering projects cause significant landscape changes and landscape transformation is an explicit representation of economic, military, ecological and social power and power is always used to justify more power.[6]

Mega-Engineering Projects in Israel

The State of Israel was founded in 1948 and from that point on many large-scale projects were planned and executed by the State through its various ministries or by other national institutions. These projects include the National Water Carrier, the Huleh drainage, the foundation of new development towns: i.e., Dimona, Yeruham, Ofakim, Netivot and in more recent times, Shoham and Modi'in, the Israel Railway, the Port of Ashdod, the Trans-Israel Highway and many others. The development and execution of mega-engineering projects in Israel occurred in stages, paralleling the development of the country and the changes in the Israeli society.

The initial stage, during the first decade of statehood, was characterized by little planning and relied mostly on vision and national ethos. That ethos was based on the Zionist ideology and belief that science and technology will solve practical problems, help build the country and replace the lack of natural resources. The national projects executed in this period were driven by the sense of urgency typical of the Zionist movement in those years, a sense that it is imperative to do the work of creating a nation and building a modern state immediately, without delay. Examples of mega-projects executed during this stage are the Huleh drainage and the first wave of new development towns.

The Huleh project included the drainage of the lake and the swamp in the Huleh Valley. The project's major goals were the creation of arable land and the prevention of malaria. (Various aspects of the project will be discussed in greater detail later in this book.)

The second stage of large-scale project design and execution occurred during the 1960s and differed from stage 1 in that it was based on much more accurate planning centralized in the hands of the government, was inspired by Prime Minister – David Ben-Gurion – and was carried out by a group of professional planners including renowned architect Arieh Sharon and others. The motivation during this stage of mega-projects was of building a modern social democratic state that by central planning national scale projects will bring prosperity to all. The ideology behind all the national projects executed during that period was collectivist, social-democrat and centralist. It was based on the belief that to achieve the goals of the Zionist movement, central planning and equal distribution of resources and opportunities were fundamental and essential elements. Projects executed in that stage included the National Water Carrier and the second wave of new development town construction.

The third stage, from the end of the 1960s and into the 1970s, was characterized by a change in attitude based on somewhat differing ideologies and motivations. The economic issue also became more prominent. This was a factor to be taken into account when initiating a mega-project, but national goals were still viewed as important and motivating. The third wave of new towns, such as Carmiel and Arad, were products of the third stage.

The last stage, continuing to the present day, is based mainly on economic considerations, privatization and the benefiting of sectors close to wealth and political power. The Trans-Israel Highway is a mega-project of this stage. It represents the process of privatization at its strongest, the highway being the largest transport infrastructure ever built by Israel and including a toll road, built and operated by a private consortium. Even for modern times and in a country as developed as Israel in the first decade of the new millennium, this effort represented an enormous national engineering project. The Trans-Israel Highway will be detailed and analyzed below.

Among the most prominent mega-projects of the new state was **the National Water Carrier**. It best represents the centrally planned project of a social democratic government. Water shortage was, and still is, a severe problem in Israel. There is not much water in the region and existing sources lie partly in Syria and Jordan. The extensive agricultural lands in the southern part of the country were served by insufficient reservoirs. Though the main water reserves were in the north, the tracts of agricultural land there were smaller. The solution adopted for that problem was to transport water from the north to the south. The plan called for conveying water from the northern watershed to the springs of the Yarkon River and from there southward, to the area of Kibbutz Magen in the northwest Negev. This part of the project was called the Yarkon-Negev Line.

The National Water Carrier crossed Israel from north to south and formed the main artery connecting all regional water projects in the State. In this way, it became possible to completely control all the water in the country and to convey it efficiently wherever it was most needed and for an equal price, regardless of location.

Early plans for that substantial, large-scale project were made before the establishment of the State, but detailed planning started only after the founding of the State in 1948. The execution commenced in 1953 and was concluded in 1964. The carrier is 130 kilometers in length and consists of a system of giant pipes, open canals, tunnels, reservoirs and large-scale pumping stations. Up to 72,000 cubic meters (19 million U.S. gallons) can flow through the carrier each hour, totaling 1.7 million cubic meters per day. Building the carrier presented a considerable technical challenge as it traversed a wide variety of terrains and elevations.[7]

The railway system infrastructure in Israel has its source in the Ottoman period. The Jaffa-Jerusalem railway began operating in 1892. The Hejaz line, with an extension to Haifa, called the Jezreel Valley railway, was built and inaugurated in 1905. Major railway development was undertaken during World War I, when the eastern and southern railways were constructed by the Ottomans. During the war, the British Empire, while advancing on the Ottomans, built and repaired numerous railways.

Starting in 1917-18, the British updated and modernized most of the existing railway lines extended, and connected them to those of adjacent countries and built new lines in Jaffa and Jerusalem. After World War I ended, the British nationalized all railways in Mandated Palestine, and created the Palestine Railways Company.

With Israel's independence in 1948, Israel Railways was created as a successor to the British company.

In the first years of the state, rail passenger traffic grew rapidly until the early-to-mid-1960s, at which point traffic began to fall off due to improvements in the road infrastructure, increase in the automobile ownership rate and lack of investment in the rail network. That trend reversed somewhat in the 1990s when a wave of railway infrastructure development began, leading to a resurgence of the railways' importance within the country's transportation network. In the first decade of the 2000s, the Israeli railway network traversed approximately 1,000 kilometers to 1,250 kilometers.

During this period, the Israeli government embarked on a major push to upgrade the existing rail network as well as construct a number of entirely new lines. Thus, a major government long-term plan came to life, including connection of almost all cities in Israel to the rail network.[8]

The Port of Ashdod is one of Israel's two main cargo ports, the other one being the Port of Haifa, initially built by the British during their mandate in Palestine.

The Port of Ashdod is located in Ashdod, about 40 kilometers south of Tel-Aviv, adjoining the mouth of the Lachish River. Its establishment significantly enhanced the country's port capacity. The port is a major point of entry and exit for both cargo and tourists.

The need to open another deep water port arose in Israel's early years, when it became clear that the expansion of the existing ports of Haifa and Eilat could not ensure efficient handling of the increasing volume of import and export cargoes. The Port of Ashdod remains one of the few deep water ports in the world to be built in the open sea, and its construction involved great engineering challenges. The decision on the location and the construction of the port was preceded by a maritime and climatic survey which confirmed the engineering feasibility of its construction.

For a number of reasons, the location of Ashdod was chosen, although there was no natural gulf there: it meshed with the state's concept of population dispersal and the establishment of urban centers in the southern part of the country; it shortened substantially the overland transport of cargoes to and from the southern and central part of the country; the source of main exports such as oranges from the Rehovoth citrus groves and potash from Sodom were much closer to Ashdod than to Haifa; it was close to existing transport arteries; and it was close to the industrial and production centers of the country, as well as to Tel-Aviv, the commercial center.

The physical design of the port began in 1957-1958 and the cornerstone was laid on July 1961. The construction was based on a long-term development plan. Breakwaters were built to create a harbor where quays could be built and developed in stages. The port began operations on November 1965 and in 1966 the construction of the two breakwaters – the southern one of 2,200 meters length and the northern one of 900 meters length - was finally completed. In the following years, the development of the port continued with the construction of more quays and in 1998, the cornerstone was laid for the Jubilee Port – a significant expansion of the original Port of Ashdod.[9]

The foundation of New Towns – Since its establishment as a state, Israel has been one of the most prolific countries in building new towns. That fact had its roots, not only in the need to settle the newcomers as quickly as possible, but also in the conception that it was the right way to build a nation and consolidate a community. The prevailing worldview was that settling population in new towns spread over large areas was the right and best way to assert sovereignty over that area and "Jewify" it. The term used was "creating facts on the ground".

That process was not usually an economic or social justifiable step, but the other considerations mentioned above were by far more important. After Israel was declared an independent state, large waves of immigrants started to arrive at a rapid rate. One of the most acute and immediate problems was the dispersion of the population over the largest area possible.

In 1948, the population of Israel was 870,000. Most of the Jewish population segment – 75% – lived in the main cities, Tel-Aviv, Haifa and the central plain, which formed only a total of 11% of the country's area. By 1952, the population had doubled and by 1972, more than three million people lived in Israel. The viewpoint of the government was that it was necessary to fight the natural tendency of the Jewish population to crowd into the country's center and thus, a policy of dispersal was to be implemented. That view was embraced by the country's planners and applied in their work.

Soon after the Declaration of Independence was proclaimed, architect Arieh Sharon was named Head of the Planning Department. His first task was to prepare an Overall Master Plan for Israel, which he accomplished in approximately one year. That Master Plan became the main tool for the leadership of the country in their work of shaping a new cultural landscape for the young nation in the making.

The idea of the New Town was a basic element of the Sharon Plan – as the Overall Master Plan was called – and starting from 1950 it became policy.

One of the long-term goals of the Plan was to deal with the issue of the dispersal of about 2,650,000 expected inhabitants. Based on the guidelines of the Sharon Plan, 400 agricultural settlements were established in the first decade of the State's existence, but the gist of the Plan was the foundation of the 'New Towns'. During the 1950s and 1960s, more than 30 New Towns, initiated by the State, were built in Israel. The following reflected three prevailing Zionist tenets:

First, the dispersal of population – the whole country or at least most of it, was considered a frontier zone and in order to keep it under control, one of the means was the spread of the civil population over an area as large as possible.

Second, the tendency to disregard the existence of the local, native population and the wish to "Jewify" the whole territory of Israel as much as possible - the foundation of new towns largely ignored the existing Arab settlements.

The third Zionist tenet was the concept according to which building of a new nation had to be based on agricultural settlements and agglomeration of population in big cities was to be avoided. The new towns were seen as preventing that process.

The New Towns idea reflected the Zionist ideology of central government, including planning. The Zionist movement considered that the planning of the country had to be done according to the guidelines of the ruling political party.

The ideology of centralism was spread by every system and by every means: education, media, cultural landscapes, etc.

One of the most prominent expressions of centralized government was the effort to base the building of the country on rural, not urban, settlements and agricultural occupations and to develop the periphery more than the center.

The Zionist ideology of solidifying a new nation by creating a strong bond between the "New Jew" and the land – his territory – and by working the land with Jewish hands rejected the idea of large, modern cities that were considered an "anti-Zionist" phenomenon.

After the state establishment and the great waves of immigrants arriving at a rapid pace, new needs and problems required new solutions.

The main purposes of the New Towns concept were: the dispersal of population according to State guidelines, Jewification of as large a part of the country as possible, control over urban congestion, and regulation of intense agricultural development in the coastal plain.

Also, physical planners of Israel used the concept of New Towns in order to shape the new urban landscape of the country in such a way so that it could sustain a technologically modern and progressive social-democratic state.

The construction of new towns continued through the years to the present-day, although in recent years the pace became much slower. All governments, regardless of their political affiliation, embraced that project, although architectural styles changed with political tendencies and interests, with general fashion and other influences.[10]

The mega-projects of **the Huleh Drainage** and **the Trans-Israel Highway** will be discussed further on in greater detail.

Changes in the Israeli Society

Human societies undergo changes with time, due to natural, internal evolution and also, under the influence of external events and trends.

The Israeli society took the path similar to that of all other societies and even more so – it changed at such a rate that there is almost no resemblance between it now and the society of the first two decades of Israel's existence.

In the first decades after Israel's foundation, the society structure was characterized by a collective identity, considered in those days "an ideological sanctity". The Israeli collective identity was based first and foremost on the Zionist ideology. The consolidation of the Israeli collectivist identity was influenced by the Zionist ideology and by the movement's attachment to Eretz Israel as the Biblical territory of the Jewish people.[11]

Hence, in order to understand the development of Israeli society and its contemporary structure, we have to analyze and explore its beginnings – the basic properties of the Zionist ideology and of the Zionist settlement processes in Eretz Israel.

The Zionist movement developed in the 1890s in Eastern Europe. Its ideology was similar to other national movements that developed in Europe and even Asia at the same period of time, such as the romantic perceptions of nation, territory and past that developed in most of the 19th century European nations. Furthermore, other events had great influence on the development and the shape the Zionist ideology took, such as the social, economic and cultural crisis of the Eastern Europe Jewish community – crisis closely connected to the changing processes of the surrounding society.[12]

But there were significant differences between Zionism and other national movements: the Zionist movement aspired to a Jewish home for the Jewish people in Eretz Israel and not wherever Jewish people lived; it praised the revival of the Hebrew language although that was not the language in use in the existing Jewish communities; it differed in its national historical perception – opposite to other national movements, which tried to prove the continuity of the past and the present of their territory, the Zionist movement emphasized the historical break between the Diaspora and Eretz Israel. All those factors made the Zionist movement, beyond a national one, also a revolutionary movement whose essence was to rebel against the existing status and build a new society and a different culture and not only to consolidate the existing status in a new frame of nation-state.[13]

The Zionist movement developed a national ideology in modern terms of national aspirations and targets and built the infrastructure for the creation of a Jewish nation in the modern sense of the concept "nation". Around that infrastructure, processes of organization, institutionalization and conceptual development were set in motion. The Zionist ideology, beyond creating the collectivist identity of the Jewish-Israeli society, outlined the society structure, determined its extent of affiliation to the movement, its territory boundaries and the nature of the regime and culture of that society.[14]

Zionist ideology had a decisive impact on other social motifs; it created social values and norms, group insights, hierarchies, social relations and symbols.[15]

The establishment of the State of Israel was the Zionist dream come true. Israel, leaning on the political parliamentary-constitutional tradition of the Zionist movement, became a democratic, constitutional, parliamentary state. Politically, after the state establishment, the decades of the 1950s and 1960s were characterized by the hegemony of the "left" – the Labor Party that ruled the country and which had a significant impact on the economic system of the young nation.

The economic system that developed in those first two decades included three main elements: the sector of the Labor movement concentrated around the Histadrut (General Federation of Labor), the civil sector and the government sector. It was a political economy, not only influenced, but in fact – dictated by politics, by the political party in power.

The economy was characterized by an ideology of collectivism and equity, while stressing work for the good of the community, the collective. The expressions of those ideology guidelines were the facts that national and social considerations were decisive in economic decisions; a significant place in the Israeli economy was occupied by organizations belonging to the collectivist system; the ideology of those organizations being based on large public commitment and, at least in part, on equity.

The economic system was an open system, characterized by three central collectivistic factors: the economic development was ideologically considered as part of the national tasks and only slightly as pure economic interests; the state and its collectivist organizations, such as the Histadrut and the Jewish Agency, had a central and decisive role in directing the economy; part of the sectors, especially the government sector and the Labor party sector, emphasized the collectivist aspect of the economy, the symbols being the kibbutzim, moshavim and the Histadrut organizations, such as Sollel Boneh, Kur, Shikun Ovdim, etc.

In this period of time the government sector underwent considerable development and included many large and strong government enterprises, civil services systems, local authorities systems, etc.[16] The decisions regarding national enterprises such as national projects were based on national goals; immediate economic profitability was a very weak consideration, most considerations were strongly connected to the elite view of long run national interests as well as internal political consideration of maintaining the dominance of the Labor parties.[17]

In the middle of the 1970s, more precisely in the year 1977, a political changeover occurred and the Labor party was replaced with the party of the "right" as the ruler of the country. The parties of the right led by the Likud were both believers in the free market economically, as well as believers that all of the Biblical Land of Israel needed to remain part of the State of Israel. They opposed the concept of territorial compromise. The question of whether or not to agree at least in principle to territorial compromise in the West Bank became one of the main subjects of Israeli discourse and the single largest issue repeated in Israeli politics, while the difference in economic approach were largely glossed over.

After that surprising political shift, a new identity had to be created based on different components. Being stimulated by the occupation of the Biblical territories or the Palestinian ones, the territorial aspect of the Zionist movement and nationalist ideas moved to the core of the political discourse in addition to the adoption of a neo-liberal economic worldview.[18] All those formed the central core of the new Israeli identity definition and became the main subject of the public discourse.[19]

At this stage, deep changes connected to the transition of political power and the loss of the Labor party hegemony lead to radical changes in the economic and social systems of the country. These showed that the agenda of Labor had run its course and in its place other economic and social patterns found their way in the Israeli society.

The above mentioned changes in the Israeli society occurred as a result of internal events, such as the wars of 1967 and 1973 and the political changes, but it is not possible to separate them from external, global happenings that influenced the world economy as well as Israel's. Examples of those events include the global oil crisis, the "détente" between the big world powers, the fall of the communism, etc.

The collectivist ideology and the state centralist economy underwent significant changes after the political change over of the seventies. In fact, changes toward a free market, decentralization and social differentiation started beforehand, in the years after the 1967 Six-Day War, but at the beginning of the 1990s they gained momentum considerably.

The collectivistic and egalitarian aspects started to fade away. A new ethos developed - an ethos of free markets and "pure" capitalism, which advocated a radical market ideology of almost unrestrained competition and privatization. Those economic tendencies were embraced by political parties of both sides — right and left. That policy was tilted toward the business sector, supporting wealth against labor. An expression of the new capitalist ideology of the Israeli market was the change in the orientation of the old central, collectivistic organizations, such as the Histadrut institutions – Kur, Sollel Boneh, etc., which became capitalist corporations similar to any private one. A similar phenomenon occurred in the Kibbutzim and Moshavim. Many underwent privatization processes that completely abolished the collectivist ethos that had been typical of the 1950s and 1960s.

All those economic changes brought with them significant modifications in the Israeli social order. One of the most important results of the economic changes was the development of a growing gap between the different social classes. First, some sectors, such as hi-tech employees, became more in demand and more moneyed than the others. Then, exposure to globalization brought on unemployment which, in turn, increased the economic and social gap between more fortunate and less so.

That situation brought Israel to the beginning of the 21st century as one of the most developed countries technologically, but also one of the countries with the biggest gap between rich and poor. The gap is also significant between the country's center and its periphery.

So, the Israeli society of the 2000s is completely different from the one of the 1950s, the early years of the state establishment. The ideologies of the state's first two decades tried to consolidate frameworks independent and unique to Israel. The deep changes in the economic ideology and system that occurred afterwards, transformed completely the social order also. The new economic system took after foreign ideologies, embraced by the outside world.[20]

The collectivist identity, typical to the Israeli society in the 1950s and 1960s faded and was replaced by personal, individual interests and benefits. Sectorial issues, that existed also beforehand, but were overpowered by national and collective interests, rose and became problems to deal with and try to solve, for instance religious and ethnic issues. Also, the issue of human rights became important and central in the public discourse and it brought up the development of the civil society and the possibility of critical activism – civil society organizations watching over, criticizing and demanding changes in government decisions regarding the public at large.[21]

At the end of the 1980s and the beginning of the 1990s, Israel started to blend into the universal globalization. The main factor which made it possible was its transfer to the post-industrial era and specifically – the rapid and intensive development of the hi-tech industry.[22]

Globalization is often generally defined as networks of interactions over part or all continents.[23] As such, the term refers to a number of deep changes and ramifications in the political world: growing universal political bonds, diminution of local space and time as the basis of economic life and resemblance of cultural life over the globe. Globalization embraces a vast meaning, including a wide variety of connections between countries that go beyond economic relations.[24]

Thomas L. Friedman defines globalization as *"the inexorable integration of markets, nation-states and technologies to a degree never witnessed before – in a way enabling individuals, corporations and nation-states to reach around the world farther, faster, deeper and cheaper than ever before..."*[25] This definition has a political aspect as well. Influenced by the reduction in costs of communication and transport, nevertheless globalization is based on the decision of national governments to participate in a universal economy and in an "open market" global system.

Generally speaking, globalization is minimization of the significance of location, place or territory in people's life. It means a spread of universal relations among people, beyond boundaries of countries, distances, time zones, etc. It changed the meaning and importance of social space.

Before the spread of globalization, territorial locations defined the term of "place" for people; in the globalization era, relations of all kinds – economic, cultural, etc. – among people exceed territorial boundaries; in fact, they exist in a "transworld" space.[26]

In order to understand and absorb the impact of globalization, we have to accept the claim that *"globalization is as much an ideational set of claims as it is a material set of practices,…globalization cannot be comprehended adequately without considering the ideational dimension of social life."*[27]

The process of globalization for Israel had positive and negative impacts for the economy, the society and the space of the country.

Socially, the transition to globalization caused the end of the collectivist narrative with its national, bonding, recruiting, austere and unifying identity and its substitution by a narrative of an individual, instant achievement and consumer oriented and hedonistic identity.[28] The hegemony of the political "leftist" elite passed, step-by-step, into the hands of the wealthy, the oligarchs who, hand-in-hand with the politicians, ran the country.

Globalization brought with it also a deepening of the gap between social classes, an increase of the inequality in the Israeli society. One of the factors to cause that phenomenon was the withdrawal of the public sector from the economic life of the country.[29]

The Israeli economy changed drastically in character because of the globalization of the country and the influence of economic universal processes.

After the establishment of the state, the Zionist movement developed a unique kind of socialism, in which concepts of collectivism and redemption of the land and labor – specifically Jewish labor – formed the basis and the foundation of the country's ideology.

During the 1980s and 1990s, under the influence of external factors and internal events, political and economic, that ideology started to change in the direction of a freer, more open market and embracing concepts of a neo-liberal society.[30]

New laws were legislated to strengthen the neo-liberal tendency by emphasizing the rights to private property. The new laws were based on neo-liberal concepts and principles that strengthened the separation of the private sector from government interference and regulation.

Gradually, Israel underwent a fundamental change, which, step-by-step, transformed it from a collectivist state with a mobilized Jewish society and centralized economy into a neo-liberal society with an economy based on a free market order.[31]

The transition from collectivism to liberalism meant a transition from public centralism to private centralism. Those changes were largely influenced by the universal globalization processes.

In economic terms, globalization, according to Uri Ram, is a set of forces which seek *"a well integrated, though internally diversified and unequal, planetary system"*. In the era of globalization, in neo-liberal regimes, the state releases the power and the hold it had on markets; its only economic activity remaining the opening of the country's markets to the world at large. In that situation, markets are shaped and conducted by international factors, forces and processes. That condition meant the retreat of the state as an active and influential factor in the economic life of the country. Therefore, the Israeli state has gradually reduced its weight and role by intensifying privatization and conceding regulation of the markets.[32]

Hence, during that period, the Israeli economy took a direction of emphasizing the private sector to the detriment of the State's and the Histadrut's economic power and influence. Like other countries of the Western world, Israel's economic tendency was to shun away from a Keynesian model toward a free-market one. The most visible sign of that tendency in Israel was the withdrawal of the State from the public services sector and the return to "recommodification" of services that were once "decommodified".[33]

Due to globalization, Israel's physical space also underwent significant change. Tel-Aviv and its closest peripheries became "world city" and functioned as post-industrial Israel's main anchor in the global economy. The "closest peripheries" sprawled further and further and the central part of the country – Gush Dan – became the core of the Israeli economic life. Tel-Aviv and the closest surroundings continued to strengthen economically, which contributed to the rise in prices, particularly those related to real estate. Whoever could not afford the high costs, moved further from the core and so, the sprawling of peripheries intensified.[34] In this context we ask how were mega engineering projects being decided upon, publicly debated and constructed under the social democratic hegemonic political economy of the 1950s and how were they being decided upon, debated and constructed under the neo-liberal political economy of the 2000s. In addition, we ask how their social and environmental externalities were considered.

The Structure of the Book

The major question discussed in this book is whether there is a link between large-scale, national technical projects and the social structure and culture of the community that gave birth to them.

We seek to find out if that link exists, if it is symbolic of the social system of the time, whether it is mutual, in what way and at what extent it manifests itself.

In this book we analyze two mega-projects referring to two periods of time in the Israeli society's history: the 1950s – the first decade of the State's existence, and the 2000s – current days. We chose one large project, symbolic of its time: the Huleh Drainage in the 1950s, and the Trans-Israel Highway in the first decade of the third millennium. The projects are detailed in Chapters 1 and 2. Both projects were large-scale, especially for a country as small as Israel. The execution in both cases required enormous financial resources and involved a complex technical operation. They were both very much typical of their times in the Israeli society of the respective periods. The Huleh drainage was the flagship project of the young State of Israel in the 1950s, a large-scale, intricate project of first-class national importance; the Trans-Israel Highway was the largest transport infrastructure project executed by Israel – even in the 2000s, when Israel was already a well-developed and a not-so-young country anymore. The Trans-Israel was considered a special national enterprise. The Highway was a large-scale project, from the core of Tel-Aviv to the northern and southern peripheries, involving high costs and with a significant impact on all aspects of life. For each project of its time, we ask if there was a mutual influence between the mega-projects executed in the given period and the characteristics of the Israeli society at that time. We concentrate our analysis on specific domains of society's life in Israel and the link between those domains and the mega-projects executed in the two chosen periods of time.

The specific domains studied here, and having a chapter dedicated to each one, are: national ideology (Chapter 3), the process of decision-making (Chapter 4), the public discourse (Chapter 5), nature conservation and environmental protection (Chapter 6) and social justice/injustice (Chapter 7).

We seek to verify if there was a mutual influence between each domain and the mega-project executed in each period of time and if it was – in what way and to what extent.

Of note is that previous works on the subject of mega-projects dealt almost solely with the environmental aspect and their impact on the environment and earth's surface; the present work, while not disregarding the environmental issue, emphasizes other aspects of society's life and that emphasis defines the specific questions raised in the present study. We raise the question how did the cultural landscapes change due to large-scale national projects and if changes in the Israeli society can be read and understood by analyzing the mega-engineering projects of the time?

In general, we looked for the relationship between the social structure in Israel, in each one of the two periods of time studied here and its relation to the mega-project executed in the respective period of time. We sought to provide some insight into the possibility of researching and analyzing a major national engineering project executed in a given period and try to learn from that about the social structure, the practices and, if possible, additional aspects of that society during the specified period of time.

We based our research on letters, newspapers articles, protocols, reports, archive films and other original documents, from archives and libraries, as well as previous studies by other researchers, regarding the two chosen projects. In addition, we used a few personal interviews with people involved in the projects.

The Huleh Drainage

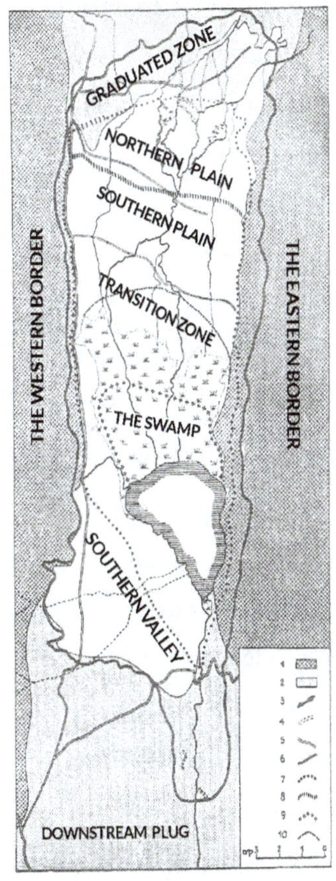

FIGURE 1
The Huleh Valley Map
before the Drainage
Source: Livne M., "The Huleh
Drainage – Advantages and
Disadvantages",
Ecology and Environment, 4, Vol.1,
August 1994.

Historical Background

The Huleh Valley extends from the Hermon slopes at the north to the settlements of Korazim and Rosh Pina to the south. The valley is approximately 30 kilometer long and 6-7 kilometer wide (Figure 1). In the center and the south of the area, a large swampy lake was formed in the Pleistocene era, by lava that flowed from the Golan volcanoes and blocked the stream of the Jordan River. The Jordan passed through this obstacle, creating a steep canyon. Originally, the river flowed in a narrow streambed, between the north extremity of the canyon and the south end of the lake. That streambed was sufficient to carry the summer water flow, but was not enough for the quantities of the rainy winter season.

Hence, in winter time the level of the lake waters rose by 1-2 meters and covered about 7-8 square kilometers of area at the north of the lake. Other rivers around the lake also overflowed and inundated the areas around them. The vegetation and the silt formed in the flooded areas captured the water and stopped them from receding to the rivers' beds. Thus, the swamps were created that varied each year insofar as duration and geographical extent.[35]

The Huleh Valley is limited by high rifts – in the east – the Golan Heights and in the west – the Naftali Mountains. At the south, the valley borders with the Korazim Heights, higher than the Huleh, but the Jordan River caught the valley's waters at the south in a narrow channel that dug its way between the Heights of Korazim and the Golan. The valley drained to the south, on a slight slope. The general direction of the Jordan Valley was the descent to the south from the Jordan sources toward the Sea of Galilee (Lake Kinneret) and to the Dead Sea. But around Kfar Hanasi, the surface rose significantly, about 200 meters above the bottom of the valley and caused the Huleh to form a closed crater. The Jordan River was left with a narrow passage and a depth capable of draining most of the crater except the last 2-4 meters in depth. The narrow width of the river caused the drainage of the winter rains to last several months. The relation between the bottom level of the valley and the exit level of the river through the obstruction was defined by the interrelations of four processes: the uplift tendency versus the drop tendency of the river bottom at the crack area, and the uplift tendency versus the drop tendency of the valley bottom.

Until recently, the main factor for the formation of the lake and the swamp was considered to be the basalt plug that blocked the water exit from the valley to the south. The other factor was the size of the channel dug by the Jordan into the basalt plug. The water flow was more than that channel could drain out of the valley, so that the water excess created the lake and the swamp.[36]

Today a different explanation is considered valid. On the short run of tens of thousands of years, significant changes occurred on the bottom level of the valley, more significant than the ones that occurred on the bottom level of the Jordan channel at the crack area. Those processes of continuous sinking of the valley bottom, on one hand, and the continuous filling up of the valley with sediments, on the other hand, are the main reason for the creation of the lake and the swamp in the Huleh.

The base of the valley, as it was found from drillings 100 meters deep and more was the result of opposite and concomitant processes of sinking and filling up, occurring at a rapid rate.

According to the way the sediments sank, there were interchanges between the lake and the swamp. Usually, chalk and shale and peat sank in the swamp. The different layers sank on top of each other, but also side by side so that the borders between the lake and the swamp changed from time to time. The pattern of those processes is obvious in the way the sinking material appears – not in regular, horizontal layers with a constant thickness but in lenses of peat with varying thickness.[37]

The peat is rich in sulfates (2% of its total weight). The peat was formed because the oxidation rate was not rapid enough to consume the organic matter from the swamp. Regarding the plug in the south, the recent theory says that it was formed by tectonic activity that brought an uplift of the soil and the basalt spill contributed very little, if at all, to the plug.

The process of the Jordan channel formation by erosion of the soil was a very slow one and so it contributed much less than considered at first to the formation of the plug.[38]

Before the drainage project commenced, the area permanently covered by water spread over about 1,400 hectares and a papyrus swamp extended over 3,100 hectares.[39] The valley and the lake constituted a rich habitat for many plants and animals. From ancient times people were attracted to the valley for that very reason. Israel is located at the intersection of two continents – Asia and Africa – and is also relatively close to Europe. Yet in contrast to these areas, a much more diversified flora and fauna, from almost all over the world could be found in this region (Figure 2).[40]

FIGURE 2
Fauna and Flora in the Huleh Valley before the Drainage – 1941
Source – Livne M., "The Huleh Drainage – Advantages and Disadvantages", *Ecology and Environment,*
Vol. 1, August 1994.

Findings dating back to ancient settlements were found close to the Benoth Jacob Bridge, near Ma'ayan Baruch and on the shores of the Huleh Lake.[41] The location of the valley close to the "sea road" made it important politically and economically. Two ancient cities laid in the valley in biblical times: Dan in the north and Hatzor in the south.[42]

In the 19th century, the Jewish settlement in Eretz Israel was renewed and with it, settlements were established in the Huleh Valley: Ysud Hama'ala

(1883), Metula further away (1884), Mishmar Hayarden (1890) and Mahanaym (1898). At the beginning of the 20th century more settlements were added in the area: Kfar Gyladi, Tel-Hay and Ayelet Hashahar (1916). The expansion of the settlements in the valley brought on the idea of the necessity to drain the swamp in favor of those settlements.[43]

At the beginning of the 20th century, the Huleh Valley included the lake of about 130 hectares and the seasonal swamp of about 470 hectares, at the north of the lake. The area was covered by papyrus plants. Because of the fluctuation of the groundwater level by 1.5 meters between the summer and winter peaks, the surface area of the swamp varied between 800 and 470 hectares.[44]

During the Ottoman period, most of the Huleh Valley was the private property of the Turkish Sultan (giftlik land). The Sultan treated it solely as a source of revenue and leased the land as a concession to the highest bidder. The concession owners imposed fishing and pasture taxes on the local habitants and, as payment for land leasing, received a large proportion of the swamp's papyrus crop.

After 1908, when the Sultan lost most of his powers, the concession switched hands a number of times. The land was leased to a French company with its main offices in Beirut, for the exploitation of the papyrus crop. In 1910, the land was leased to two rich Syrian merchants who lived in Beirut – Sarsock and Bayhum – in exchange for payment and for the promise to drain the lake and the swamp. The idea of draining the Huleh Valley was an old one, dating from the beginning of the 19th century. The two Syrians did not drain the Huleh and from them the concession was transferred to the agricultural Syrian-Ottoman company in exchange for the same promise - to drain the swamp.

When the Huleh Valley became the property of the British Mandate, the British approved the concession on condition that the agricultural Syrian company immediately begins the drainage works. But this company, too, was unable to honor its commitment and did not implement the drainage project.

At the end of 1934, the concession was purchased by Joshua Hankin for the Palestine Land Development Company (PLDC or Hachsharat Hayeshuv). PLDC promised the British government to allocate, after the drainage, 1,500 hectares of the drained land, to Arab inhabitants of the region.

During the British mandate period, two plans for the drainage project were prepared. In 1936, by British recommendation, a drainage plan was ordered with the British company Rendel – Palmer – Tryton. A second plan was prepared by a Jewish Agency engineer – Dov Koblanov – who had gained experience in swamps drainage works in Kabara. In that era, the swamp represented "a dark, frightening place, swarming with plants and sickness"[45] and the draining of swamps was considered, not only by Zionists but by the whole world, the triumph of mankind over nature and the harnessing of nature to humanity's needs.

The execution of the drainage project was entrusted to JNF and PICA (Palestine Jewish Colonization Association), but a number of factors – the Arab rebellion during the years 1936-1939 (the tartza"v-tartza"t events), the Second World War and the War of Independence – along with the country's economic situation, conspired to delay the execution of the drainage project till Israel's independence.[46]

The Concept of the Drainage

The outcome of the War of Independence evoked a strong feeling of national pride for the Jewish people in Israel and also in the Diaspora. Part of it was due to the perception that, until the beginning of the Zionist Movement activity in Eretz Israel, the land was desolation and nothingness and the pioneers made the emptiness bloom, developed the soil cultivation and drained the swamps. After Israel's independence, projects previously consigned to the realm of dreams during the Mandate, became important national goals that could be implemented.

The Jewish National Fund (JNF) found itself confused and lost when all at once its main reason of being – "purchasing of land for the Jewish people in its country" – ceased to be an issue. As a result, it began to look for other goals, to emphasize secondary tasks and to define new, additional assignments. In this way, at its jubilee, the JNF declared the Huleh drainage its top project. It was considered the most prestigious project of the new young country.[47]

The Huleh drainage was the record achievement of the new country. The project involved planning, financing and execution of a vast and complex engineering project requiring coordination on a national level. An old Zionist dream was becoming a tangible reality and it offered the settlers of the Upper Galilee, old and new, thousands of hectares of arable land. The expectations were that the drained land, in the water rich environment of the valley, would become the granary of Israel and contribute to the economic and social stability of the settlers.[48]

The drainage project was the continuation of the Zionist activity that brought the pioneers to Eretz Israel to make the desert bloom. The project was regarded as revolutionary. In those days, the topic of soil cultivation was regarded much like today's view of hi-tech industries, especially given the background of food shortages that were rampant in the first years of the young country coupled with the intensive demand for income resources for the first and large [successive] waves of newcomers.[49] The Huleh drainage project was treated with great enthusiasm by the public. It became a symbol for the Zionist concept and the Zionist slogan of "conquering the desert".

The young country saw in the Huleh drainage a project of prestige and excellence. That attitude was easily understood, taking into account an important fact: the establishment of the State of Israel brought with it a crisis in the Zionist movement as is the case whenever an ideal finally becomes a reality. The JNF also faced a crisis when its main goal and mission – purchase of lands for the Jewish people in its country – became obsolete; with the establishment of the State more than 90% of the land became the property of the Israeli government and the JNF went looking for a new raison d'être. So, the Huleh drainage project was chosen as the first project to be executed among many development projects necessary to the economy of the new, young state.

Formal Goals

The Huleh drainage project had clear and defined goals that were publicly proclaimed:

◆ **Malaria prevention** – for a long time, considered the main and most important reason. In fact, malaria had been eradicated from the Huleh valley before the drainage began, mostly thanks to the work of Dr. Mar from Rosh Pina, who brought the pesticide DDT to the country. Nevertheless, even after the malaria disease was eradicated, this remained an important issue in the eyes of the public.

◆ **Additional arable land** – though a lesser goal at the beginning, this was revealed later on, as the biggest achievement of the drainage. The use of peat for soil cultivation was not a sure thing. Even the soil of the lake bottom was an uncertainty for agriculture because of its limestone content.

Under the pressure of the mandate government, 150 hectares of the reclaimed land were to be allocated to the local Arab population. Hence, the expectations of additional land for cultivation were not large. The results were surprising: both the lake bottom and the peat soil were suitable for agriculture although their cultivation involved many problems and the profitability was low. Nevertheless, eventually the reclaimed land produced reasonable crops. The Arabs of the Huleh

Valley fled the area during the War of Independence so that the 150 hectares due to them remained part of the land for Jewish settlements.

◆ **Additional water** – according to estimates and in absence of data and measurements regarding evaporation in the valley, some 28 million cubic meters were saved due to a decrease in evaporation (from 68 million cubic meters before the drainage to 40 million after the implementation of the project).

◆ **The peat exploitation** – thoughts and plans had been presented regarding the peat and its utilization for different purposes such as organic fertilizer, raw material in the chemical industry or as fuel. Those plans were never more than an idea or a small scale experiment because digging out the peat meant in fact – creating a new lake.

◆ **Energy** – another idea brought up in connection with the Huleh drainage was the production of energy by exploiting the descent of the Jordan waters into the Sea of Galilee. The issue was dropped because of economic and political reasons; the idea was raised and discarded a number of times.

◆ **Transport** –in spite of the declarations and the good intentions, the drainage project did not bring any revolution in the transport system of the Huleh valley. It facilitated the building of the south-north road at the eastern side of the valley at the foot of the Golan Mountains and even then, a narrow, twisting, forsaken and insignificant road, with solely a local contribution.

No other road was built over the reclaimed land, nor along the valley neither across it.[50]

The Drainage Execution

In the year 1951 the JNF prepared itself, with the help of the Diaspora Jews, to start the Huleh drainage project. It was the first engineering national project for the young, new State of Israel.

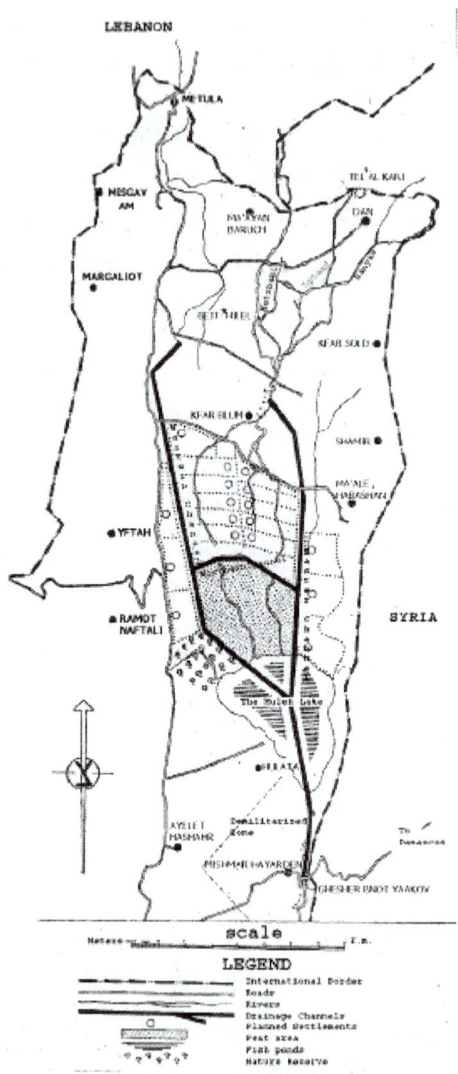

FIGURE 3 – The Huleh Drainage Plant Map
Source: Karmon Y., *The Huleh – Past and Present*, Ma'arachot, 1958.

The main core of the project included two extensive engineering feats: shifting the Jordan riverbed to the eastern and western sides of the valley into drainage channels that carried the Jordan waters to the downstream of the river, and the opening of the basalt plug that blocked the lake exit. Those procedures brought on the regular flowing of the Jordan waters and its tributaries to a drop in the groundwater level in the valley region. Figure 3 depicts the drainage plan map.

Tahal, as the national company for the management of the national water resources, was chosen to design the details of the project and its staging. That decision was made by the commission established by the government, in the first year of its existence – December 1948. The role of that commission was to examine the issue of the Huleh drainage. The commission members were: Prof. Broer from the Technion, Eng. Blas from the Ministry of Agriculture, Eng. Berchyau from the JNF, Eng. Koblanov from the Jewish Agency, Dr. Cohen and Dr. Roth from the Ministry of Industry and Commerce and Dr. Carmon from the Ministry of Agriculture. The commission adopted Eng. Koblanov's solution: two separate riverbeds for the Jordan River – one on the east side and the other on the west side of the lake.

The commission presented its final report to the JNF in June 1949. The follow-up of the execution of the drainage works was assigned to a restricted commission, composed of the members of the first one as well as Eng. De-Leo of the National Potash Company.

The plan included two main parts:

The first part was deepening of the Jordan, in order to lower the water level, so the lake could be emptied. The second part was creation of a channel system descending to the Jordan, at such a slope so that water would not remain in the valley.[51]

The drainage project was executed in three steps (Figure 4 on next page):

FIRST STEP (March 1951 – March 1953): The deepening of the Jordan riverbed, south of the Huleh Lake, so that all the water coming from the north and flowing to the Sea of Galilee would pass through. The deepening works were 4.5 kilometers long, between the south end of the valley – the Churi Orchard –

and the Benot Jacob Bridge, nearby Mishmar Hayarden. The deepening of the Jordan riverbed eliminated forever the main source for the Huleh swamp.

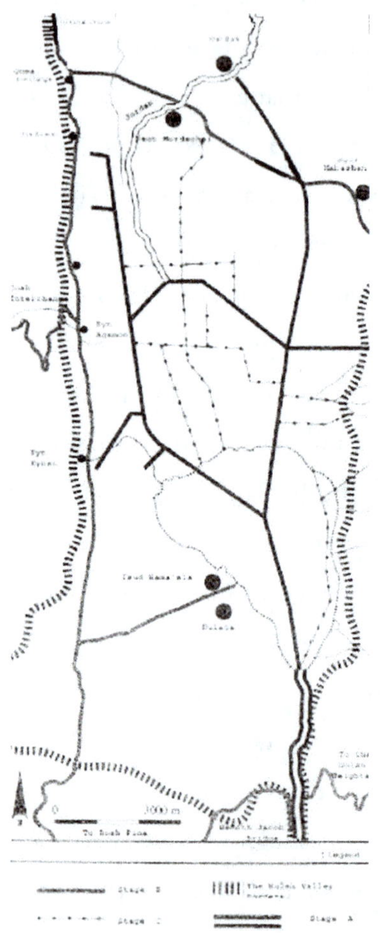

FIGURE 4 The Huleh Drainage Execution Map
Source: Karmon Y., *The Huleh – Past and Present*, Ma'arachot, 1958.

SECOND STEP (Summer 1953 – Summer 1955): The swamp drainage and the prevention of valley flooding in the rainy season. That was accomplished by the digging of the main drainage channels: the eastern channel which replaced the Jordan riverbed – 19.5 kilometer long and 50 meter wide and the western channel – 16 kilometer long and 20 meter wide. Those two channels were north-south oriented, were connected by another channel and met at the center of the previous Huleh Lake. There they connected with the widened Jordan riverbed. In fact, those two channels replaced the riverbeds of the Jordan River and the Tura River, at a lower level than the original one so that flooding of the surrounding areas will be prevented during the rainy season.

THIRD STEP (**Summer 1955**): The completion of the digging works and all preparations in view of the final drainage. That included the building of bridges over the channels, connection of all the channels to their outlets and preparation works for the Huleh reserve.

In October 1957, the barrier of the southern outlet of the Huleh Lake was removed and the lake and the swamp were emptied of their water.[52]

Many problems arose during the execution of the drainage project:

Political Problems: Serious difficulties developed between Israel and its neighbors - the Syrians (to be detailed below). Syria opposed strongly the drainage project, both formally, by complaining to the U.N. Security Council, and by sporadic acts of violence such as shooting at the drainage workers. During the preparation of the detailed border line between the British Mandate and the French Mandate in the Middle East, at the beginning of the 20th century, due to the stubbornness of the Borders Commission British representative - Newcomb – the whole of the Jordan River was included in the British zone. In fact, the border line was traced along a strip of land east of the river. So, the border line was some 0.5 kilometer east of the Jordan talweg and both river banks belonged to Eretz Israel and later – to the State of Israel. Nevertheless the Israeli military grip on the eastern narrow strip could not materialize in a hostile atmosphere – an armistice without peace – so that actually, the Jordan River was the border between Israel and Syria. Areas at the east of the Jordan, even the Mishmar Hayarden zone and other small but significant areas for the drainage project were declared a Demilitarized Zone and that caused many problems during the execution of the drainage project. That subject will be discussed more in detail, further on in this study.

Technical Challenges: many problems and difficulties arose during the execution of the project either because of the political conflict with Syria, which caused complications for the execution processes, restrictions on the location of the mechanical equipment and interruptions in the drainage works, or because of the technical difficulties encountered by field conditions – dredgers broke down on the basalt rock, workers and mechanical equipment suffered from Syrian attacks. Mechanical equipment owners refused to rent their tools and only the Prime Minister's – Ben-Gurion – intervention and the activation of an obligatory order helped recruit the necessary equipment.[53]

The Huleh Peat

The peat is a kind of soil created from residues of plants accumulated under water in anaerobic conditions (lacking oxygen environment). It consists of matter in the form of a net, which retains water inside.[54] Already during the early stages of the Huleh project, the existence of peat in parts of the lake soil was known and that knowledge raised great expectations of a natural raw material to be exploited and taken advantage of in various ways. Investigations regarding the amount of peat and its exact emplacement in the Huleh Lake were carried on from the very early stages of the drainage project. One of them was conducted by Professor Leo Piccard, Head of the Hebrew University Geology Department and Director of the Israel Geological services. Professor Piccard found deposits of peat at a depth of 30 meter and 80 meter, deposits with a high content of nitrogen that made them valuable as fertilizers.[55]

Another investigator was Dr. Govrin who worked under the supervision of the geologist Salomonike, as mentioned in a letter to the Secretary of Industry and Commerce.[56]

The expectations of benefits from the Huleh peat exploitation were great, even more so considering how poor in natural riches Israel was. From the very beginning, when the project was just in its cradle, the use of peat for multiple purposes became an important issue.[57] For example, it was assumed that the peat could be used as fuel due to the gas swamp it contained.[58] In June 1949, The Huleh Drainage Committee recommended in its concluding report to continue and complete the tests on peat properties – physical and chemical – and also to perform quantity tests.[59]

The JNF, which was responsible for the project implementation, considered the peat exploitation as an important component of the project and referred to it as follows: "The project will enable the use of peat from the Huleh area for the benefit of agriculture, the chemical industry and heating."[60]

The second stage did not include the commercial exploitation of peat but it did cover peat conservation by preserving the special conditions necessary for the peat to keep its qualities, not deteriorate and so, loose its value.[61]

It was known then that the peat consisted of 80% - 88% water. The drainage of the Huleh Lake brought with it the danger of the peat losing its humidity and becoming hard, or even burning. As such, it was of primary importance to preserve its humidity.

At first, the peat was considered an efficient fertilizer and physical qualities soil improver. Its role was to increase the soil water pull and to keep heat conditions constant inside the soil. As a fertilizer, it could be used in its natural form, or after being improved by some industrial processes, as floor padding for cowsheds and henhouses. Later on, considering the lack of local raw materials for energy production, the idea of using peat as a fuel began to form and became more and more attractive. Well known was that in other countries, peat was used as a fuel in industries, to heat boilers, in power stations (in Russia and in Ireland, for instance), in blocks, iron, lime industries, etc. Tests were performed in order to find the compatibility of the peat as a fuel, but the results were inconclusive.[62]

Other studies indicated that its utility as a fertilizer was preferable.[63] One article noted that when the Huleh drainage project would be complete, *"Israelis may then exploit an estimated 4,000,000 tons of peat from the swamps as fuel or as fertilizer and cultivate 4,000 acres of new farmland and 5,000 acres of improved land."* [64]

Peat as a Fertilizer

A number of tests and experiments were performed on the Huleh peat in order to determine its specific properties as well as its efficacy in various uses. It was obvious from the start that the Huleh peat differed from the European or American varieties. Despite all the efforts, it was difficult for scientists and researchers to arrive at a final and definite conclusion regarding the peat properties and its usefulness.

Documents from the period of 1952-1957 contain repeated references to tests and experiments performed with the peat, but the results were inconclusive.

The experts that undertook those tests confirmed the commercial value of the peat on a single dimension: they determined that the peat could serve as an efficient fertilizer, provided that nitrogen be added to it. In laboratories, technicians succeeded in adding the correct amount of nitrogen through a chemical process. Also, about five tons of peat were to be sent to the Dutch laboratories for further examination.[65]

Some intensive studies on that matter were done in the laboratory of The Agricultural Research Station in Rehovoth, a branch of the Israeli Ministry of Agriculture. Reports of those ongoing studies were prepared and sent to that Ministry.[66]

A number of scientists worked on tests on the Huleh peat such as Reifenberg and Moshicky, who described the chemical composition of peat of the Huleh swamps in 1941; and Schallinger, who worked on a vast research regarding exploitation of the Huleh peat for agricultural use as a fertilizer. After such efforts and published articles, it would have been reasonable to expect that the value and usefulness of the peat would be well established and that only implementation remained unsolved.

Nevertheless, contemporaneous documents and articles showed that questions and doubts about the peat and its commercial value kept arising and troubling all involved. Some of the problems referred to the fact that the peat soils were not homogenous, but rather were mixed with mineral soil sediments. Still, everyone seemed convinced of the peat's value as a raw material.[67]

There was much experience with peat use in the world and attempts were made by JNF, the Ministry of Agriculture and others involved in the matter, to take advantage and learn from that experience. Consultants were brought from oversees to study the Huleh peat and advise about the best and most efficient ways to use it.[68]

In 1949, the report of the Huleh Drainage Committee talked about ongoing experiments on the peat.[69] In 1953, a notice in Israel Digest mentioned more detailed examinations of the peat properties in the future and at the same time, it talked about utilization of the peat for different uses.[70] Other documents showed the same phenomena – studies and experiments of the peat throughout the 1950s.[71]

At the same time, in parallel with various laboratory studies and field experiments, planning of the peat exploitation and even field works in that direction continued, without regard to the fact that there was no certainty about the value or the correct way of exploiting the material. During the first half of the 1950s, work proceeded continuously in an effort to exploit the Huleh peat.[72]

A comprehensive report was prepared, summarizing all the findings of the researches performed on the peat, up to 1957. This report was based on a few elements: the work of JNF in draining the Huleh swamps, the scientific work performed for a number of years by Dr. Salomon (Shlomo) Rabikovitz at The Agricultural Research Station in Rehovoth and the work performed since 1900 with peat in the San Joachim delta, in the U.S. state of California. By initiative of Mr. Sam Hamburg, Mr. John Zuckerman visited Israel in July 1955 and advised about treatment and irrigation of the peat soils.

Interesting in the above report were the details of peat properties: *"Peat soil is permanently subsiding ... Peat soil is in permanent danger of burning when getting dry ... Water flow in peat soil differs from water flow in mineral soil..."*[73]

The report elaborated about each of the above mentioned properties.

Misgivings and Apprehensions Regarding the Peat Value

From early stages of the Huleh drainage project, there were questions about the ways to preserve peat properties and the proper means to cultivate peat soils.

The concern was that, with the drying of the lake, the peat would dry and lose its special properties.[74]

It was obvious that work with peat soils is problematic, requiring special methods and a special kind of mechanical equipment. It was understood that it would be difficult to excavate peat by using ordinary digging machines and something special would have to be deployed to enable the excavation of the peat from areas heavily soaked by water.[75]

Despite the many studies, laboratory research and field experiments performed on the peat, during the years of the Huleh drainage, and even toward the final stages of the project, there still remained unanswered questions and many uncertainties concerning the exploitation of peat and its agricultural and commercial value.[76]

The Danger of Peat Ignition

The danger of peat ignition was known from the early stages of the Huleh drainage project.[77] There was evidence of ideas and proposals on how to deal with peat soil fires, how to try and avoid them and, if they occur, how to control them. Nevertheless, the reality proved to be less encouraging than the plans. In fact, fires occurred often in the peat soils of the Huleh and disturbed the drainage works.[78] Fires erupted in the peat area and rapidly burned out of control, causing damage to the soil and disturbances to the drainage work. The Ministry of Agriculture tried to find the root cause for the fires and the ways to prevent them. For that purpose, the Minister asked for an investigation by the Public Works Department.[79]

The investigation performed by Mr. Bartal, Public Works Department Manager, was thorough and his report to the Minister of Agriculture – very detailed.[80]

A great deal can be learned from this report on matters regarding the peat and its handling. One example was the special attention given to developing methods to prevent the peat ignition, such as channels dug especially to preserve humidity in the peat.[81] The technique used to produce peat included, as a first stage, cleaning the area of vegetation so that the excavator would reach the bare soil to dig in. Disposal of the vegetation could have been done by a regular excavator combined with handwork, but this was an uneconomical way of doing it. So instead, the vegetation was burnt and the area cleared for peat digging. There were specific instructions on how to effectuate the vegetation burning so that the fire would stay under control and not spread. These included watering the soil beyond the separation channels, disposing of the papyrus in some places by handwork, having special supervisors present while burning the vegetation and so on.

The instructions were followed to the letter but on September 28th 1955, the vegetation burning became a raging fire spreading out of control over more and more areas. Mr. Bartal's investigation found that the cause of the incident was the strong wind with unusual vortexes that occurred that day and winds that blew the coals of papyrus and the ashes to further areas causing ignition of the vegetation there. Efforts were made to control the fire, but it was in vain and the fire spread fast.[82]

The investigation pointed out that the real danger of peat ignition arose from the subsiding of the water level as a result of the Huleh drainage work that caused the drying out of the vegetation and of the upper layer of the peat. The danger increased during the summer, when groundwater level decreased every day.[83]

Despite the investigation and all its important findings, the peat ignition continued to be a problem, difficult to prevent or even to control.[84]

Fires kept on bursting in the Huleh peat soils and were a problem and a disturbance all along the way, for the Huleh drainage works and for the farming of the Huleh soils.[85]

Special Treatment of the Peat Soils

The peat soils were difficult to work with and required different treatment and special attention.

> Peat areas do not come into being in the world in a uniform way and the structure of the organic matter in the Huleh not necessarily will be similar in structure and composition to other peat areas in the world. The treatment of the peat areas must be individual, by learning the local conditions for local exploitation…Also, there is no guarantee that the whole peat area is uniform.[86]

Awareness of that, among other reasons, caused JNF to sign the contract with the American company 'Construction Aggregates Corporation' to perform the drainage works in the Huleh, including protection work for preservation of the peat properties.

The digging of the peat soil was difficult and problematic and required special mechanical equipment.

> In addition, modern special equipment is required for work in the peat soils, equipment that cannot be purchased by small settlements.[87]
>
> …I talked to Mr., … an expert in agricultural equipment from the Technion.
>
> I explained to him the problems that arise from ploughing the peat soil and I proposed to him the following principle of machinery.[88]
>
> …The company (Construction Aggregates Corporation) is getting ready to bring special equipment in order to perform the above-mentioned work (Channels digging in the peat soil).[89]

Movement of the heavy machinery existing in Israel, on peat areas, is impossible because the allowed pressure in these areas is no more than 2.5 pounds/square inch. So, in order to ready the peat soil and to construct an irrigation system on it, it will be necessary to bring equipment from abroad.[90]

Even the use of peat as a fertilizer was not a simple matter of digging and spreading it on the fields. It required previous treatment of the peat in order to improve its effect on the soil.

The use of peat for agriculture was problematic, either as a fertilizer to enrich other soils or as a fertile soil itself.

> In peat soils, regular irrigation methods – sprinkling and flooding – are not possible because wet peat soils are not workable for farming.

Peat soils sink 10-20 centimeter a year. This fact makes very difficult the built of permanent constructions on peat soils and requires special means of irrigation and drainage of the area.[91]

Of the plan to prepare the peat soil for farming, a lot was based on the experience acquired on the peat soils of California, in the Sacramento – San Joachim delta. More than that, it was recommended by Tahal to use consultants from abroad in order to take advantage of the experience accumulated there with peat soils and in order to avoid local problems.[92]

In sum it may be noted that a lot of knowledge about the problems of using the peat was accumulated during the works on the drainage. However, the ideological enthusiasm and the belief in the power of science to solve any technological problem drove the JNF to start the projects based on the optimistic assumption that problems will be solved along the way.

‪2‬

The Trans-Israel Highway

The Trans-Israel Highway is the largest and most important Israeli transport project of the first decade of the twenty-first century. It gives definite priority to the private car over any other means of transport.[93] The highway is slated to become the main interurban axis of the country, in the North-South direction. In addition to its role as an interurban major highway, Road 6 is expected to service the Gush Dan Metropolis (Greater Tel-Aviv) as an outer ring of the area. For that purpose, latitudinal roads and interchanges were planned along the central part of the highway.

Yet, the Trans-Israel was one of the most controversial projects of the country, raising strong reactions from all strata and sectors of the population, oppositions as well as support, on every aspect of the day-to-day life. The project met with great support from special-interest parties, such as economic developers, investors and real estate developers. On the other hand social and environmental activists and landowners opposed it fiercely.[94]

The highway was planned to start a little south of Be'er-Sheva and continue to the north, a few kilometers east of the shore, to the north, to the Tefen region and the border with Lebanon. Road 6 was planned as a speedy multi-lane expressway, its junctions to other roads – by interchanges only.

The defined and publicly presented purposes of the highway were as follows:

◆ To create a quick and effective connection of the Galilee and the Negev to the country center – Gush Dan and Jerusalem (shorten distances between the periphery and the center of the country).

◆ To help with the government plans for the dispersal of population and employment centers.

◆ To create the main transport axis for the traffic from the east to the urban centers of the coastline.

◆ To facilitate the increasing traffic at the center region and especially at the Tel-Aviv Metropolis.

◆ To create an international transport infrastructure that will enable a continental connection between Israel and its neighbors, once peace is achieved.[95]

The Trans-Israel Highway, as the main traffic axis of the country, was destined to have a significant impact on the trends and magnitude of development of many of the Israeli society life systems. That impact included land uses of the near (and also not-so-near) areas along the highway's route. It was supposed to cause changes in existing plans. Its effect on open, green spaces and on the country's landscape was to be crucial and on the quality of life of the nearby settlements – significant.

The Highway Concept

The concept of the Trans-Israel, passing through almost all the country, from north to south, was brought up for the first time in the 1960s. A preliminary planning, a physical marking on maps and a legal authorization were accorded to the highway for the first time in 1976, when the government approved the National Outline Plan for Roads and Railways – NOP 3 (TAM"A/3). On the drawings of that national plan, a line was marked for the Trans-Israel Highway route. The overarching idea was that the road would be part of the solution to the traffic congestion in urban areas, would help disperse the population from the coastal zone to the north and the south of the country and would, by extension, also encourage creation of new sources of employment.

The highway's route was traced also in the Regional Outline Plan of the center (TAMA"M/3) and of the south (TAMA"M/4), plans that were approved in the 1980s.

The transformation of the road to a national highway by the name of Road 6 occurred at the end of the 1980s. During that period, the large number of immigrants arriving in Israel from the former-Soviet Union was the incentive for the government to prepare the NOP 31 (TAM"A/31) – the National Outline Plan for Construction, Development and Immigration Absorption. That plan was finally approved in January 1993. Road 6 was part of that plan as part of the solution to the immigrants' absorption and the dispersal of the population.

The forecast of 200,000 immigrants arriving every year for the next five years required the creation of thousands of new jobs and their dispersion to sites all over the country. In that connection, the planners of NOP 31 had to deal with and find a solution for the transport infrastructure, considering the already lagging state of that system. Part of the highway's route was changed and segments were shifted to the east, toward the so-called "green line". The NOP 3 steering committee recommended including in NOP 31 only the segments that were approved already by the government in the framework of NOP 3. The decision was that NOP 31 would become the leverage to promote roads of national importance. For that purpose, detailed design of the above mentioned segments were included in the NOP 31.

The National Council for Planning and Construction decided to promote an additional plan, NOP 31A for roads – (TAM"A/31A), that would include segments of Road 6 and the latitudinal roads connecting to those segments. In order to speed up the construction of Road 6, NOP 31A was prepared and approved on a detailed design level.

At the beginning of 1991, the Public Works Department, which was then responsible for the project, prepared a viability study of the Trans-Israel Highway, based on the traffic data available at the time. The results showed economic viability of the highway.

In June 1992, the National Council for Planning and Construction dealt with the segments presented to her by the steering committee and decided to require an environmental impact statement for some parts of those segments. Also the decision was taken to hand over the NOP 31A to the regional committees and for them to present it to the public and report back on the public's review and their observations and comments.

During the year 1993, many objections and reservations accumulated regarding the highway, some from local authorities and other public institutions and others from private citizens. Because of the many objections to the Trans-Israel plan, an investigator was nominated in order to formulate recommendations regarding the findings of the environmental impact statement. A special subcommittee was appointed to deal with those recommendations. The chosen investigator was Gidon Vitkin, a former judge, and his recommendations were presented in the end, to the National Council for Planning and Construction. Vitkin rejected the NGO IUED's (Israel Union for Environmental Defense) request for a general impact statement for the whole project.

In November 1992, in order to hasten the project implementation, the government decided to establish a government company – the Cross-Israel Company Ltd., subordinated directly to the Prime Minister and not to the Minister of Infrastructure, as would normally have been the case.

In 1993, the Cross-Israel Company ordered a new feasibility study, which was prepared by MATA"T (The Transport Planning Center Ltd.). The goal was to again verify the economic profitability of the highway and to analyze the future traffic loads that would be generated by the new highway.

In 1994, the NGO IUED (Adam, Teva Ve'Din) required that an overall environmental impact statement (EIS) be prepared, referring to the whole project and not only to segments of it. The general EIS was to be based on objective interdisciplinary scientific tests under the supervision of an environmental consultant. The IUED claimed that the data obtained from those tests was not available before to the Cross-Israel Company, the National Council and the public at large.

In April 1994, the National Council for Planning and Construction endorsed its June 1992 decision against an overall EIS and settled for an impact statement for only some of the highway's segments. At the same session, the National Council decided that there was unquestionable necessity to the highway and that other transport solutions such as the railway were complementary and desirable but not substitutes. The National Council decided as well to establish a team of professionals, one of them the representative of the Israeli EPA, to accompany implementation of the highway project, including supervision of environmental issues.

In June 1994, the IUED (Adam, Teva Ve'Din) submitted a petition to the High Court of Justice, and the Court instructed the defendants to present in 60 days their arguments for refusing to prepare an overall EIS for the whole project.

Meanwhile, the feasibility study ordered by the Cross-Israel Company was accomplished and the results corroborated the highway's viability. The study's findings and the recommendations resulting from them urged all involved in the project – the ministers of transport, infrastructure, finance and construction and housing – to promote the passage of the Trans-Israel Highway law by the Knesset.

The day after the High Court's decision regarding the comprehensive EIS, the government approved, in a special meeting, the "Trans-Israel Highway - Road 6 - Law". The purpose of that law was to enable the Cross Israel Company to take immediate possession of the appropriated public land for the road without a court order. The government empowered the ministerial committee for legislation issues to determine the criteria for the land compensations magnitude; but if their decision was not to satisfy the expectations of the farmers and the Arab villagers, owners of the appropriated land, the matter could be brought before the Court and so, prolonged for a considerable amount of time.[96]

Once the Trans-Israel law was approved, the Minister of Construction and Housing gave order to the Cross-Israel Company to start immediately the preparations for the highway construction. He also instructed the Israel Land Authority to look for alternatives for the appropriated land for cases in which monetary compensations would not solve the problem.[97]

In 1995, the Knesset approved an additional law regarding the Trans-Israel, the tall road law that determines that the central part of the highway will be a toll road.[98]

Also, it was decided that a private consortium, chosen by bid, will finance, execute, operate and maintain the highway as a toll road, for 30 years.

In January 1998, the consortium Derech Eretz Highways was chosen as the bid concessionaire. It was composed of three partners: Canadian Highways International, Africa-Israel and The Ministry of Construction and Housing.[99]

In 1999, construction work began. At the same time, the anti-highway protest activity of the environmental activists, the "Greens", intensified.

In November 1999, a new manifest was published: it demanded a stop to the highway execution and a call to verify anew its profitability. The manifest was the result of an unusual cooperation between politicians from right and left wings, six ministers and the Knesset chairman – a total of 57 Knesset members. They were joined by 33 non-parliamentary organizations. In September 2000, the Movement for the Road 6 Stopping was founded; it included Knesset members from across the whole political spectrum – right, left and in-between. Various other Israeli public personalities, such as actors, writers, television celebrities and scholars joined the movement.

This group focused on the social problems anticipated to result from the highway and not on the environmental issue.[100]

The Highway Route

The south end of the highway is in the Be'er-Sheva region, from there the road continues to the Kyriat-Gat surroundings, east of Kyriat Gat, to the interchange by the same name. From there, the route continues, in the center part of the country, along the railway, reaching the Ben Shemen interchange, east of the city of Ramleh; there the highway runs to the east of the railway, it joins the road 444 route and reaches the towns of Rosh Ha'Ayin, Kalkilya and Tul-Karem, at the interchange of Tul-Karem.

The Highway continues to the north, surrounding the urban center of Gush Dan and crossing the national latitudinal road system; from there, at the foothills to the Eyron junction and further on, on the north-east side of Hadera, to the junction with road 70 (the Yokne'am Road or Wadi Milek Road) and reaching Yokneam. At that location, the highway bifurcates: the western branch, on the east side of the Zevulun Valley and the northern part of the coastal plain up to Shlomi and Rosh Hanikra, close to the Lebanon border; the eastern branch – to Ramat-Ishai, the Beit-Netufa Valley, the Golani Junction and Amiad.[101]

Figure No. 5 (on the next page) shows a graphical description of the highway's route.

In the following chapters, the two national projects will be analyzed with respect to specific aspects: national ideology of the times each project was executed, the process of decision-making, the public discourse that developed around each project, the impact of each project on the environment and the attitude toward nature conservation and environment protection in the respective periods and the issue of social justice or injustice in regard with each project.

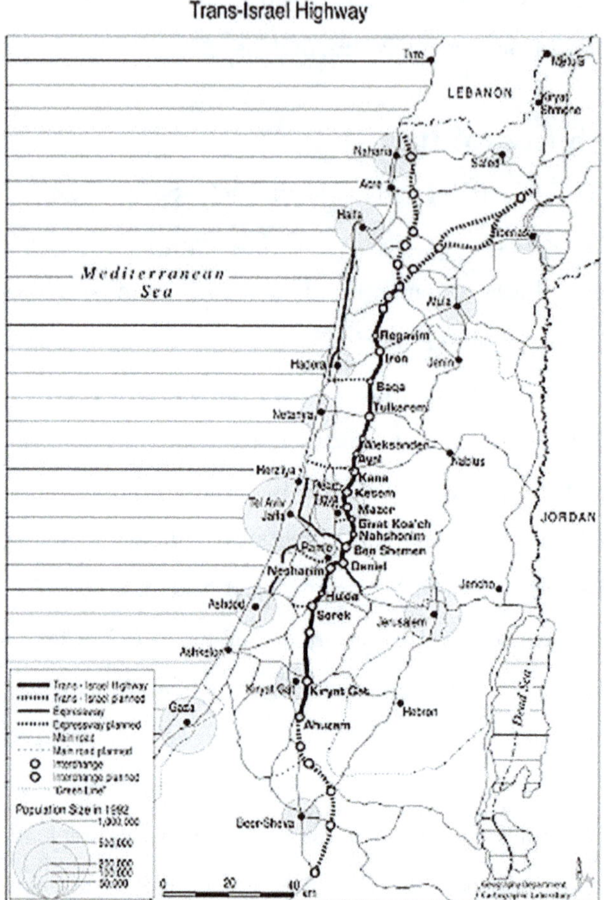

FIGURE 5 – The Trans-Israel Highway Route
(Note: The map reflects the planned route and population sizes during the nineties,
the key period in the project's design and approval)
Source: Garb Y., *Constructing the Trans-Israel Highway's Inevitability*, Israel Studies,
Vol. 9, No. 2, Summer 2004.

❧ **3** ❧
National Ideology

A. The Huleh Drainage

Zionist Attitude to Nature and Environment in Palestine/Israel

The first waves of immigrants to Eretz Israel/Palestine and specially the second and third waves (Aliyot), at the beginning of the 20th century, had grown up and been educated with the concepts of nature and environment, but upon their arrival in Israel/Palestine, they left behind the beliefs of their countries of origin.

Inspired by the Bible, they perceived the Promised Land - Eretz Israel - as their true homeland and they made great efforts to promote an emotional and physical attachment to it. But the land, when the newcomers arrived from Europe, did not resemble the images in their dreams of "The Promised Land". So, these pioneers found a bewildered nature in Eretz Israel but not a hospitable environment. Based on their notions of environment, as they knew and learned it in their countries of origin, they perceived the new land as desolate, strange and alienated. As a result, their perception of the nature around them was as an enemy, of sorts.[102]

The immigrants faced a natural environment totally unfamiliar and different from their expectations. They regarded the sandy dunes, the desert and the swamps as a threat to their survival. They suffered from the conflict arising from the contrast between the imagined environment and the experienced one.[103]

One of the factors to the sense of desolate wilderness toward the land was rooted in the romantic worldview toward nature they brought from their countries of origin.

At the beginning, the first immigration waves adopted a romantic attitude toward nature and environment in the new country. They considered that their redemption and transformation into a new people, a real nation, similar to the ones of the Western world was dependent upon forming a physical bond with the land by working it with their own hands. But despite their efforts, standards of living remained low and the adaptation to the new country - difficult.[104]

Zionism's attitude to land became ambivalent. On one hand, bonding with the land expressed an essential connection between environment and people. On the other hand, the land existed in order to be developed. The slogan of "making the desert bloom" reflected this ambivalence. It showed the importance of being connected to the land, but not to the land as it was. It did not value letting the desert remain as it was found, but rather changing it into something else.[105] The bond to the land was an essential element of the Zionist ideology. In fact, it embraced Heidegger's view that a people cannot exist as a nation without a bond to a particular land. This notion was very influential in central and eastern Europe, from where most immigrants came.[106]

So, the attitude and the mentality changed and a new ideology was developed by the Zionist movement. Nature was described in political speeches and in school textbooks as "nothingness", "emptiness", "desolation" and "dreariness", and the message was that this nature had to be "conquered", "suppressed", "made to flourish" and "civilized" in order to transform it into an environment.[107]

In order to connect with the land, to create a more hospitable and familiar environment, to become a nation united with its territory, the pioneers had to change nature and create an environment which will correspond to their views and expectations, as Cronon referred to in his article *"In Search of Nature"* in *"Uncommon Ground – Rethinking the Human Place in Nature"* [108]

The means to achieve this goal, in the Zionists' views, was to give the highest priority for land-use to housing and agriculture. The former was necessary to accommodate the large-scale immigration that followed the state establishment; the latter was the expression of Zionist ideology on the aspired way of life – rural settlements and farming. According to Heidegger, human beings must build and create settlements not only to have a place to live in or a roof over their head, but also in order to replace their homelessness with a feeling of "home", security and attachment to their surroundings.[109]

The Zionist ideology toward nature developed into regarding nature as an obstacle to be overcome, subdued, conquered, covered in concrete or asphalt or drained like in the case of the Huleh swamps. This attitude toward nature, land-use and policy to transform the environment was characteristic of "frontier" societies in other parts of the new world.

For the new immigrants in the young state, the main challenge was to change the existing nature, which they considered hostile, and "civilize" it. In their minds, that meant building and cultivating – covering the land with concrete and pavement for settlements and with farms for agriculture.

Conquering nature and transforming the desert in a green and prosperous land, also had a moral aspect – it was expected to create a new type of Jew, completely different from the Diaspora one – physically strong, free and capable of living from manual work.[110]

The widespread and persistent attitude of the Zionists was that working the land was getting close to nature and that this closeness would create a new kind of person – stronger and healthier physically and mentally. In this way, the Diaspora will be forgotten and the new type of Jew will be born. Along with immigration to Israel, agricultural settlement and working the land were the fulfillments of Jewish nationalism and of the Zionist dreams.[111]

Redemption of the Land

Biblical phrases such as *The Land Shall Not Be Sold Forever For the Land Is Mine (Lev. 25:23)* inspired the ideology of making the desert "bloom", conquering the wilderness and redeeming the land. These conceptions became the slogans, the foundation of Zionist activity in Eretz Israel, before and after the establishment of the State.

The idea was to create an environment in the new country that would give the immigrants a feeling of belonging, a sense of roots in a new homeland, of placeness. An example of this was the planting of forests that would suggest those of Europe and in so doing, change the natural surroundings to mimic one more familiar to the newcomers. The act of reshaping the outer world into an environment based on Jewish perception of the landscape was regarded as highly important in the Zionist adaptation to the land.[112]

> What are we seeking in the land of Israel? To redeem it…and to give rebirth to our people. The two are not separate tasks but two sides of the same issue. There is no redemption of the Land without the redemption of the people, and there is no redemption of the people without the redemption of the Land. Buying lands with money is not enough as long as it is not cultivated by Jews.[113]

In the last years of the 19th century, the concept of redemption became connected to Eretz Israel. Purchasing the lands owned by local Arabs was a financial-economic deal and its transfer into Jewish hands – part of the redemption. The purchase was a necessary condition for land redemption and "Israel revival", but not a sufficient one. To build settlements, populate the land and work it and develop agriculture, all by Jewish hands, were as necessary as the ownership of the land.

Redemption was for the sake of the people, it was redemption from foreigners and from desolation, attended by land cultivation and general progress.

> Redemption of the land in modern times is the purchase, reclamation and settlement of land in Eretz Israel by the Jewish

> National Fund, by private individuals and organizations and later, by the State of Israel.[114]
>
> Our world hinges on redemption of the land. However, the land can be redeemed in two ways: via legal channels and via settlement. Trough the first way one gains rights on the paper, but actual rights can only be attained by means of the second way.
>
> The legal concepts are transitory, and the mouth that prohibits things today is the same one that permits things tomorrow. And only "holding" rights last forever, and the holder is the labourer.[115]

The religious Jewish ideology also emphasized the duty of Jews to settle the land, to own it and work it with its own hands and by those means - redeem it.[116]

Stage by stage, "redemption of the land" became for the Zionist movement, a synonym for acquiring land from non-Jews and building Jewish agricultural settlements upon it. On a higher level, the notion of "redemption of the land" was looked upon also as the key to the redemption of the Jewish people, its transformation into a nation and its growing roots into its territory – Israel/Palestine.[117]

The Zionist ideal was that agriculture was a noble and healthy occupation, not only economically, but also spiritually. The goal of developing a type of Jewish peasant permeated the education system. It became a noble activity and more than a means of making a living, it was considered a means of creating attachment to the land and getting close to nature.

Even pioneers who had embraced "white collar" professions in their country of origin adopted these ideals upon arrival in Eretz Israel. And so for the pioneers, the agricultural settlement became the desired new life style in The Promised Land.[118] Though refined by the Zionists, these ideas about the land were, in part, derived from contemporaneous European and American sources.

One of the ideological streams that influenced Zionist thought was the French physiocratic school which claimed that only the cultivation of land could improve a society's material value and that the only source of that value was nature. The physiocrats considered nature and land the most important elements in human life and agriculture the most desirable and proper way to make a livelihood.[119]

The first waves of immigrants believed that agriculture should form the basis for the economic development of Israel. Henri Near named this phenomenon "the agrarian deviation" of the Zionist Labor movement.[120]

The "agrarian deviation" became the ideology of the Labor Zionists and "working the land" – an ideal. It was an expression of the spirit of the times. The 'spirit of the times' is the set of beliefs and concepts forming the infrastructure and the basis of the general thinking of a whole group of people at a given historical period.

The Holy Bible, too, influenced the agrarian deviation. The Jewish society in the Scriptures was an agrarian one featuring, in particular, shepherds and their sheep and the aspiration of the immigrants was to restore these elements to their newly-reborn society in Israel.

In light of the concepts developing in Europe in the 18th and 19th centuries and influenced by them, Zionism was a romantic movement with two facets - one of its facets was nationalism and another one – the idealization of nature and agriculture. "The early waves of immigration to Palestine were characterized by a romantic attitude to nature and a glorification of rural life."[121]

In Israel/Palestine, the public rhetoric was based on the hegemony of the agriculture over any other occupation. The concept was that agriculture work would create an elite, morally and politically superior citizenry.[122]

The redemption of the land became the basis and the myth of the Zionist ideology. At first, it meant simply to acquire the land from the ownership of non-Jews, but after a time its meaning broadened, including treatment and improvement of the soil (*hachsharat hakarka*)[123] for agriculture and working the land using Jewish hands.[124]

The Zionist movement felt a strong and urgent need to create myths, symbols and rituals in order to support and sustain the immigrants' integration in their new country. The environment was, as a result, politicized and manipulated to a drastic degree.

The immigrants that came from Europe regarded the local environment – dunes, marshes and swamps – as hostile and threatening. They described it as "desert", "nothingness", "emptiness", "desolation", "neglect", "ruin", and so on. Therefore, they felt the environment had to be "conquered", "suppressed", "made to flourish", "blossom", "be civilized" – so it would become more familiar and hospitable.[125]

This concept about local nature and landscape and the attitude toward the environment became part of the Zionist ideology concerning the settling of Israel by the immigrants.

The Zionists differentiated nature from culture and treated nature by scientific means and measurements and especially by according it economic value. Their belief was that their way of acting and changing nature by technological means will develop and intensify their bond with the land.

They gave a conceptual touch to their pragmatic approach to nature by adding notions of "kibush hakarka" and "kibush ha'avoda"[126] in their ideological platform.[127]

Hence, the Huleh drainage was the Zionist way of "kibush hakarka", of conquering and subduing nature in order to meet the needs of immigrants, creating land for cultivation from wild, unprofitable swamps.

The Ethos of Development

The ethos of development originated as a solution to the needs and hardships of the immigrants, in the late 1930s and also after the Second World War. It became a necessity for absorbing and integrating, in a short period of time, a great number of immigrants including Jewish European refugees from the

Nazis and Jewish refugees from Arab countries. Also, after the establishment of Israel, development was the answer to the pressing needs of the new independent state. *"Development was equivalent to success in the co-operative effort to master the alien environment…"* [128]

With time, the notion of development was considered in a larger framework. The ruling elite in Israel wished to transform the natural environment, the local landscape, into a "civilized one" as an expression of their success in building the new state and the new nation.

> They wished to transform the dunes into wheatfields and the
> bare hills into mountains covered by woods in order to reflect
> their values of physical work, the return to nature and the
> transformation of the Jewish soul on the Jewish soil.[129]

But the Zionists had an ambivalent attitude toward nature. On one hand, they remembered the romantic feelings of the past and, on the other hand, they adopted the practical, useful attitude for the future. In order to build the country and the nation, they strived to exploit the environment and its natural resources and on that basis, to create a modern economy and find solutions for the needs of the new state.[130]

Thus, later development became the legitimation for the Zionist idea and even an end in itself. Those who dared oppose development were considered opponents of the very core of Zionism.

The basic principles of development consisted of three definite activities: afforestation, draining swamps and building settlements.

The first immigrants who came to Palestine between the 1890s and the 1920s purchased the cheapest land they could afford – the marshy lands in the valleys. Their first task was to prepare this land so it could be cultivated. So, they drained the swamps and used the land for agriculture. After a while, these acts became an integral part of the ideology of building the country.[131]

Draining the swamps was a vital objective, its necessity not to be questioned or doubted. It was considered as one of the acts to complete the redemption of the land, the first one being its purchase from non-Jewish hands.[132]

So, in Israel, the Zionist movement became *"an assault on a desolate wilderness, a conquest of the desert, an attempt to make the desert bloom. The latter meant the abolition of the emptiness, of nothingness."*[133]

> ...the ethos of development, of conquering nature, of transforming the wilderness into a fruitful soil, which was an ideal and an aspiration, became the dominant ideology of the Jews in Israel from the 1910s until the present time. This attitude, and the policy of 'immigrant absorption', of supplying jobs to the immigrants who were unemployed... all brought about the ethos that development was of necessity one of the cornerstones of any government's policy. It even became an official ideology, reflected in posters, propaganda and programs of education, by which it was also promoted.[134]

The Zionist movement viewed agricultural settlement as an instrument for realizing the Zionist aspirations. Therefore, rural life and agricultural occupation constituted a central national narrative.[135] This narrative created a distinction between urban and rural sectors. In most cases, the rural sector was identified with cooperative and communal settlements such as Kibbutzim and Moshavim (cooperative farms), based on collectivism. That way of life placed the nation, i.e., the collective not the individual, at the centre of the discourse and the individual was required, even expected, to advance the collective or national interests at the expense of one's own for that purpose.

Hence, in the years after the new state's establishment, the Israeli society was a mobilized one; meaning that the public embraced the worldviews of the elite that had complete hegemony over the country. The perception was that the governing elite took care of the people and every decision was made in the interest of all. Public opinion accepted the elite hegemony unquestionably. The democratic process consisted of free elections of the people's representatives and the decisions of those representatives were accepted by all, in every aspect.[136]

In Kellerman's words: "…most of the population agreed, freely or otherwise, with the national emphasis on rurality and cooperativeness that was put forward by the ruling establishment."[137]

It was in this atmosphere that the Huleh project was embraced by almost all (with a few exceptions - as it will be discussed further on) without any questions, doubts, objections or adversarial comments.

The draining of the Huleh swamp represented the embodiment of the Zionist effort to change nature and conquer it by transforming it into something that can be used and benefitted from. It was considered the chief wonder of the Zionist project.[138]

David Ben-Gurion, the first Prime Minister of the new State of Israel, was personally responsible for pushing forward the project.[139] The acclaimed goals of the project, the justifications presented to the public, the rhetoric around it and the framing will be discussed in other chapters of this work. But beyond them were ideological and political motives, stronger than the technical aspects of the issue.

The ethos of development and the emphasis on agriculture, as detailed above, were the ideological basis of the effort to drain the Huleh swamp. Possibly, an additional incentive existed for the strong wish of the Israelis to implement the Huleh drainage project and that was to control and have sole use of the Jordan River waters. The problem of water was and remains a major one in the Middle East and the Huleh project was not the only fight over this issue.

Though no official documentation claiming that statement was found in the Israeli archives, some private manuscripts and foreign articles imply as much.[140]

> … Israel used legalistic tactics to implement a carefully planned policy whose quintessence was the imposition of Israeli sovereignty over the DMZ. The strategy behind this policy was to drain the Lake Huleh marshes, win exclusive control of the Sea of Galilee, and complete Israel's Natural Water Carrier, a project whose aim was to divert water from the Jordan River to the northern part of the Negev desert to the south.[141]

Draining swamps, as afforestation and building new settlements, was imbedded in the Zionist conscience and in the public mentality so deeply that no questions arose about the real necessity of the Huleh drainage or any other deficiencies or damages the project could cause.

Politically more reasons existed to implement the project than to question it. The Huleh Lake and swamps were located on the border between Israel and Syria. Part of the Huleh valley was in the Demilitarized Zone, as established by the Armistice Agreement.

Settling the frontier zone with Jewish settlements and specially in an unclear status area like the Demilitarized Zone, developing agriculture in this area, were acts meant to enforce the Israeli presence on the frontier and emphasis the Israeli sovereignty in this zone. That subject will be further developed in the chapter about frontier considerations (the Israel-Syria conflict) regarding the Huleh drainage.

The most important and dominant factor in forwarding the Huleh drainage was the government itself. The first deliberation on that subject occurred in the government session on the 29 March 1950 when the topics discussed were the Huleh concession, the urgency of the project and the causes for its delay.

The project was considered essential to immigrants' integration in the new land and the potential it offered them to make a living. Ben-Gurion informed the session's participants of the rumor that numerous immigrants were expected from Romania, Hungary and Iraq. The Huleh drained area could afford a place for new settlements and work for many of those newcomers.[142]

The second decisive factor in the Huleh drainage implementation was the Jewish National Fund (JNF). It was a dominant and active institution before the state's establishment. Its main role was to acquire as much land as possible for Jewish ownership and to raise money from donations and any other sources to that purpose. But after 1948, when Israel became an independent state and almost all the land – about 95% – was nationalized and in the government's hands, the question arose whether there was still need for organizations such as the JNF whose main role had been the acquisition of land. This question became even more relevant when the Basic Land Law of 1960 was enacted, creating the Israel Land Authority which was given the task of managing and administrating the state and the JNF land, as well as absentee owners' property.[143] The JNF became unsure of its future and its role in the new state. It was even unsure of government support.

In a session of the JNF Board of Directors, one of the participants said:

> In my conversation with The Prime Minister, he talked with great sincerity and raised the question of the JNF's future, mentioning its intense activity in settling the land and building the country. But the government treats the JFN as a stepdaughter and the general tendency among the government's members is to ignore the JNF activities.[144]

The JNF felt it had to fight for its survival. In its book – "Kama" – A. Granot expresses these feelings explicitly:

> After the state establishment, much confusion prevails in the Zionist movement regarding the role of the Zionist Labor Organization (HaHistadrut HaTziyonit) in general and particularly – the place of the Jewish Fund in the Zionist activity. The claim is no secret: is there any necessity

> or even any demand to acquire land for money when the
> Israeli government is in the possession of lands available
> for settlement...
>
> ... until two years ago, the tendency in the Zionist circles
> was to transform those thoughts into reality; and the practical
> conclusion was the requirement to abolish the JNF, or at least,
> to merge it with Keren HaYesod into one Zionist fund.[145]

The 23rd Zionist Congress defined additional roles for the JNF, roles according to the ideology and the spirit of the times. It was not enough to acquire land, it was no less important and necessary to treat and prepare this land for cultivation. As mentioned above, the preparation of the land included afforestation, swamp drainage, and rock removal.

The JNF made afforestation and swamp drainage its most important activities in the new state. It received the blessings of the Zionist Congress for these activities.

> The roles of the Fund (JNF), approved by the congress
> authorization are now, in addition to acquisition of the land "in
> any form and in any way", preparation of the soil, afforestation
> and other developing activities. Land redemption is not
> completed unless it is accompanied by freeing the land from the
> desolation chains. To this purpose a forceful battle is required
> against the curse of the land, an inheritance of generations
> of neglect and a wrong and deficient way of cultivation. The
> first and most important part of this battle is improvement of
> the unfitted soils for agriculture ... The soil improvement is
> executed by a few ways: drying the swamps, drainage of the soil
> and removal of excess groundwater that impedes cultivation.[146]

In accord with the Zionist Congress decisions, the JNF kept acquiring every piece of land available, but also started to treat and prepare it for cultivation:

But only acquiring the land is not enough. Every Zionist knows that the land of Eretz Israel is not all good soil. In fact, most of it is poor quality soil, not fit for agriculture.

In preparing the land and generating the soil, JNF fulfills the Zionist movement's mission...[147]

Frontier Considerations

Even if the primary motive of the government to advance the Huleh drainage was embedded in the Zionist ideology (the bond to the land, swamp drainage and land cultivation), there were additional incentives to the project. The valley was situated on the border with Syria, so it was a frontier area. The Zionists had strong convictions about frontier zones. The perception was that settlements and Israeli activity – like cultivating the land – in these zones were most important for security and political reasons: to emphasize Israeli sovereignty and to create facts on the ground in the disputed areas.

As Avraham Granot, a leading Israeli policy-maker regarding land issues, put it:

> The settling of the mountain is necessary for economic and security reasons. It is situated on the frontier and borders with Lebanon, Syria and the Jordan State.[148]
> We tend to purchase most of the land in the Huleh region. … From a political point of view, these lands are important because they border on three sides with other countries.[149]

The mindset of the Zionist movement toward the frontier settlements and their role and importance for the state was expressed by the first Prime minister and Minister of Defense of Israel in the following statement:

> Most of the conquered areas are unsettled and vacant and our borders are long and outstretched. Solely the army cannot watch over them. We have to build a line of frontier settlements

> along the border with Lebanon, Syria and the triangle … These
> settlements are a basic condition for the state's safety.[150]

During and after the War of Independence, David Ben-Gurion introduced the concept that frontier settlements (along the borders) were necessary not only in order to keep stronghold over the Israeli peripheral zones, but also as a reinforcement of the defense system of the country. The frontier settlements became an integral part of the military network and of the defense infrastructure. Their role was to fill in for the non-ability of the army to place regular solders along the borders permanently. Therefore, in the fifties and even later on, the army had a planning office working in coordination with the other Israeli settlement authorities: the Jewish Agency, the (civil) Planning Office, JNF, the settlement movements. The army was involved in defining the location of the settlements and their space deployment, their size and boundaries, the land for cultivation and other allocated means so that every settlement could be self-sufficient. The army was involved also in the choice of the founder core members of each frontier settlement and its decision was that those members will be young and experienced in cultivating the land. The Army equipped them with arms and transmission equipment and prepared them to protect the settlement from enemy attacks. In fact, the frontier settlements were part of the defense system as much as part of the civilian life of the country.[151]

The decision to start the implementation of the Huleh drainage project was taken at the beginning of 1951, by the Ministries of Foreign Affairs and Defense, only after serious considerations of the project consequences regarding military and defense aspects. The Prime Minister himself was involved in the matter. The discussion was sparked by the proximity of the project to the Syrian border and the fact that part of the work had to be done in the demilitarized zone. The Ministry of Foreign Affairs considered the project so important that it justified the risk of a conflict with Syria in the framework of the Armistice.[152]

From the military point of view, the Army regarded the project as an opportunity for Israel to affirm its sovereignty on disputed territories. This reason, in the Army's opinion, was more important than any economic or agricultural one.

In the Armistice Commission, Israel was represented by Army members. They claimed that the Huleh concession was obtained before the War of Independence, so that any work done on its territory could not be considered a violation of the Armistice Agreement.[153]

In any case, the Huleh drainage project gave birth to a series of frictions that developed in a conflict, diplomatic and on occasions even military, between Israel and Syria.

The Syrians saw themselves as involved in the Huleh drainage project long before Israel. In June 1914, the Imperial Ottoman government granted a concession to two Arab merchants – Muhammad Omar Bayhum and Michel Sursock – for the drainage of the land in the Huleh area. The two merchants formed the Syro-Ottoman Agricultural Company Ltd. in order to implement the terms of the concession. The Company was Syrian; nevertheless, its seat was in Beirut and it was registered as a foreign company in Palestine as of the 27th of May. On 3 October 1934, the Syro-Ottoman Agricultural Company Ltd. transferred the concession to the Palestine Land Development Co. Ltd.[154]

During the time the Huleh concession was in the Syrian company's hands, the two merchants failed to comply with the Ottoman requirements to drain the swamps and develop the land. But the idea of the drainage was a known fact, it was discussed in various circles and no opposition to it was expressed by any party at that time. Thus, when preliminary works for the drainage began in 1950, like the Jordan dam repairs and land surveying on both sides of the

Jordan, they were made with the full knowledge and help of the United Nations forces and also with the approval of the local Syrian commandant who ordered his forces not to interfere with the drainage works. So, in the period between July 1949 and February 1951 no animosity [around the subject of the drainage works] developed between Syria and Israel in that region.[155]

Nevertheless, frictions began soon enough between the two parties. The official explanation given for the conflict was the 1949 Armistice Agreement and the problems that arose from some of its terms. As early as 1949, within the framework of negotiating the armistice agreement, Israel and Syria disputed the borderline in the Huleh region. Israel tried to make the British-French agreed upon Syrian-Palestine border from 1922 the new border between them. Syria refused and demanded that the truce lines be used instead, in view of the fact that several small areas in Palestine were under Syrian occupation. As a compromise, these areas, in addition to two other small areas of Palestine territory under Israeli occupation, were made into a demilitarized zone (DZ), *"pending final territorial settlement between the parties"*. The DZ meant that the armed forces of both parties were not allowed to enter and no military actions of any kind and size will take place.[156]

The Huleh bordered the Middle DZ situated between the Sea of Galilee and the Huleh Lake. It included the narrow strip between the Jordan River and the international border and also small areas west of the Jordan River. South of the Huleh Lake, the DZ became larger, into a triangle shape. This DZ included 4 Palestinian villages: Al-Didara, Kirad-Al-Baqqara, Al-Batiha and Arab-Al-Smalna and one Israeli settlement: Mishmar Hayarden. Two additional Palestinian villages – Kirad-Al-Ghannama and Yarda were adjacent to the DZ border and were considered part of it.

In conclusion, three DZs were designated in the agreement (see Figure 6 on the next page).

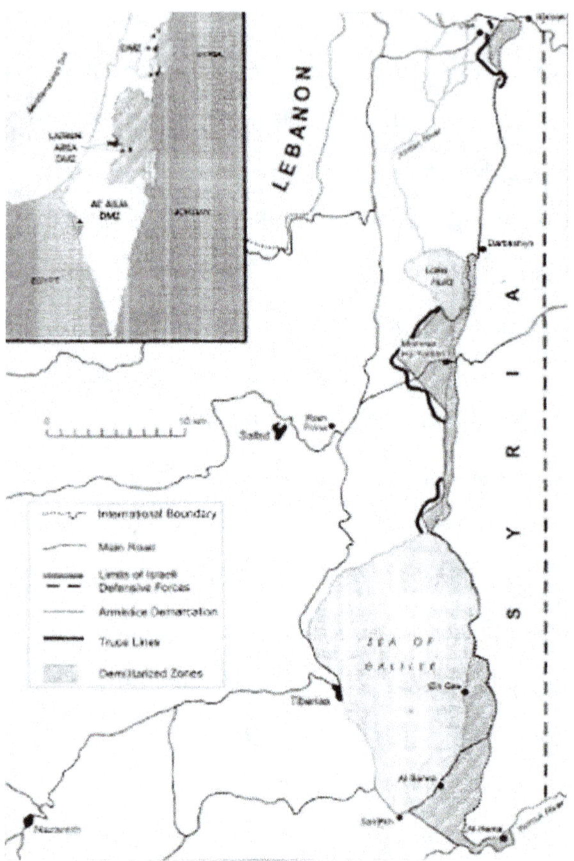

FIGURE 6 - Locational Map of the Demilitarized Zone in Northern Palestine According to the 1949 Israeli-Syrian Armistice Agreement

Source: Ghazi-Walid Falah, *War, Peace and Land Seizure in Palestine Border Area,* Third World Quarterly © Third World Quarterly, Vol. 25, No. 5, 2004, reprinted by permission of Taylor and Francis Ltd., www.tandfonline.com on behalf of The Third World Quarterly.

The General Armistice Agreement (GAA) also stipulated:

◆ The Mixed Armistice Commission (MAC) was responsible for the agreement.

◆ Normal civilian life in the area was to be restored.

◆ The agreement was not to prejudice in any way the final rights of either party in the final settlement, the agreement being only of military and not political considerations.

◆ No military forces of either party were allowed to enter the DZ.

The DZ was from the first a hotbed of friction and tension between Israel and Syria. Sovereignty over the DZ remained an unsolved issue, pending a final agreement between the two states but meanwhile, the three areas were the focus of border tensions between Syria and Israel.[157]

The differences between the parties were centered on a few key issues: the legal status of the Zone, the drainage of the Huleh Lake and the Israelis agricultural work in the Zone.

As noted before, many of the tensions that developed in the DZ were based on the parties' differing interpretations of the GAA.

Israel claimed that the agreement dealt with military issues only and did not refer in any way to political and legal matters. Israel felt completely sovereign in the zone regarding civilian matters, with the understanding that it did not have to ask Syrian permission for any civil activity intended to be undertaken there. The only acceptable restriction was the prohibition against bringing military forces into the DZ.

On the other hand, Syria maintained that neither it nor Israel had sovereignty over the DZ and that the Security Council had to enforce the armistice in the zone. In Syria's views, the MAC had the authority to interpret and allow or interdict certain activities in the DZ. Neither party was to be allowed to take any unilateral action in the zone, like the drainage or other projects, even if said project did not include police or military forces or indeed, any kind of military action. Syria felt it was to be consulted on all significant activities in the zone and any development was not to be implemented without her permission.

The views of the responsible UN officials on the status of the DZ were different than most of the Israeli ones and similar to most, but not all, of the Syrian positions.

Regarding the drainage of the Huleh swamp, the UN officials held that Israel should have requested permission of the MAC Chairman for the project.

They disagreed with the Syrian view that its consent was also required and that the project contradicted the GAA because it would alter the military status quo in the DZ.[158]

The first Syrian opposition was raised on the 5 January 1951, when the Syrian delegation addressed the Chief of Staff of the MAC with the request to open the dam on the Jordan River (built and in use from 1933) to avoid flooding the local Arab lands in the DZ, around Ayn-Tyna and Sayde and to ensure compensations to Arab land owners that suffered damages because of the drainage works.

On 15 January 1951, Israel began excavation works on the west side of the Jordan, as part of the drainage project. On the 27th, the Syrians lodged a complaint to the MAC on the work carried out on Arab-owned land, by Israelis not living in the DZ. According to Syria, these works were a violation of the GAA, paragraph 5(2). The excavation works continued and on 4 February 1951, for the first time, the local Syrian Commandant threatened to open fire on the drainage workers. The Israeli answer was that the works were civilian, designed to restore civil life in the DZ to a normal status and if Syrian forces were to open fire on the drainage workers, Israel would return fire.[159] The drainage works continued on the west bank of the Jordan River without any Syrian interference, but was accompanied by many complaints as well as open opposition on the east bank.

The Israeli position was that it would not discuss the matter with the Armistice Commission because it was solely the responsibility of the Chief of Staff, General Riley, to decide on the issue of restoring civilian life to normal in the DZ. Israel also declared that it was willing to pay compensations to all individuals who would suffer any damage as a result of the drainage works.[160]

In the Armistice Commission meeting that took place on 21 February 1951, both sides agreed to address the issue to General Riley, to determine whether the drainage works in the Huleh area constituted a violation of the Armistice Agreement (paragraph 2). Though Riley's answer did not refer solely to the Huleh drainage question, it elaborated on the issue:

◆ Israel would have no military benefit from the drainage.

◆ The Huleh drainage is an essential project.

◆ The dam built at the Jordan outlet from the Huleh wetlands that causes floods on part of the DZ lands, impedes returning civil life to normal in this zone and so is in violation of paragraph 5 (2) of the Armistice Agreement (the dam was built in 1933 and was in use even before the conflict).

According to General Riley's view, *"any laws, regulations or ordinances in force prior to the GAA which affected any areas included in the DZ are null and void (in a revised wording 'are held in abeyance')."* Accordingly, the Huleh Concession of 1934 was not to be considered valid in the new circumstances. Therefore, the opinion of the United Nations Forces Chief of Staff was that the drainage works may continue only after an agreement is reached between the Israeli and Syrian delegations, and only then. Riley's conclusion was that the Palestinian Land Development Co. Ltd. is to be ordered immediately to stop work until an agreement is finalized.[161]

Israel contended that this ruling was, on principle, *ultra vires*, contrary to the practice of the past two years, and absurd in its consequences, putting the area and its inhabitants in a legal vacuum and creating *"an island of anarchy dedicated to the maintenance of a swamp".(S/2084, 10 April 1951).*

The Government of Israel explained its position in the following:

> Only two distinctions characterize the demilitarized zone from the rest of Israel territory; first, that no activities of a military character are permitted in the former, while no such restriction affects the latter; second, that in regard to the latter, the

Chairman of the Israel-Syrian Mixed Armistice Commission possesses the authority explicitly defined in article 5.

The "civilian nature" and non-military character of the work in what is admittedly "territory under Israel control" excludes not only any Syrian right of objection, but also any theory that this work is affected by the jurisdiction of organs or persons charged with the implementation of the Armistice Agreement.[162]

Israel was asked to stop the drainage work on private Arab lands, in the Demilitarized Zone, until the Commission meeting. A few days later, Israel began work on the east bank of the Jordan despite the protests of U.N. forces and the U.N.'s stated direction to work only on the west bank.[163]

On 25 February, the army commenced an operation code-named, "Two banks of the Jordan River." Its purpose was to ensure the safety of the workers on the eastern bank of the Jordan and to create facts on the ground in the DZ. The enemy was defined as the Syrian army and the Arabs living in Kirad-Al- Baqqara, Kirad-Al-Ghannama and the owners of the Churi grove.

More than any other, the Israeli voice most insistent that the drainage works will continue on the eastern bank was the Army, which saw it as a declaration of sovereignty on the DZ. That is, from the Army's point of view, the importance of the Israeli-Syrian conflict on the Huleh was not the drainage itself, the struggle over water resources or Israel's image abroad as a modern country, but rather, control of and sovereignty over the DZ.

Meanwhile, the Chief of Staff tried to reach an agreement between the Arab landowners and the Palestinian Land Development Co. Ltd. concerning the compensations to be paid.

On 15 March, Syrian forces penetrated the Demilitarized Zone and opened fire on the Israeli workers. Israel and U.N. representatives reached an agreement to stop work on the 16 March and resume on the 23rd, in the hope that during this cooling-off period, the Chief of Staff would come to terms with the landowners regarding the compensations to be paid to them. Unfortunately, this did not happen, mostly because of Syrian pressure on the landowners. Israel was required to continue waiting for the Chief of Staff's decision and not to resume the drainage work, despite the agreement permitting resumption of work on the 23rd. Israel saw this as a breach of the Armistice Agreement. Israel resumed the drainage work and for this, was treated as the violator of the Armistice Agreement.

Israel's position was: accept of the Chief of Staff's decision regarding the compensations, even without a formal agreement, but refuse to accept his decision regarding continuation of the drainage work. Syria's position was: cessation of any drainage works and requirement the commitment of both sides to accept the decisions of the Chief of Staff on the matter.

Syria, too, was interested in extending its control over at least part of the DZ. On 27 March, the drainage work resumed, south of the Churi property, on the west bank of the Jordan River. With it, the Syrian fire on the workers resumed as well.

At the same time, the DZ's Arabs began to flee to Bakara. Meanwhile, Israel and Syria continued firing at each other in the Demilitarized Zone and filing complaints against each other to the Security Council.

On 30 March, the Israeli government met to discuss the problem. Attending the meeting were the Prime Minister and representatives of the Army, the Ministry of Foreign Affairs and the Palestinian Land Development Co. Ltd. The Government embraced the Army's call to show sovereignty over the DZ but, at the same time, decided on a policy of avoidance of acts that could be interpreted as provocations toward the Syrians.

The decisions taken were as follows:

◆ To continue the drainage work.

◆ To avoid activity in the DZ that could be interpreted as aggressive, but to return fire if fired upon.

◆ To evacuate the DZ's Arabs.

◆ To ensure that armed Syrian forces will not penetrate the DZ.

On the night of 30 March, 800 Arabs from the DZ were evacuated. Meanwhile they themselves forwarded a letter to the Israeli Prime Minister, asking to be removed and permanently relocated.

On 1 April the U.N. representatives met with the Israeli Army Chief of Staff and explained that Israel's refusal to participate in the Armistice Agreement Committee's meetings were jeopardizing its existence and paralyzing the work of the U.N. forces.

Despite the Government decision to avoid provocations of the Syrians, on 4 April 1951, the army sent a military patrol, disguised as policemen, to Al-Hama, to supervise the area.[164] The Deputy Chief of Staff, Mordechai Maklef, was the only one to approve the mission. No government authority was involved in the decision to send the patrol to Al-Hama. The Syrian forces opened fire and killed six of the Israeli soldiers. The Minister of Foreign Affairs, Moshe Sharett, complained about the mission to the Prime Minister, contending that the incident would jeopardize the efforts to solve the conflict diplomatically at the Armistice Commission.[165] The Al-Hama incident became a turning point in the Syrian-Israeli conflict as it marked a change from the struggle over a drainage project to a struggle over sovereignty over the DZ. The Army's intention in mounting the Al-Hama mission was to demonstrate its absolute authority over the DZ area.[166] In that case the army intervened in a matter outside its military jurisdiction and made a decision in a political domain and acted upon it.

The issue of the sovereignty over the DZ caused some internal friction between various Israeli government agencies and the military. All sides wished for the same thing – Israeli sovereignty over these disputed areas – but differed on the ways and means to achieve that goal. The Army considered itself entitled to take decisions and act independently in the matter that otherwise would be entirely in the purview of the state – the Ministry of Defense and/ or the Ministry of Foreign Affairs. These Ministries argued that the Army had no right to interfere in state decisions and act on its own.

Minister of Foreign Affairs Sharett used the Security Council decisions as a pretext to initiate meetings with General Railey without the presence of Army representatives. By that method, he intended to retrieve for himself and to his Ministry the power to decide the course of action in the DZ. That behavior created frictions between him and Chief of Staff Yigal Yadin.[167]

At this juncture, it seemed that the Huleh drainage project embodied different goals for different people. For the Army, it was first and foremost a means to affirm Israel's sovereignty over the DZ. For the Ministry of Foreign Affairs, the project was a showcase to present Israel abroad as a modern, advanced country. For the Prime Minister and others in the government, it was the way to ensure more settlements, advance agricultural development and solve part of the struggle for water resources.[168] Israel agreed to participate in the Security Council meetings on the condition that the only subjects to be discussed in those meetings would focus solely on complaints of both sides relating to violations of the Armistice Agreement and would not, on any account, include claims concerning civilian issues in the Demilitarized Zone.[169]

There were two major issues in the Syria-Israel conflict concerning the Huleh project:

The way in which each side viewed the Demilitarized Zone. Israel's position was unambiguous: the DZ was extra-military, but was not extra-territorial; it was completely and definitely under Israel's sovereignty.[170]

The true problem surrounding the issue was the desire of each side to move the international borderline in the Demilitarized Zone to its advantage. Israel wanted to establish its sovereignty in this area and define the final borderline on the east bank of the Jordan River. Syria wanted to take advantage of the conflict around the Huleh work and push the borderline to the Jordan waterline.[171]

The Arab-owned land – some 28 dunams – that stood in the way of the drainage works, in the Demilitarized Zone.

Israel tried to solve the problem by means of compromise. It offered to buy, lease, exchange for other lands, or pay compensation for the privately-owned land that interfered with the project's progress. At some point, the Arab landowners would probably have agreed to come to terms with the Israeli offers, but the Syrians pressured them into refusing any deal.[172]

In order to affirm its sovereignty over the Demilitarized Zone and solve the problem of the private lands that impeded the progress of the drainage work, Israel decided to transfer the Arab families that owned those lands to other Israeli regions, outside the Zone.

In conclusion, it is clear that at least part of Israel's treatment of the local Arabs in the Demilitarized Zone had little to do with the problem itself and a lot to do with political interests, some of them completely unrelated to the Huleh drainage work.

B. The Trans-Israel Highway
The Trans-Israel Highway as a Neo-Liberal Project

The Trans-Israel highway was a very controversial infrastructure project. It represented the most neo-liberal, privatization-oriented activity of the government and as such, it raised strong reactions from both sides – supporters and opponents and everyone in between.

Neo-liberalism is an economic and political philosophy that emerged in the 20ᵗʰ century as a reaction to some of the economic turmoil earlier that century. Neo-liberalism is an ideological outgrowth of liberalism. It tends to minimize the role of the state and maximize the private business sector. It seeks to transfer control of the economy from the public to the private sector, under the assumption that it will produce a more efficient government and improve the economic stability of the nation. Neo-liberalism favors privatization over direct state activity; it considers economic profit the most important, even the decisive factor.

The rise of neo-liberalism influenced the Israeli polity as well, so that the Israeli society of the 1990s was characterized by the development of values consistent with neo-liberal tenets. Those values brought on significant changes in the political, economic, social and legal systems as reflected by the deregulation of markets, privatization and human rights legislation that took place in the middle of that decade.

Those neo-liberal values, which were promoted by the private sector in the industrial domain, opposed the collectivist Zionist-socialist ideologies that had dominated the early stages of the Histadrut's (The Federation of Jewish Labor) existence. Historically, the values of Jewish collectivism and the redemption of land through labor (Hebrew labor) formed the basis of the Zionist socialism that dominated Israeli politics from the founding of the state.

Nevertheless, in the 1990s, Israel underwent radical changes that gradually transformed it from a collectivist state with a mobilized Jewish society and centralized economy into a more individualist economy with a tendency to free markets. In Israel, as in other Western countries, the Keynasian economic regime was pushed aside and replaced with a free market-oriented economic system. Individualism, economic benefit, competitive markets and efficiency became the new ideology and the cultural norm.

The far-reaching privatization process that has been taking place in both the Histadrut and the public sectors caused profound changes in the Israeli economic structure. Considering the history of the State – the long tradition of Hebrew labor and collectivism as central Zionist values, the historic role of the Labor Movement and the Histadrut in the events leading to the founding of Israel – Israeli neo-liberalism seems fraught with contradictions.[173]

The process of privatization in Israel was accelerated by internal changes and by external, international developments as well. The internal events included socio-political changes, namely the rise of the Likud party to power in 1977, the financial crisis at the end of the 1980s including the bankruptcy of two large public companies – "Koor" and "Hasneh," and the 1985 financial plan for stabilization of the national economy.

The external developments that influenced the Israeli privatization included the international expansion of the neo-liberal ideology in the West as well as in Third World countries. Other influences were the collapse of the Communist bloc, demographic changes in the Western countries and the spreading of globalization all over the world.[174]

The process of privatization was very controversial and created quite a stir among supporters and opponents alike. The supporters of privatization claimed that the private sector is more efficient because it has to function in a free and competitive market. In order to survive in such an environment, it has to continuously strive to improve quality and cut costs. Public enterprises have no such incentive to improve efficiency. Also, by privatizing public services and infrastructure, the government can save on the investment they require from public funds.[175]

The claims of the privatization opponents were that the private sector has only one interest in mind - to maximize profits. If that means depriving the lower classes of support and welfare help, so be it. The private sector has no social responsibility toward the weaker segment of the population, their only responsibility and concern is toward the shareholders or owners of the company. If necessary, quality will be compromised, in order to keep profits up. It is essential to show immediate profit as the shareholders cannot wait for eventual profitability.[176] In its later phases, the process of privatization in Israel became oligarchic when, in addition to increasing control by the wealthy over economic and social life, their involvement and interest in politics intensified.[177]

For opponents of privatization, public infrastructure privatization is especially problematic. In their view, it means renunciation by the government and the people of the right and the means to initiate and to make changes in the public system if need arises. And that is in conflict with the basis of democracy.[178]

The problems are especially evident concerning the privatization of transport infrastructure. The transport system is a mass network that requires an overall look. Privatization of segments of the system impedes the coordination between those parts and reduces the efficiency and the safety of the system as a whole. Also, the transport infrastructure is not profitable. In order to make it attractive to the private sector, (i.e., profitable) the government must add special bonuses to the franchisee – low purchase price, guaranteed profit, some cost-sharing, etc., as will be detailed further on, regarding the Trans-Israel Highway.[179]

Proponents of the Trans-Israel Highway project were mainly the government representatives and the interested parties that were going to benefit from the highway – financial profits from the toll fees, real estate value increasing, and so forth. The opponents were more diversified and included politicians, parliament members of different parties, some political parties from the opposition (the only thing they agreed about), artists, academics and intellectuals, some celebrities and, of course, many ordinary citizens. But first and foremost, the "green" organizations opposed the Trans-Israel Highway because they considered it an environmental and social catastrophe.

The opposition to the Trans-Israel Highway may have been vocal on the environmental issue but, in fact, it included a variety of quality-of-life elements.

Their claim was that the project was controversial; the decision to implement the project was taken in the absence of a national transport master plan. Yet, the highway was executed despite strong protests by different organizations, which felt that not enough preliminary planning and environmental studies were performed and not all necessary economic calculations were executed to verify the road economic viability.[180]

The proponents' claims also touched on a variety of issues. Based on the neo-liberal ideology of the times, they argued mostly about the economic and transport benefits of the project.

The Economic Aspect – in comparison with other developed countries, Israel was much behind in the transport domain. The political changes of 1977 led to the installation of a government that reduced considerably the investment in transport means, and caused a serious decline of the public transport.

In the Rabin-led social democrat party era that followed, large investments in infrastructure in general, and in the roads system in particular, were made in an effort to improve matters, reduce gaps and improve public transport. Despite all that was done, the congestion on the roads remained one of the highest in the world. The Public Works Department (MAA''TZ) prepared a feasibility study for the highway and determined that a road system including the Trans-Israel Highway would result in significant reductions in travel time and in automobile operation costs. That study showed the economic viability of the road.[181] In the opinion of Nehemia Strassler, the financial editor of *Haaretz*, there was a direct connection between the Trans-Israel road and economic growth, employment and welfare.[182]

The Transport Aspect – supporters of the project claimed that a number of benefits regarding the transport would be gained from it. First, it would encourage transport infrastructure development.[183] In comparison with other developed countries of the Western world, Israel had the highest congestion on its roads and the lowest number of private cars per 1000 population. But the number of cars was constantly going up, as a result of population growth from natural causes, massive immigration from former USSR and the rising of the standard of living.[184]

Second, Route No. 6 would ease traffic congestion in the densely-populated center (Gush Dan). The road was designed to detour away from the country center on the east side and permitting travelers from Jerusalem to Haifa or from Be'er-Sheva to Netanya, to reach their destination without passing through Gush Dan. That would decrease the Gush Dan (country center) traffic by 15%, a significant decrease for traffic congestion and travel time. The Israeli Planning and Research Institute for Transport, in a report from 1998, concluded that without Route 6, the road system would collapse. It claimed that the Trans-Israel Highway was indispensable and had to be implemented, along with the development of the rail system. The report noted some reservations regarding the road; nevertheless it found that the benefits (such as the connection of the country's South to the North, and the addition of eastern accesses to the Metropolis of Tel-Aviv) were convincing.[185] The access traffic to the highway will connect by interchanges without traffic lights, limiting congestion at the on-ramps to Route 6.[186]

Third, the transport service level of the road system would be significantly improved. At present, that service level is lower than in other Western countries, lower even than Holland and Belgium, countries with small surface areas, like Israel. The number of vehicles increases at a faster rate than the increase in roads so that the service level of the road system worsens with time. The heavy traffic and the associated congestion impacted negatively on the economy, including hundreds of thousands of working hours wasted in traffic jams, a drastic increase in car expenses (fuel, repairs), increase in air pollution from extended periods of emissions because of longer travel times, and undesirable changes in land use caused by heavy traffic-associated inaccessibility to some areas.

In Strassler's words:

> There is no argument that Israel's transport infrastructure is very much behind. Road-Kilometer wise, we are at the lowest level compared to Europe, half of Portugal. The congestion on the roads is one of the highest in the world; the number of working hours wasted in traffic jams is huge and so is the number of traffic accidents that occur because of the lousy infrastructure.[187]

All the above made the implementation of Route 6 plans a necessity.

According to the Cross-Israel Highway Company and the Derech Eretz Consortium, the implementation of the project would also help develop the public transport system.

> It (Route 6) will enable quick and easy connection to the mass transportation system, because of the possibility to build on the interchanges areas train stations, where drivers will be able to park their cars and continue their way by train, which will function in parallel with the Trans Israel Highway.[188]

The Trans-Israel Highway prompted much resistance that encompassed the various sectors of the population, including politicians – some of them in public office, intellectuals and "white collar" professionals – including experts in that field, such as engineers and urban planners, "green" organizations and ordinary citizens.

The opponents of the project raised concerns across the board and they countered the claims of the supporters point for point.

The Political Aspect

The development of the neo-liberal ideology in all aspects of daily life - Route 6 was considered by the opponents to represent much more than another road; it was a political statement about the way the country was going to continue its development; it symbolized the deep change in the development and the political economy ethos of Israel. After the State's establishment, the development of the roads system was an integral part of the Zionist project. The building of transport infrastructure was based on the ideology of modernization, conquest of the physical space by the Jewish population, settlement and sovereignty over the territory. In those years, the development of the transport system occurred under the socialist collectivist ethos. The roads system planned by Arieh Sharon in his Israel Master plan of 1950 was meant to assure accessibility for the periphery and the border settlements. The development of every infrastructure item was a new statement that the people, by its representatives and the national institutions, would be the ones to build the country.

In a sense, the Trans-Israel Highway was a contradiction to that ethos; it was a political statement about the way and means the country was going to continue its political and economic development.[189]

Political benefits unrelated to transport issues – The road project was used by politicians to achieve other goals, political benefits, totally unrelated to transport. For example, Shimon Peres aspired to create, by means of Route 6, a connection between Egypt and Syria, with Israel as the bridge in between, should a peace agreement and a "New Middle East" configurated. That was considered, by some, to be a colossal waste of resources for an event that might never occur.[190] Ariel Sharon, who at the beginning of the 1990s was the Minister of Housing, strove to reinforce the Jewish settlements on the other side of the "green line", by means of Route 6.[191]

The privatization tendency - Within the framework of the dominant global ideology of neo-liberalism, the tendency to privatize as much as possible, not only industrial plants and different kinds of businesses, but also national infrastructure, dovetailed nicely with the Trans-Israel Highway project.

Privatization started in Israel in the 1950s in the industrial domain, continued in the late 1970s with residential neighborhood construction and penetrated the municipal services in the 1980s. It reached its climax in the 1990s, with privatization of the most attractive item: national infrastructure. Route 6, as a toll highway and a BOT (Bid, Operate, Transfer) project, was the expression of that climax.[192]

The connection between wealth and political power - Many private and public factors were of the opinion that one of the main reasons for the stubborn support of the government in regard with the Trans-Israel Highway – that is, financial and procedural support – was an economic one; powerful corporations were to gain substantial profits from the highway construction and those corporations held great wealth and were in a position of putting remarkable pressure on the government in order to obtain its support.

> Netanyahu and Baron found in it (the BOT system) a perfect fulfillment of their radical neo-liberal perceptions. By chance or perhaps not by chance, that system fit the interests of some of their close connections.[193]

The thesis that the main reason for the government support of the highway was to better with the interests of the wealthy was reinforced with time by some facts:

Although Route 6 was planned to stretch from the Galilee to the Negev, for a length of approximately 300 kilometer, the first segment to be constructed was in the center of that expanse, the 90 kilometer from Gedera-to-Hedera. That fact contradicted the government claim that the main reason for the construction of the highway was to bring the periphery closer and ease its accessibility to the center.

The division of roles between the two main players – the State-run "Cross-Israel Highway Company Ltd." and the private consortium "Derech Eretz" – was odd, if one considers first and foremost the public interest. The role of the state company was to negotiate with the owners of land that would need to be acquired for the highway. That is, cover the purchase, expropriation or compensation necessary to obtain the land, prepare the plans for the road and obtain the necessary statutory approvals. Those activities were paid for by the State; they were costly and not profitable.

The consortium "Derech Eretz" received a strip of land "clean" of any complications in addition to the final and statutory approved plans of the road. All it had to do was to construct the highway and charge the travel fees. Who were the components of the big corporation "Derech Eretz"? One of them was the Ted Harrison Group, which controlled "Shikun Ovdim", "Shikun U'Pituah", "Solel Boneh", the "Even V'Sid" quarries, etc. - in other words, one of the biggest construction and infrastructure corporations in Israel. Another partner was "Africa Israel Investments Ltd.", a huge real estate company, which specialized in money generating real estate – construction and marketing of shopping malls, industrial zones, offices buildings, medical centers and residential neighborhoods.

Thus, it was obvious why "Derech Eretz" began the highway construction with the Gedera-to-Hedera segment, that being the most commercially attractive and money-generating segment of the project, and postponed to an undefined latter date the peripheral segments.[194]

Intensive, money-generating real estate development along the central segment of the highway occurred almost before the highway construction was completed. The "Derech Eretz" consortium itself initiated, from the first beginning, real estate development along the road – including a huge industrial zone of some half-million square meters at the Kassem junction, the "Global Village" near the Ben-Gurion Airport.

It seemed that, although the highway was presented to the public as a national transport solution for the Israeli traffic problems, its main reason for being laid in the real estate development benefits it would bring to some wealthy and powerful corporations. It was not clear how much benefit would be achieved for the nation's transport infrastructure, but it was evident that other benefits would flow to several large companies – the companies that stood to build the highway and collect the toll fees, the ones that will develop the land on either side of the highway and transform those areas into lucrative real estate and so on.[195]

> The link between wealth and political power and the influence of the wealthy on the government representatives is obvious and evident...[196]
>
> A lot of people will get rich: real estate sharks, bankers and businessmen, civil engineers, contractors and others...[197]

The Economic Aspect

Almost all of economic underpinnings regarding the Trans-Israel Highway were criticized and disapproved by those opposed to its construction.

The economic viability of the project - Feasibility studies conducted on the project did not prove its cost-effectiveness. Professionals and experts in the field disagreed about that subject. They even disagreed about the transport models used in the aforementioned studies. Some of the criticism was directed towards the basic assumptions of the studies and suggested that the traffic forecasts were implausible; that the investment in lateral connecting roads and the damages to the tourism industry and to other fields, because of the highway, were not taken into consideration, and so on. The argument went that if the project would have been shown to be cost effective beyond any doubt, the government would not have given financial guarantees to the franchise company.[198]

The opponents also claimed that it was not possible to refund the investment, cover the maintenance and also make a profit from the Trans-Israel Highway, under the conditions established for the project. The research prepared by the Cross-Israel Highway Company, which included the analysis and the study of similar cases in other Western countries and from professional literature, showed that the tolls on roads of the same order of magnitude were never able to cover the full amount of investment and maintenance the roads required.[199]

Urban and regional development in undesirable sites and directions - With Israel being a country small in area, the land development trend was towards dense urban settlements, high buildings and intensive use of public transport. The chances were high that the Trans-Israel Highway would influence urban development in entirely different, undesirable directions, such as industrial zones and commercial centers along the route's highway instead of the city centers; additional development of the country's central region instead of the Galilee and the Negev; promotion of suburban sprawl. Those damages were not taken in account when the economic viability of the project was analyzed.[200]

Escalation of private cars use and slowdown of public transport development - The opponents of the highway maintained that Route 6 would encourage the use of private cars among those who can afford to pay for gas and maintenance on a regular basis; for these people accessibility to the country's central region will be much easier. But the low-income population, who will not be able to use private cars for day-to-day transport, will not benefit from the new highway.

The government would have no incentive to invest in public transport development. Public transport will be in competition with Route 6 which, if not profitable, will result in the government being required to pay the "Derech Eretz" consortium the financial guarantee according to the contract terms.[201]

Public transport development is crucial to the economy development due to its efficiency in land use and due to its accessibility to all segments of the population.[202]

Also, the financial guarantee to "Derech Eretz" to which the government committed itself, created a conflict of interests between the private consortium and the government on one side and the public on the other side. The consortium would have no interest in decreasing the toll fees of the highway in order to encourage more people to use the road; their profit was guaranteed by the contract terms. For its part, the government would not be interested in developing the public transport, for reasons as explained above.

The public at-large, on the other hand, needs a public transport system well-developed, convenient and financially accessible to all.[203]

The Trans-Israel Highway, as planned, would be expected to cause sprawling of the suburbs, increases in air and water pollution, the wasting of valuable and scarce land, and increases in gas demand and importation of that resource. All of these would negatively affect the Israeli economy.[204]

The more roads that are constructed, the more the vehicle fleet on those roads increases, making more roads necessary – that is, a never-ending, vicious circle.[205]

A burden on the State budget and on public funds - The government maintained that the Trans-Israel Highway would not be a burden on the public funds due to the fact that the entrepreneur consortium would finance its construction. So the public was presented with the assurances that the highway would be a perfect solution for the extant traffic problems and would, at the same time, save public money. The opponents, of course, claimed that all the above was simply not true.

Even before the highway construction began, hundreds of millions of shekels were spent by the government on items connected with the highway that were included in the State's part of the agreement: compensations for land expropriation, lateral connecting roads to the highway and their interchanges, relocation of existing infrastructure, planning and statutory approvals and the financing of the state company "Cross-Israel Highway". Furthermore, the government was under obligation to cover the losses of the franchisee, "Derech Eretz", if the highway turned out to be unprofitable.[206]

No solution for the unemployment problem - The claim by the government that the highway, being a national large-scale project, would help solve at least part of the unemployment problem, was disingenuous. The work on the highway construction was temporary, and based on past experience; the workers employed for that kind of labor were foreigners.[207]

If public transport was to be developed, in contrast, it would provide a significant and permanent pool of jobs for many workers in associated professions.[208]

The Transport Aspect

The highway cannot solve the traffic problems - The Trans-Israel Highway, as a national, large-scale infrastructure project, was first and foremost built as a transport project. Its initial objectives, as declared and presented to the public by the government, were to enhance Israel's transport system by way of enlarging and developing the roads network and relieving the traffic congestion on existing roads. The opponents to the project attacked those declared objectives, by claiming that the construction of a new road, even a multi-lane, fast highway and extending it to almost the whole length of the country, would not solve the traffic problems in Israel. It would, instead, contribute to suburban sprawl, increasing of the gap between rich and poor, undesirable regional development, significant environmental damages, and so forth.

Israel had no experience with a comprehensive transport solution and especially not with commuting on a daily basis. The Israeli approach had heretofore been expressed by the equation: transport = roads (private vehicles), rather than transport = a mix of solutions – private vehicles, trains (long distance, trams and subways), buses, maritime and air transport and bicycles.[209]

In the 1970s, the attitude toward transport mechanisms changed in Western Europe. The Western European countries came to the realization that adding more roads would only increase the number of vehicle and will not ease traffic jams. So they *decreased* the pace of road system development, even stopping it entirely in some cases. Instead, they developed a different approach: the promotion of public transport by developing the mass transportation system and synchronizing its different components.

The main reason for this change was the belief that the rate of road development will never catch up to the rate of growth in vehicle number. Moreover, development of the road system will lead to an increase in the number of private cars, boosting their use and amplifying the traffic. The European experience suggested that there were three reasons against excessive road system development:

- ◆ Roads are a boost to suburban sprawl – highways and interchanges are magnets for residential subdivisions and industrial zone development. Residing in suburbs requires private car ownership and usage because there is no economic viability in public transport development for small residential developments.

- ◆ The bottleneck effect – the number of entrances to a big city is a constant (Tel-Aviv has 21 entrances), and the number of cars that can enter the city, per time, must also be constant. By constructing more roads to the city (i.e., to the same 21 entrances), we can "widen the bottle" but not "the neck", so that the traffic jams will still be there.[210]

◆ The illusion of a quick, easy accessibility – a new, fast highway attracts more traffic to it. In Israel, this fact is questionable but in countries where there is competition between the roads system and the rail, this fact is an accepted truth.[211]

A good example and an extreme case for the equation "more roads - more jams" is the city of Los Angeles. It is the most paved city in the U.S. in length of road per capita, and the highest rate of cars per capita – more than 1,000 cars for every 1,000 inhabitants and the most jammed in the U.S.[212]

The Trans-Israel Highway will prevent, or at least delay public transport development. The construction of the Trans-Israel Highway will prevent, or at least delay for a long time, the development of the mass transportation system. That, for different reasons, among them, the more important being:

◆ The government will have no incentive to develop public transport, so as not to create competition to Route 6. Intensive use of the highway will save the government payment for revenues to the "Derech Eretz" consortium, so the lesser the competition, the better for the government budget.

◆ The government budget for transport will be low because of the high investment in all items connected with Route 6 that were financed by public funds, such as lateral connecting roads, interchanges, land expropriation compensations, planning and statutory approval, etc.[213]

The public funds allocated for Route 6 did not leave room for public transport development, especially for the Israel Railway, which is much more efficient and necessary than the Highway.[214] For that reason, there were not enough public funds left for the creation of a subway authority and the budget allocated to Israel Railways was a tenth of what the Railway management asked for.[215]

The real solution for the Israeli traffic problems lies in a comprehensive and synchronized development of mass transportation system, including: upgrading of existing roads and interchanges, construction of a suburb rail system, construction of subways in the large cities, creation of public transport routes, etc.

Instead of all that, the only solution, which is not a solution at all, offered by the government was the construction of the Trans-Israel Highway. The fact that only public transport, and not additional roads and highways, can ever ease traffic congestion has been a known and accepted fact, for some time, in other Western countries.[216]

The development of a comprehensive public transport system will have not only traffic advantages, but also significant environmental, social and economic ones.[217]

The main objectives of the Trans-Israel are to connect the Galilee with the Negev and to create a 'belt' around the center (Gush Dan). Those objectives are contradictory – the development of transverse roads with interchanges and intersections, usually east-west, will make the traffic north-south more difficult and will create an unnecessary criss-cross roads system in the country center.[218]

Most experts in the field of transport, in Israel and in the Western world, are of the opinion that more roads will not solve traffic problems and that the real solution lies in the development of public transport systems.[219]

> Hashimshoni (the Head of the Israel Institute for Transport Planning and Research) is of the opinion that the Trans-Israel is important as a metropolitan transport axis, but as opposed to the Cross-Israel Company people, he is convinced that the highway's advantages depend on the development of the public transport. According to him, it is necessary to create a rail system, such as the one that functions today between Ashdod and Rehovoth to Tel-Aviv, to intensify

significantly the trains' traffic and to equip them with more modern engines. "If we construct Route 6 without developing the rail transport, the future development will be impeded." says Hashimshoni, "because it will not be possible to keep free the area surrounding the Trans-Israel Highway. Even if the planners will try to keep it free, the planning institutions in Israel, being under political pressure, and mayors and Heads of Local and Regional Councils, will push for development and construction." The efficiency of the rail transport depends on centralized development of residential and industrial areas so that rail passengers, leaving the train station, can reach easily their destination and not on sprawling of the construction, which will decrease the mobility potential of the rail passengers. Meanwhile, there are no budgets for the rail transport but big funds are allocated not only for the construction of the Trans-Israel Highway but also for the operation of the toll road on the central section of the Trans-Israel.[220]

The Social Aspect

The periphery will not be brought closer to the center - Contrary to the claims of the government that were presented as one of the main motivations for the promotion of the project, the expressway will not help the periphery, nor the low-income class that lives there. The periphery will not be brought closer to the country's center.

Entrepreneurs will not invest in enterprises located in peripheral areas, solely due to their location along the new highway. The easy access to be created by the highway for the Galilee and the Negev to Gush Dan will be solely to the advantage of private car owners, specifically those able to afford the expenses (gas, maintenance, toll fees) associated with daily travel by private car. Low-income residents of peripheral areas will not have the resources to do this and, hence, with derive no benefit from the Trans-Israel.[221]

The fact that the first section of the highway scheduled for construction was the segment between Gedera and Hedera, was a central objection of project opponents and the basis for many protests.

That fact alone contradicted the government claim that a principle objective of the Trans-Israel was to help the peripheral areas of the country. More and more, it appeared that the main reason for the project was to create an outer ring road around Tel-Aviv in an effort to ease the traffic congestion in the central region.[222]

The opponents to the highway did not believe the other sections of the road would be built at all, suggesting that the Galilee and the Negev were never going to benefit at all from the new highway.[223]

The development of employment resources will continue in central Israel and not in the peripheral regions of the country - With uncertain probability for success, entrepreneurs will not be enticed into taking the risks associated with new investments in peripheral areas, especially when more attractive opportunities will arise in more accessible central Israel locations alongside the new highway. Even before construction began, plans for use of land along the central section were being prepared and pressures exerted to release those lands for commercial use. Again, no help for the country's periphery. On the contrary – it will increase the gap between it and the center.[224]

The Trans-Israel Highway was, in the eyes of many of its opponents a pivotal factor in the process of deepening the social gap between the wealthy and the poor. The argument was that the road will intensify suburban sprawl and, as a result, the use of private cars – characteristics of the wealthier classes.

As previously stated, one had but to look at the example of Los Angeles.[225]

Thus, Route 6 can be expected to help only those with private cars and the means to use it on a daily basis. The poor, the old, students, new immigrants, the Orthodox and other socio-economically weaker segments of the population – those who generally lack access to private cars – do not stand to benefit at all from the new expressway.[226]

The "Pretzel" phenomenon - Opponents of the project maintained that the Trans-Israel would intensify the vicious circle of suburban development which leads to deterioration of the inner-city and then results in greater suburban sprawl and so on. That phenomenon is known as "the pretzel effect" and is considered a negative influence on the social equilibrium of a country. Vis à vis Israel, it violates the averred government policy regarding population dispersal. Also, the urban sprawling along Route 6 would be expected to cause more and more rural settlements to morph into urban ones, at a time when more cities are not needed in Israel.[227]

For opponents to the project, one had only to look at the examples set by American cities:

> [A] worse catastrophe will be caused by the side effects of the highway. Many cities in U.S. are like a pretzel: the center deteriorates, is abandoned to crime and drugs and is emptied of population. The business development centralizes along the belt roads outside the cities and the suburbs sprawl further and further and cover whole regions of open land.[228]

Increase in travel by private cars and its impact on the social gap - The Trans-Israel will increase the use of the private car and dependence on those vehicles. That fact will have a major impact not only on transport but also, and more important, on the social equilibrium of the population. It will deepen the gap between the "haves" and the "have-nots". The dependence on the private car for day-to-day mobility promotes the provision of services that differ from those in city centers, construction of private houses which require large areas, less emphasis on public transport, none of which provide economic benefit for small peripheral communities.[229]

Conclusions

In the 1950s, Zionist ideology and its associated worldviews dominated the country. The objectives and the ways and means to achieve them were clear-cut and unequivocal. Mega-engineering national projects, such as the Huleh drainage, were a direct result of that ideology. Those projects were carried out in accordance with the accepted beliefs and vision, as expressed by the country's leaders.

Because draining swamps was considered a national goal and one of the activities necessary for nation-building, questions of technical problems, economic viability or national necessity did not arise, nor were they considered or examined. It was taken for granted that swamps were to be drained. It seemed that the goals were adjusted to the project and not the other way around.

The Israeli society was a mobilized one so the public accepted the leaders' decisions regarding state affairs and national projects almost without question.

In the first decade of the new millennium, as a result of internal and external changes, the Israeli society had come to differ substantially from what had existed in the era of the founding of the state.

The circa 1950s national ideology of collectivist socialist Zionism was replaced by the neo-liberal ideology with its most salient characteristics: privatization, reduction of state involvement in the economic life of the country and the promotion of private enterprise.

Mega-engineering national projects, and the Trans-Israel Highway is definitely one of them, reflect the changed worldview and ideology of the current leaders. It symbolizes the ideology of neo-liberalism with its tendency to privatization of even the most vital projects such as transport infrastructure.

Mega-engineering national projects, both in the 1950s as well as in the 2000s, reflect the spirit of their times and the prevailing ideologies and worldviews. That the ideology and worldviews underwent modification over those five decades is no surprise as it reflects the inevitable political, economic, and social changes that occur as a nation grows and matures. Both projects served additional goals to the stated ones. While the Huleh drainage served national-security purposes as viewed by the military elite, in the case of the Trans-Israel Highway economic interests of large monopoly corporations interests were served by the project. In both cases, the political elite cooperated with those elites. If this observation is valid, it symbolizes the transition of Israel from a "military state" as identified by Ben Eliether to a neo-liberal state.[230] Thus, national mega-projects are fundamentally faithful to the spirit of their times and to the motivations relevant at the time of their execution.

The Process of Decision-Making

The Process of Decision-making Involving the Huleh Drainage

On 26 December 1948 the Ministries of Agriculture and Commerce and Industry established a common committee for the planning of the Huleh drainage project.[231]

The role of the committee was to guide the project planners on several questions:

- To what extent will the drainage be directed to benefit soil cultivation by means of modern machinery?
- In what way will the drainage be executed so that it will enable peat exploitation in the concession area?
- In what way should the drainage and the irrigation of the concession area be planned so it will match the utilization of the surrounding zone?

The committee included 4 engineers and 3 government representatives: Prof. Jacob Braver from the Technion, Eng. Simha Blas from the Ministry of Agriculture, Eng. Alhanan Berchyau from the JNF, Eng. Dov Koblanov from the Jewish Agency, Dr. A. Cohen and Dr. B. Roth from the Ministry of Commerce and Industry and Dr. Yehuda Karmon from the Ministry of Agriculture.

The committee dealt with the progress of the Huleh project planning, the examination of peat use possibility, papyrus growth and its industrial use, legal issues regarding the concession, etc.[232] The committee asked two different engineers to prepare the drainage plans: Werber and Koblanov. The basic requirements were: lowering of the groundwater to enable intensive mechanical agriculture and at the same time, keeping the groundwater level high enough in the deep peat soil to enable its digging and utilization. The committee met 18 times and it decided to adopt the Koblanov proposal. Koblanov had a large experience with draining swamps from the Kabara drainage. The committee submitted its final report on June 1, 1949. One month later, the government established another, technical committee, charged with supervising the drainage project implementation. That committee included the same members of the previous one and in addition - Eng. Abraham DeLeo from the Potash Company.[233]

Other committees were established by the different government Ministries, not necessarily in coordination with each other, so that sometimes they worked simultaneously and even arrived at contradictory conclusions.[234] At the same time, the Jewish Agency decided also to appoint a committee for the Huleh region planning. There was no coordination between this committee and the technical one, so the conclusions and the decisions were sometimes at odds, as had happened with the issue of the fish ponds establishment.[235]

In 1950, the drainage plan was approved by the technical committee mentioned above. The plan was examined also by the national planning committee.[236]

All the various committees dealt with the drainage plans on a principle basis and the question of a formal, more detailed approval of the design kept arising from time to time. On 15 November 1950, at the Board of Directors meeting of the JNF, the issue was plainly expressed in the following sentence, as noted in the meeting protocol:

> Concerning the Huleh drainage plan, that its consequences
> will be a complete change of the Jordan and the Merom
> waters morphology, a basic question arises: is the JNF Board

of Directors allowed to take upon itself the decision without
receiving first the approval of the most important institutions
of the country – the Knesset and the Government.[237]

The period of time discussed here is previous to the planning and construction
law legislation, in 1965. At these times, the only legal basis for the approval of
the planning process was the Planning Act from 1936.[238]

Although the planning and construction law was not yet legislated and
the planning process was still not regulated, efforts were made to supervise
the drainage planning and to find a formal way of approval procedures
for the project. For that reason, the government committee was named, a
committee that provided the basic planning approval. The planning was also
supervised by the governmental superior drainage committee – a technical
committee representing the National Council for Planning and Construction.
That committee dealt with the technical details of the plan.[239]

Although some effort was made to accomplish a kind of regulatory
and supervisory process for the drainage planning, approval for the project
execution, the "go ahead", was made in fact by one party only – the leaders
of the country, the government and especially by the Prime Minister Ben-
Gurion, as it is duly recorded in contemporaneous government meetings
protocols.[240] No other entity was involved in the process of decision-making;
as befitted the mobilized society that was Israel of the 1950s; there were no
organized parties to oppose the project or be involved in any other way in the
decisions regarding the drainage. If there were opinions that differed from
the rulers' ones, they were vaguely and humbly expressed, but was in no way
taken in account in the decision-making process.

The Process of Decision-Making Involving
the Trans-Israel Highway

The 2000s in Israel define an era of regulated planning and construction
procedures. In 1965, the Planning and Construction Law was legislated and

from that point on, the procedure for any construction project was clear and defined. Changes and additions were effectuated from time to time, such as the compulsory Environmental Impact Statement that accompanied each construction project, but basically the process was established by the law.

The Trans-Israel Highway was a national project, of significant magnitude – the largest infrastructure project of the country – ever. As such, it went through the regular process, step by step, according to the Planning and Construction Law.

The highway was included in two National Outline Plans – NOP (T'AMA) 3 and NOP (T'AMA) 31; NOP 3 was approved in 1976 and with it – the Route 6 alignment from Be'er Sheva in the south to Barkay in the north; in 1989 an amendment to that plan was approved and with it the continuation of the alignment to the north. The alignment was integrated also in Regional Master Plans – Central Region RMP (T'AMAM) 3 and South Region RMP (T'AMAM) 4 which were approved during the eighties. The upgrading of the road to a national highway, by the name of Road 6 occurred in 1990.

The preparation of NOP (T'AMA) 31 – an integrated national outline plan for construction and development for the purpose of immigrant absorption – started in 1990 and was approved by the government in 1993. That plan included the Trans-Israel Highway alignment. In order to move forward as quickly as possible with the execution of the Trans-Israel, which was considered an urgent necessity as a solution to traffic difficulties, NOP (T'AMA) 31 A for roads was prepared and approved, including the design of parts (14 sectors) of road 6; it was also presented to the public, through Regional Councils, in order to solicit public comment. Viability studies and traffic analysis regarding the highway were conducted more than once (in 1990 and in 1993).[241]

The highway's plans were discussed in 60 meetings of the National Council for Planning and Construction, a few times in the Finance and Economics

Committee of the Knesset and approved by three governments.[242] Even the opponents of the project had to admit that the planning and the statutory approval of the project were done "by the book".

> In terms of the legal aspect, there was no fault in the planning and the approval process. The road was approved by every statutory forum and all High Court of Justice petitions against the highway construction were rejected. The whole process was open to the public...[243]

Research regarding the conflict around Road 6 was prepared by the University of Haifa in 2002. The research studied, among other subjects, the process of decision-making in some aspects connected with the Trans-Israel Highway. It found that regarding planning and public involvement, the decision-making process was proper, correct and fair to the public. The approval process was conducted according to the Planning and Construction Law and even more than that: even though there was no compulsory public presentation, the road being approved as part of a National Outline Plan, the public was given the chance to view and remark on the road plans. Special investigators were appointed to deal with the many observations and claims of the public. The public and the "green" organizations were given the opportunity to present their opinions and claims to the committees dealing with the road, even to participate as members of those committees.[244]

In other aspects, the decision-making process was less adequate. Regarding the transport issue, the process was deficient; there was no thorough examination concerning the highway necessity and the development of a comprehensive transport system; no studies on the impact of the highway on land use and on public transport were conducted. Also no one tried to examine the public willingness to pay for a toll highway.[245]

Criticism regarding the decision-making process was raised by representatives of the "green" organizations. They asserted that the process never included the examination of the necessity of the highway construction and its impacts; those issues were never discussed by the National Council of Planning and Construction. The National Council implemented the government decisions and did not deal with the essence or the necessity of the project as a solution to the transport problems of the country. The structure of the decision-making process did not make possible a connection between all concerned parties. There was no opportunity of the highway alternatives examination and of interdisciplinary discussions between concerned parties and/or professionals. Despite that criticism, the whole process was conducted according to the law.[246]

Being initiated and supported by the government, the project received special attention; some of the issues were discussed in government meetings and some processes were expedited.[247] The implementation of the project was facilitated by the government involvement, such as the establishment of the Cross-Israel Company, the definition of its roles, the order of execution of the highway's segments and so on. Of extreme importance for the project was the legislation by the Knesset of two laws – the first regarding land expropriation and the second – declaring the highway a toll road.

The first of the two laws, legislated in 1994, was of a significant importance for the project. It enabled the seizure of land necessary to the highway's construction before the compensations process was finalized. It was a drastic law, affecting private property rights, but it meant a quick way out for the implementation of the highway.

Indeed, the Trans-Israel law was properly approved by the Knesset and apparently there was no flaw in the procedure it went through but, behind the curtains, there were improper details in the way things were conducted regarding the law approval.

Some of the Knesset members that voted for the law had varied relations with factors distinctly and personally interested in the highway execution.

The agricultural lobby was interested in the project implementation as an economic leverage for the kibbutzim and the moshavim situated along the highway's proposed route. One of the Knesset members was at the time a paid director of Africa-Israel, a component of the Derech Eretz Consortium; another one had a personal interest in the project since his wife's private company provided consulting services on the issue of public relations to Derech Eretz; another one was himself a paid consultant to Derech Eretz.

There were some claims and criticism in government discussions about the highway. Some remarked that no transport alternative to the highway was presented to them, an alternative other than a road, such as the railway. Others claimed that viability studies presented to the government by the Cross-Israel Company were unreliable and professionally questionable. Despite promises of the committee's heads to look into those claims and remarks, nothing was done and the Trans-Israel law was approved by the Knesset without problems and by a majority of votes.[248]

The process of decision-making was conducted according to planning laws, but other factors were no less involved in the process: on one hand, the government initiated the project, and pushed for its execution by using meanings described above; on the other hand civil society, represented by various NGOs – social and environmental – organized, acted in many ways and influenced the process, especially on the environmental issue. The media played also an important role in the process of decision-making by its intensive presence in the public discourse.

Conclusions

The Huleh drainage was a large-scale national project, outstanding for a new country in the 1950s. Despite the formal process of decision-making, the various committees that dealt with the project and the formal approvals, remarkable for the times, the basic decisions were made by the leaders who formed the Israeli elite during that period of time. In principle, the project was discussed, approved and pushed forward in government sessions as early as 1950. The real initiators were the Prime Minister and his ministers, and not the planning and construction institutions (see chapter 3 above).

The processes necessary to set the agenda – problems, politics and visible participants, were all conducted by the elite. They decided, according to the Zionist ideology dominant in the country, what were the most pressing problems on the national agenda. One of them was the drainage of swamps.

The decision-making process regarding the Huleh project followed the principle of the elites controlling the process. The elite – the leaders of the country – decided about the project according to their values, interests and worldviews. That does not mean that those interests and worldviews were opposite, or even partially different, from those of other groups of the country. It just means that the elite behaved in a patronizing way, taking for granted that they knew better what was best for the whole country.

The hegemony of the elite was clear and undisputed. In the process of decision-making regarding the Huleh project, the voices speaking against the project or even mildly criticizing it, were scarce, weak and a priory apologetic.

In its dealings with the Huleh project, the hegemony of the elite was not at risk; the policy of the drainage was in consensus with the ideology embraced by the majority of the population.

The players involved in the process of decision-making regarding the Huleh drainage were the government, the JNF and a small group of scientists and nature enthusiasts. Each one of those players had a different agenda and sometimes those agendas came in conflict with each other.

The government had first and foremost in mind the need to provide for the new immigrants arriving to Israel. It was not especially interested in preserving the JNF as a national institution. The JNF saw in the drainage project the opportunity to find a new role for itself. The scientists and nature enthusiasts regretted the destruction of the swamp habitat and strived to preserve at least a small part of it.

The process of decision-making was almost entirely non formal. There were no laws and institutionalized procedures to manage such large projects. The Israeli Parliament (the Knesset) was not involved. The main power struggle was between the JNF and the government and the last took the lead in this struggle. The implications of the project on national security and the risk for rise of conflict with Syria had deterred the JNF for making the decisions by itself. The government used also the sense of urgency in order to control the JNF. The national planning institution also became involved in the decision-making by supervising the project plans, including their support for the allocation of preservation of 400 hectares of the swamp for the reserve. By that they consolidated their authority.

The government's actions included the work of several members of the professional staff, but they remained fragmented and uncoordinated. At the end, while the government set the general goals, the JNF plans specified the details and the technical instructions for the project. The involvement of the "Greens" was enabled by including their representatives in some of the committees and by informal meetings with the leaders of the JNF.

However, despite the power struggle among the three elite groups, they all had shared the same discourse and the same solutions to the challenges set by the project, based on the hegemonic discourse of belief in the power of centrally planned solutions based on national interests and the blind belief in the power of science to solve problems. In the end, the three players united around the Zionist ethos of development by collective agricultural means and that brought to each of them achievements – the government had more land for cultivation, the JNF had a national project to execute, so it was again a most needed national institution, scientists and nature enthusiasts were able to create a nature reserve.

The 2000s find a different society in Israel, a different kind of elite and of political power relations. In the decision-making process regarding the Trans-Israel Highway, it is evident that power – political, economic, etc. – is at the base of that process and controls it. Groups with common interests organized themselves in order to lead the struggle against the highway, or at least, to obtain maximum changes on the topics relevant to them. Two coalitions were formed around the project: on one hand, the government represented by the Cross-Israel company and the Derech Eretz company, which executed the project; on the other hand, the civil society which represented the public interest. Each coalition hired its own professional specialists in order to advance its interests. The final decisions were based on the equilibrium of power between those two groups.

The connection between wealth and political power and its reflection on that project were discussed in detail in chapter 3. The adherence of the leaders, the government officials, to the upper strata shows itself in the special bills approved by the Knesset and legislated especially for that project. The project followed the process of decision-making defined by the Law of Planning and Construction and no one, even the opponents of the project, could claim otherwise. The law itself leaves room for civil society to raise their claims and the project managers allowed public involvement from the early stages of planning. Nevertheless, the officials in charge with that process used their power to influence it in a way that answered the interests of the big corporations and the wealthy of the country – the upper strata.

A few facts point in that direction, e.g. the project was initiated and pushed forward by the government, without looking for alternatives for the transport difficulties in the country; the special laws legislated specifically for that project favored the consortium in charge with the project execution on expense of the lower, weaker strata. The consortium in charge with the project execution included big, strong corporations, such as the Ted Harrison group and Africa-Israel Investments. Those corporations on one hand could put pressure on the officeholders in charge with the project and, on the other hand, could make them benefit for the cooperation. So, the process of decision-making reflects that cooperation and the preference of the officials for the upper – over the lower – strata. For example, the law of land expropriation enabled the seizure of the necessary land for the highway construction before the compensation was finally established and the Arab landowners were put in an unfavorable position in their negotiation for the compensation. The law declaring the highway a toll road favored those who could afford the daily use of private cars and the cost of the toll and disregarded the position of the others who could not afford it. Above all, the government took the risks for possible deficits in the operation of the road on behalf of the general public.

The decision-making process of the Trans-Israel project followed a formal well defined path. By the 2000s, Israel had well defined planning laws and the project followed them strictly. Researchers have not been able to find any fault with the process of approval of the project. The process included Parliament (Knesset) decisions, the required committees approvals, hearings of public opinions and reservations about the project, discussions about those reservations, etc. The public campaign against the Trans-Israel included Parliament discussions, appeals to the High Court, public demonstrations and so on. A number of society sectors took part in the public discourse. Civil society demonstrated its ability to organize, to set a policy in order to guide action and to mobilize masses for action. It gained also enough power to force the consortium to apply environmental measures of the highest standards known in Israel. However, civil society failed to question the need for the project itself and to force the consortium to apply means that required high investments.

☙ **5** ❧
The Public Discourse

In democratic regimes, the government policy and actions became, little by little, a matter of public opinion, as it is expressed by the public discourse, more than a matter of ruling power. MacIver said: *"This incessant activity of popular opinion is the dynamic of democracy."*

That theory is based on a few assumptions:

- The public is interested in government.
- The public can form a cohesive opinion.
- The public is capable of expressing that opinion.
- The public's opinion will be taken into consideration in government decisions.

Because the attitude to an issue can differ from one individual to another in a given community, public opinion is usually considered to be the opinion of the majority or of those who stand out to present their opinions publicly in that community.

In more recent years, the notion of public opinion was enlarged so that it does not have to represent the majority. The public is no longer expected to be homogenous and it can have a few, different ideas on a given issue. So "the public" can be the whole civil society of a country but also, a smaller group of individuals having a common bond about a specific issue, e.g. a geographical location, a professional union, a political party, etc.

Public discourse and public participation in the decision-making process regarding mega-engineering national projects have significance on a few levels. On one hand, some essential and basic problems can arise when the interest of the public is not identical with the personal interest of the decision makers. Although, allegedly, the decision-makers, (the country's leaders), are supposed to represent solely, or at least – first and foremost – the public interest.

However, the public discourse and the public participation in the decision-making process can facilitate the way to solve conflicts and the public opposition to the project which can, at least, delay a project, if not cancel it completely. On the other hand, even when everyone concerned is willing to have public participation and public opinion expressed regarding a national mega-project, there are technical difficulties in implementing the process. Those difficulties diminished with time due to the revolutionary development of the media.

The discourse analysis will include the narrative study and the display of the power structures that motivate and impel the way the debate is articulated and conducted, and hopefully, the core of the discourse will be exposed.

In the present work "the analysis of narratives" type of research will be used. A set of newspapers articles and other media means were collected, considered as basic data for the examination and analyzed in order to emphasize the claims about the characteristics of the Israeli society in the two periods discussed here and their reflection in the way the national mega-engineering projects were conducted.

Two aspects were considered crucial for the analysis, therefore studied with special attention – the participants of the discourse in each case, their role in the debate and its consequences; the discourse structure or core that reflected the values and practices of the society of that period.

The way the mega-projects are presented to the public, the incentives displayed by the leaders and decision makers in order to convince the public that their decisions are in the best interest of all and gain the people's support, are not always identical with the real motivations behind those decisions.

Many times the decisions made by the leaders create a conflict of interests between different sectors of the population. The goal of the leaders' rhetoric in the way they present the project in the public discourse is to minimize conflicts and opposition to the project. The presentation of a mega-project by the decision makers in such a way forms the framing of the public discourse.

Public Discourse and Public Opinion on the Huleh Project

In the 1950s, the first years of Israel as an independent state, the country was dominated by the Zionist ideology in its mobilized, collective national form. In the mobilized society that accepted the elite hegemony public debates over mega-engineering projects had remained limited. That subject was largely detailed in chapter 3 above. Nevertheless, Israel was from the beginning a democracy and as such, public opinion could be expressed freely.[249] That time there was a restricted attitude toward the autonomy of the media, especially the press, and toward the freedom of information. Until the 1960s, the state media functioned more as the voice of the government than the voice of the people. Most information about the project was dispersed through movie magazines that distributed government propaganda that appraised the project.

The few attempts of the press to recruit the public opinion and convert it in a different direction than that of the political paths were considered an intrusion into the legitimate domain of the professional politicians. Even those attempts were expressed in a hesitant and tentative way, without any indication of criticism.[250]

The way the media conducted itself was characteristic of a mobilized society. In the 1950s and 1960s, there was a lack of understanding on the part of the public regarding its rights to receive information and to express its views and opinions. The tendency to a central control of freedom of information and of speech weakened gradually, in some measure due to the Anglo-Saxon democracies – England and the United States.[251]

Media Coverage of the Huleh Project

The coverage of the press and other media means of the 1950s reflect the spirit of the times, the ideology and the issues most important in the eyes of the public. Not only the topics themselves and the contents of the articles indicate what was relevant and significant in those days, in connection with the Huleh project, but also the frequency with which some issues were mentioned, referred to and reviewed at length in the press. The issues most popular and most discussed in the press, regarding the Huleh drainage project, were not many, but they met with a high degree of coverage.

The national importance of the project and the pride it inspired - That was the most important issue and also the ideological basis and the main motivation to implement the Huleh project. It referred to the significance of the drainage for the development of the country, its contribution to the economy in general and to the agriculture in particular and especially to the realization of the Zionist ideas and aspirations of conquering nature and the wilderness as part of it. Draining the swamps was one of the most important refrains of the Zionist movement and it was treated as such in the media of those days. That formed the abstract or the setting of the narrative.

The Geva studios produced a few cinema news journals about the Huleh drainage. All of them talked about the importance of creating hundreds of hectares fit for cultivation,[252] the abolishment of the swamps plague,[253] man's triumph over nature[254] and the changes brought to the country's landscape.[255]

> The disposal of the swamp from the northern region of the country is the goal of the JNF big plan of draining the Huleh – according to the JNF journal, *Karnenu*..[256]

In the same article, the setting of the narrative is described as follows:

> The swamps of Nahalal, Hedera and the Huleh and others, marshy land in many corners of the country were one of the notions representing the obstacles of the pioneers of the new Hebrew settlement, the stubbornness, the passionate devotion and the self sacrifice of the early days. In song, story and play was expressed the approach of the pioneers to the swamp to fight it, to exterminate it and to built in its place healthy, flourishing settlements.[257]

Other articles talked also about changes in primeval orders by draining swamps.[258] So, the complication or the initiating event is, for that issue, the drainage of the swamp and it is mentioned in all the articles and the documents referring to the Huleh project.

Expressing the national pride and satisfaction in what is considered in the eyes of the writers, an important accomplishment is the implementation of a large, complex technical project – the drainage of the Huleh swamps.

> By finalizing the Huleh drainage plant, one of the biggest development projects of the country was completed, a project that changes primeval orders of the country. … The Huleh plant will be recorded as one of the largest and the most impressive accomplishments that represents faithfully how far go the development ability and the initiative potential of our people in building its national independence and how far the technical execution capacity of the Jewish worker goes.[259]

In the newspaper *Davar*, the reporter, K. Shabtay, expresses his pride in what is in his eyes a significant national achievement:

> Although I know very well that bigger and more complicated technical wonders than that (the Huleh plant) were achieved

already in the world at large, I felt something like a national
pride in learning about that technical – engineering story.[260]

The Israeli – Syrian conflict and the national security issue - Most of
the articles referring to the Israeli-Syrian conflict over the Huleh project were
simply reports and updates on the frequent events occurring almost every day
around that conflict.[261] Second, the military and security issue was regarded as
being of the highest importance for the country and its population. Last but
not least, the conflict was for Israel a test-case for its sovereignty over every
inch of its territory, especially in the DZ.

The setting of that narrative consists in the Israeli perception and
interpretation of the Armistice Agreement that in the DZ, Israel was
complete sovereign and besides letting military forces in, it could do
whatever it decided without asking permission of anyone. The undercurrent
of the dispute, as explained in chapter 3 above, concerning the fight for the
final border line, appears clearly between the lines of more than one article
in the newspapers.

> Although the Huleh drainage is nothing else than a pretext,
> due to excuse the Syrian assaults or the violation of the DZ
> principle and the Syrian trespassing, it seems that externally it
> will be smart to learn a lesson in justifications for the hostilities
> against us.[262]
>
> The editorial in your issue of May 22 entitled "A steady
> hand", which deals with the Israel-Syria border dispute, has the
> following passage: "Syria also is apprehensive lest the drainage
> work prejudice her claims to sovereignty in the area." [263]

Israel considered the Syrian opposition to the Huleh project a pretext for its
acts of hostility and found proof of that in different facts, like the fact that
some of the armed attacks of the Syrians were far away from the area of the
Huleh project.[264]

Also, the Syrian opposition to the Huleh project was considered, by Israelis as well as non-Israelis abroad, as an indication of resistance to progress and adherence to the old ways.

> The Armistice Agreement was not supposed to interfere with our normal life and the meaning of normal life in Israel is development. And development means the Huleh drainage. Although the Huleh concession was in Arab hands for tens of years, they did nothing in this matter and the concession passed into our hands.[265]
>
> In fact, I don't understand why the Syrians would care that you drain the Huleh. I believe their opposition is instinctive; the opposition of a desert man to any progress due to limit the desert borders. (an U.N. officer).[266]

The disputed area that became the heart of the Israeli-Syrian conflict around the Huleh project extended to 2.8 hectares privately owned by Arabs.

According to the Israeli press, Israel made real efforts to find a reasonable solution and compensate the Arab owners of the disputed area, but because of the Syrian pressure, the owners would not come to an agreement with the State of Israel on the matter.[267]

> We know, from reliable sources, that the Arab owners of the 28 dunams (2.8 hectares) in the Huleh drainage area are permanently under the Syrian government pressure not to sell the land to the P.L.D.C. The land owners are willing to sell the land to the Jews so that they can cultivate the rest of their lands in the DZ.[268]

The ambivalent attitude toward nature - Many articles reported the ambivalent attitude toward nature, an attitude that was typical of the period. The underlying belief was the Zionist ethos that man had to fight and subdue nature, tame and change it so that it will serve his needs, as detailed in chapter 3. On the other hand, there were already other considerations, at least on the part of a few people – scientists, researchers and nature lovers. Their opinions were expressed less loudly but they were not completely silenced. The attitude of those scientists and nature lovers was that the damage to nature by draining the Huleh was a necessary evil and that it had to be accepted. Amotz Zahavi is cited saying as follows: "It was clear that agriculture and settlement were top priority, and it was considered obvious that swamps should be drained. No one could imagine that you could say no to drying the Huleh."

> He went on to say:
>> The draining was deeply troubling to nature advocates, but it was difficult to talk about it, because anyone who spoke out was considered anti-Zionist. This (the drainage) was seen as a tremendous achievement, celebrated in writing and song. But it wasn't thought through, and the result was ecological destruction. I'm against such policies that enthusiastically promote all kinds of big projects that change the face of the land without a comprehensive assessment of their environmental impact.[269]

The struggle to subdue and conquer nature was a much used Zionist slogan, the initiating event being, in this case – the draining of the Huleh swamp. The evaluation was the necessity to create more and more land for cultivation in order to develop agriculture and to provide more means of livelihood for the immigrants.

> ... Techniques and romanticism – there is no room for both of them on the same lake. Man triumphs, nature surrender. We knew that: the Huleh drainage means economical development and national achievement. The more dunams for cultivation, the less dunams of swamps. But what can you do, the heart aches when you remember the beauty of the lake, when it was still alive, still breathing and storming.[270]

The nation's aspiration was to build on the drained lands of the Huleh thousands of cultivation farms, create a new, rich source of livelihood for people. That would be a dream come true. These sentiments were expressed in virtually the same breath with the regrets over losing the beauty, the richness and the diversification of the Huleh swamps nature.[271] There were even those who viewed the nature reserve as a loss of land for farming and that farming was far more important than preservation of nature.[272]

The preservation of nature as an issue existed even in those early days and was expressed in a few articles in the newspapers and always for the sake of nature itself and not for the sake of man.

The beauty and variety of the Huleh fauna and flora was much appreciated and its disappearance with the drying of the lake and the swamp was regretted.[273]

> Settlement expansion and conquest of the desolation – lights and shadows mingle in them. …with the drying of the Huleh, for instance, a rich natural reservoir will be wiped out and nothing will be left out of it.[274]

The same article goes on to say that the participants of the Botanical Congress decided to ask for the saving of *"valuable nature assets, most important for the education of the nation and the study of the homeland."* [275]

The Creation of the Huleh Reserve was the expression of the will to keep alive part of the Huleh nature. It represented the compromise between the view that development was first on the priority-of-importance scale for the nation, but that nature also had its value and sometimes, at least part of it was worth preserving.[276]

To preserve the unique fauna and flora of the Huleh Lake region by way of proclaiming a reserve (reservat) of 4000 dunams (400 hectares) – that is the demand of the Commission for Nature Preservation, the Botanical Society and the Zoological Society of Israel. With the draining of the Huleh swamp and the nearby flood areas, home to rare birds nesting, priceless scientific assets and esthetical values are going to disappear from our country's landscape.[277]

Other issues received some coverage in the press. One of them was the Huleh peat.

The Huleh Peat raised great expectations and was considered for a long time a treasure and a natural resource for Israel, a natural source for energy, land fertilization or a very fertile land in itself.

> Israeli scientists calculate that although this peat (the Huleh peat) contains 28 percent ash it could be used as fuel to run a 10,000-kilowatt power station for several decades. Studies now proceeding at the Rehovoth Agricultural Research Station may show, however, that this particular peat can be more economically used as fertilizer.[278]
>
> Israelis may then exploit an estimated 4,000,000 tons of peat from the swamps as fuel or as fertilizer and cultivate 4,000 acres of new farmland and 5,000 acres of improved land.[279]

The problems and difficulties that arose in the effort to exploit the peat were also reported in some articles.[280] The attitude toward peat exploitation reflected the Zionist worldview and belief that science can solve everything and action is imperative and urgent. Therefore, they preceded action – the Huleh drainage – to the results of peat research, in hope that science will find solutions to every problem arising along the way.

The activity of the JNF and its significance in the building of the country was an important topic in the press. The JNF was praised, its contribution to the development of the country emphasized, its status in the national apparatus outlined.[281]

Dr. Abraham Granot, one of the Managers of the JNF, in his article from 28 December 1950 in the newspaper *Davar*, describes in detail the new roles of the JNF in the building of the country, as a redeemer of the land and a developer for farming in addition to afforestation and other roles that the JNF held previously to the creation of the state.[282]

Also, other articles refer to the same subject – the role of the JNF after the establishment of the State of Israel. As detailed in chapter 3 above, at that time, the JNF felt unsure of its future role in the new state.[283] The Huleh drainage was the "jewel in the crown" for the JNF, the most important and significant project, after the establishment of the State. That fact was much emphasized by the press.[284]

> The Huleh plant will be the main project of the JNF in its jubilee year – so was reported yesterday at the first meeting of the Jubilee Commission, at the JNF House in Tel-Aviv, headed by the Knesset chairman – I. Shprintzak – the highlight of the development projects of the JNF until now.[285]

Criticism of the Project

The Huleh drainage was a much-praised project, the national pride of the new state and a reason for feelings of achievement and progress. In general, the media had words of appreciation and commendation for all involved in the implementation of the plan. A few articles included some comments and criticism regarding the project, especially on the topic of economic benefits (or losses) and later, on the topic of technical problems.

> Seven and a half million liras were invested in the farm and how much was spent on the land acquisition and the drainage? The interest is 700,000 liras per year and the development 140,000 liras more and at the end, the revenue does not cover the expenses. The losses are constant – about 1 million liras per year.[286]

Later on, there was some criticism on the basis of technical issues and questions about the efficacy of the plant were raised.

> The Huleh drainage was justified ten years ago mainly for the need to expand the cultivation lands. The experience acquired in those times does not ratify this presumption. More than that: the Huleh drainage prevented the implementation of the original plan of the National Water Carrier. If the Water Carrier would have been built according to the original plan, the digging of a large lake in the Huleh would have been necessary. Now we lead, even in regular years, 500 million cubic meters of water, through the Huleh to the Sea of Galilee, damage the water quality because of the salinity and we damage the water of all wells along the way by diluting them in order to attenuate the salinity of the fields irrigated by the Sea of Galilee waters.[287]

Even as early as 1950, there was an article in the newspaper *Davar* that summarized the benefits and the damages that were expected from the drainage project. The most obvious benefits mentioned in the article were the creation of hundreds of hectares of land for cultivation, the addition to millions of cubic meters of water for irrigation and the building of thousands of new farms in the area. But, side-by-side with those benefits were losses, possibly not less important, losses of a few industry sectors: the papyrus as a raw material in the paper and the weaving industry, the peat as a raw material for construction (insulation panels), pharmaceutical industry and others and the wiping out of the fishing industry in the Huleh Lake. The Ministry of Agriculture decided that the benefits were worth the losses so the drainage was to be completed; nevertheless, the reporter mentioned that some specialists still had doubts about the rightness of that judgment.[288]

In 1955, there was more criticism along similar lines. Questions were raised about the justification of the project. With the establishment of the state, millions of dunams of land became the property of the state so was it really necessary to invest 9 million liras in order to create 30,000 dunams more? Were not other issues more pressing and more vital for the development of the country?

Malaria, the curse of the Huleh valley and one of the main reasons to drain the swamps, was no longer a danger. As early as 1939, the workers of the Malaria Research Laboratory in Rehovoth, headed by Professor Mar, had cleared the swamps of the anopheles mosquitoes using D.D.T. In the years 1949-1950, there were no malaria cases at all in the Huleh valley. So the Huleh drainage had little to do with the improvement of health conditions in the region.

The conservation of water by preventing the evaporation of 100 million cubic meters of water was superfluous because the surrounding settlements were not capable of using all that water. Besides, specialists claimed that other methods were cheaper and no less efficient in conserving that amount of water. These included deepening the Jordan River bed and completing the National Water Carrier from the North to the Negev.

The most critical article claimed that the expectation that the Huleh's drained lands would be used for new settlements and the creation of 2,000 farms did not materialize. The decision, following the American consultant's advice, was to cultivate the drained lands in one large farm. The investment of 9 million liras at that period of time was much more necessary to the Jews in the Galilee and the settling of the West Galilee than the drainage of the Huleh. For the JNF, that project was very important but for the country and the whole nation, other issues were more critical and urgent.[289]

Summarizing the subjects of most concern brings us to the conclusion that the structure of the public discourse was based on the Zionist national ideology of collectivism, building the nation and the country so that any action taken in that regard was to be praised and deserving of pride. Furthermore, even the critical articles did not question the rational of the plans and did not call to preserve the whole swamp, but questioned whether this was the most effective project for development. The environmental issue existed, but was not very developed in comparison with current times and was, in any case, secondary in importance to development and progress.

The Framing of the Public Discourse Around the Huleh Project

Being that the Huleh project was implemented at a time when the Israeli society was a mobilized one ruled by an hegemonic elite, the framing of the public discourse took place mainly in propaganda movies, newspapers articles and radio programs that appraised the project along the lines of presenting it as a reason for national pride, celebration of Jewish superiority over the underdevelopment of the neighboring countries and celebration of the power of nationally centralized efforts to conquer nature for the benefit of the people. Only few articles cautiously raised criticism on the rationality of the projects and its damage to nature.

The JNF, feeling the need to justify its existence and future activity, presented the Huleh drainage as its most important project and contribution to the country building. Never publicly discussed were the JNF's internal problems after the establishment of Israel, when almost all the land became the property of the new state.

> In a conversation with the Prime Minister (Ben-Gurion), he talked overtly and raised the question about the future of the JNF, which has a huge contribution to the development of the settlement and the building of the country. But the government treats the JNF as a step-daughter and the general tendency in the government circles is to ignore that contribution.[290]

As detailed in chapter 3, the real and main incentives for the project of the drainage was the ethos of progress and development; it was the flag of the Zionist movement and swamp drainage became an important part of that philosophy. The goals of the project presented to the public by the government – the framing – consisted of malaria prevention, creation of agricultural land and use of the peat for fertilization and energy production, goals unanimously accepted by the public as part of the country building.[291]

Even the scientists and nature lovers that considered the destruction of the lake and the swamp a real loss, framed their request for a reserve in a quiet and almost apologetic way, not daring to reveal their true thoughts and feelings about the drainage project.

Almost no one talked openly and publicly about the irreversible damage to the natural habitat or the damages to the soil and water quality, the framing was expressed by asking for the reserve as a place for further research and study of unique fauna and flora, for education of future generations. The request emphasized the benefits the reserve will bring to people and especially the Jewish-Israeli community.

> The swamp area of the Huleh has a special meaning for science, because that area is unique. It is the only place, besides the Tropical Africa that has included in its flora papyrus. In that landscape many kinds of plants and rare animals find shelter.[292]
>
> The Huleh reserve, according to plans, will serve for tourist visits, for zoology and botanic researchers, school children and nature lovers that will long for a landscape corner untouched by human hand.[293]

Public Discourse on the Trans-Israel Highway

In the 2000s, the public discourse regarding the Trans-Israel Highway was defined by two phenomena – the existence of an advanced and active civil society and the very developed technical means of mass communication typical of the times. With it being so controversial a project, the Trans-Israel intensified the reaction of civil organizations, stirred up their activities and stabilized their relations around that topic.

The public discourse included many NGOs, such as the Israel Union for Environmental Defense (Adam, Teva Ve'Din), the Green Course, the Movement for Social Change from Below (Bdidut), the Moose (Ayal Koreh), the Green Wave, etc.

They all used and took great advantage of the existing methods of mass communication, especially the Internet. That enabled them to spread their views in real-time, rapidly reaching tens and hundreds of thousands of people. The web was used not only by NGOs but also by private individuals who expressed their opinions and communicated on Chat sites,[294] likely influencing one another to intensify the struggle.

The technological means available in the 2000s made for a large and comprehensive public discourse and public reaction to the highway. It enabled quick organization of protests and demonstrations; it reached large masses of people. Other means, as always, included newspapers, the radio and the television. However, the web played a major role and changed the rules of the game in speed of reaction and number of people involved.

The public discourse around the Trans-Israel showed several interesting characteristics. Almost all reactions to the project dealt with taking stands, supporting or criticizing/opposing the project. Most of the supporters were the interested parties in the project execution – the Cross Israel Company, the Derech Eretz Consortium, people working for them or employed in other ways for the project. Even the scholars that made their opinions public in supporting the highway plan were involved in some ways, as consultants or otherwise, in the project. But mainly, public discourse evolved around opposition to the project and criticism of its every aspect.

The majority of newspaper articles or other documents from the web, professional journals, conferences and others, dealt with more than one topic, usually all the controversial issues regarding the highway. The documents that dealt with just one issue were scarce.

NGOs that existed before the initiation of the Trans-Israel and had a specific objective, when dealing with the highway, embraced all issues. For instance, the NGO *B'didut,* the Movement for Social Change from Below, was a social movement that usually dealt with class problems but in this case, it covered everything – environment, economics, politics, transport; the MaTa"H (The Center for Educational Technology) Virtual Library – published articles relating to almost every aspect of the highway project.

The green organizations that usually concentrated on environmental protection, sensing that social issues were more "attractive" and had more impact in the struggle around the highway, dealt with them at least as much as with environment problems or even more.

In general, the social aspects were much emphasized in every discussion and became a central issue for the opponents of the Trans-Israel in their struggle against the project, along with political, economic, transport and environment concerns. The basis for all discussions on those subjects, one that formed the setting or the background of the narrative was the fact that in the 2000s, Israeli society was dominated by a neo-liberal government whose trend was toward radical neo-liberalism and spread of privatization to more and more sectors.

> The process that brought it (Road 6) into life at the end of the 1990s and the beginning of the 2000s represents a revolutionary change in the development ethos and the political economy of Israel in the last decade of the 20th century.[295]
>
> The privatization, that started in Israel in the 1950s in industry, continued at the end of the 1970s into housing construction, infiltrated in the 1980s into the domain of municipal services, reached in the 1990s the most attractive cookie jar rim, the national infrastructure.[296]

Many articles emphasized the link between wealth and political power in connection with the Trans-Israel Highway, as an expression of the neo-liberal tendencies of the government.[297] The complication or the initiating event of the narrative was in the process of planning and construction of the highway, from the initiating concept, in the 1970s, through the planning and statutory approval and the special laws legislated to facilitate the project and finally - its execution.

A few articles chronicled the process the highway went through from concept to actualization.[298] The two laws legislated specifically for the Trans-Israel, were also mentioned in the newspapers, as part of the process of the project implementation.[299]

Almost every article, document and any other form of expression, included the opinion, namely the criticism concerning the highway and its potential negative impact. It was almost impossible to find a neutral article, one that just conveyed facts without taking a (usually negative) stand regarding the project. The criticism, as analyzed in chapter 3 above and chapters 6 further on, covered all the relevant aspects – political, economic, transport, social and environmental.

Newspaper articles and various NGOs documents on the web discussed the expected damages from the highway. They doubted the economic viability of the project and the financing of land expropriation, planning and statutory approval by public funds, although the project was presented to the public as privately financed. The highway was going to increase the dependency on the private car and discourage use of public transport and, anyway, the government was going to avoid investment in the development of public transport in order to decrease competition to the Trans-Israel. The highway was going to intensify the sprawl of suburbs, the development of industrial and employment centers in places that already were developed instead of improving the situation of the periphery – the Negev and the Galilee.

The most damages were going to occur to the environment where the list of problems was the longest: waste of land resources – agricultural land covered by asphalt, landscape damage and loss of green space – green areas destroyed in order to make room for the highway, air pollution, groundwater pollution and noise nuisance because of the heavy traffic on the highway, fauna and flora damage because of loss of natural habitat, etc.

All the above problems were detailed and analyzed in many newspaper articles and the disapproving opinions were explicitly expressed.[300] Looking back on the issues discussed in the various media, the obvious subjects that formed the core and structure of the public discourse were typical of a neo-liberal society – no national ideology was involved besides the ideology of economics and profits raised by the coalition of capital owners and government on one hand, and of social and environmental issues raised by civil society on the other hand.

At first, the struggle of the various NGOs - social, economic and environmental, was directed against the project implementation and the aspirations were to have it completely scrapped. When it became clear that the project was indeed going to be executed, the "green" organizations continued the fight in order to minimize the damages they believed would accrue from the highway's construction. In the end, ecological and other aspects were taken into consideration, much more than what was originally intended, attributable directly to the civil society struggle.

Looking at the public discourse as representative of two opponents in a conflict, we can assign the government, the companies involved in executing the project and all other factors benefiting from it – consultants, planners, etc. to one side and all the NGOs and other organizations dealing with environmental and social issues – Adam, Teva Ve'Din, B'didut, Green Course, etc. to the other.

Each framed its side of the discourse, presenting every issue with an eye towards convincing the opponents to adopt its point of view.

On the economic issue, the proponents claimed that the project would save money for the public funds, the highway being a BOT project, executed and maintained by a private company. That was the framing narrative, trying to convince the opponents that a privatized, toll road would benefit the public financially. The ideology and the real incentive behind it, was the tendency to privatization, even of basic infrastructure, in an atmosphere of radical neo- liberalization.

The wish to 'do good' on the part of powerful elements such as the Derech Eretz consortium, was not mentioned by any of the project's proponents, but was also part of the ideology and incentive to build the Highway. Viability studies were prepared in order to demonstrate the economic profitability of the project.

> In the frame of the feasibility study, a viability examination of road 6 was prepared by Ma'atz (The Department of Public Works) which will be expressed by saving on traveling duration and operation costs of the cars moving on a road network that includes road 6 versus one without it. The study shows that the investment in road 6 is very profitable.[301]

The social benefits of the Highway were presented to the public in such a way that the weaker strata of the population would accept the road as a benefit, an improvement in their situation. The road, it was said, will bring the periphery closer to the center of the country; it will facilitate employment for the population and accessibility for that population to the cultural institutions of Tel-Aviv and Gush Dan.

> The road initiators claim that the Highway has social benefits. According to them, the road will bolster the periphery by bringing it closer to the center and in that way, it will fulfill a social goal. …It will help employment by facilitating speedy movement of people and merchandise from the north to the south.[302]

Environmental protection was a much discussed issue, dealt with and for which most efforts were made for changes and improvement.

> At the beginning of the month, the company Derech Eretz proudly notified the public that she will be the first in Israel to adopt the Geneva treaty of plants conservation. The treaty stipulates that countries have to avoid using plants that are not local and can cause ecological damages. ..Derech Eretz says that until this day the treaty was not applied in Israel but she will make a point of not planting any strange kinds of plants on the road shoulders.
>
> ...Now the company tries to convince that the road will not have a negative impact. She changed the road route in the Gevaton area, next to Rehovoth, so as not to damage the nature reserve; in the Kfar-Saba area, the company acted in order to close an unregulated solid waste site and she plans to restore it; the highway route was changed in a few more places in order to avoid nuisances of noise and close to the settlement Bath Hefer, in the Sharon region, " in the framework of a long and sensitive dialog" – in the words of Derech Eretz – she took care of a problem born of the closeness of the highway route to the settlement's borders.[303]

Writing in the journal *Green, Blue White,* Darel-Fosfeld and Prujinin explained and detailed, item by item, the measures that were taken by Derech Eretz to protect and preserve the environment and build a "green" road.[304] They, of course, were consultants to Derech Eretz, on the subject of environmental impact. That does not mean the facts they mentioned were untrue, just that some of them were not completely accurate. In any case, the "green" institutions considered that what had been done by Derech Eretz on that subject was far from sufficient.

Another issue addressed by Derech Eretz was the subject of archaeology. The consortium financed a comprehensive archeological study along the alignment highway.

> First a systematic and rigorous development study was performed along the whole highway alignment and afterwards full archeological excavations were conducted in every place that was an archeological relic declared officially by law or undeclared at all… The Antiquities Authority worked hand in hand with Derech Eretz. The consortium was not a typical entrepreneur, which looks at archeological excavations as a necessity imposed by law and which tends to minimize as much as possible its damage in time and finances. Derech Eretz is a serious institution which sees afar and understands the true importance of the scientific research of what could be destroyed by the construction of the highway.[305]

All that contribution to the environmental protection and preservation was in fact the framing of the public discourse on that subject by the interested parties in the execution of the highway. The facts may be true, but the real reasons and motives behind it all was the realization that it was much easier, cheaper and quicker for the consortium (and the other interested parties) to finance the studies, adjustments and minor changes in order to cooperate with the demands of the "Greens" rather than fight them.

In fact, when those demands required significant investment, the consortium fought against and refused to include them in the highway plans. For instance, one of the disputed issues was the tunneling beside environmentally sensitive areas along the route, such as the segment in the Ramoth-Menashe region, between the Barkai interchange and Road 70. This region is rich in unique natural and landscape elements. Derech Eretz was asked to tunnel the highway segment that passes through this region, but they agreed to do that only for a very short length, since tunneling is a much more expensive alternative than building overland. The issue had to be brought in front of the High Court of Justice to be decided.[306]

The opponents of the project, the environmental and social organizations, developed an agenda of their own in framing the public discourse around the highway so that as many people as possible would rally to their cause. They concluded that social arguments were more "attractive" to the public than the environmental ones; they therefore put the social arguments front and center. Even organizations that had, heretofore, dealt solely with environmental issues now placed social issues on their agenda for public discourse. That does not mean, of course, that the environmental problems were forgotten or neglected.

The claims that the highway construction will create new employment opportunities for the weaker strata or that the periphery population will be brought closer to the center were strongly refuted:

> The highway provides work mainly for foreign workers and will bring benefits to foreign companies at the expense of the land owners, farmers and rural settlers which will have their land expropriated for much less than its market value.
>
> Road construction is a temporal source of employment, while public transport requires a large pool of steady professional workers.
>
> The highway will have the opposite effect: instead of developing the Galilee and the Negev, suburban economic centers will be developed along the central corridor of the road.
>
> In the peripheral zone of the country, which allegedly is the main zone to benefit from the highway, the number of private car owners is twice to three times smaller than in the center. That is true also for the Orthodox and Arab populations.[307]

The economic aspects of the project were also attacked in many forms. The accuracy of the viability studies performed on the project was criticized and the conclusions doubted; claims that the highway will prevent or at least delay public transport development were raised; the argument that state budget and public funds were not to be burdened by the highway construction were completely refuted based on the fact that the government covered (from public funds), many items connected to the road (land expropriation compensations, interchanges execution, planning, etc.) as detailed in chapter 3 above.[308]

Even if most or all facts were correct, the motive framing the discourse was opposition to the privatization trend and the radical neo-liberalism of the 2000s as well as opposition to the government's estrangement from all social and welfare activities.

The "Greens" framed their argument around their demands for changes, adjustments and other specific requirements in order to preserve the environment and minimize damage from the highway. The real motive underpinning this was, of course, that the environmental and social NGOs were completely opposed to the project itself and considered the highway a poor solution to any of the economic, political, transport, social, and environmental points of view. Only when faced with the reality that the highway was inevitable, in spite of their struggle to stop it, did they revise their activities from simple opposition and protest to demanding specific concessions.

Conclusions

Analyzing the public discourse of the 1950's surrounding one of the largest national projects – the Huleh drainage – readily reveals the structure of the society, the basic ideology that constituted the platform of public decision-making and the attitude toward the environment and its preservation. The subjects of the narratives were a live testimony to those conceptions, but also the frequency of their appearance in the media and the way and tone of the little criticism the project met with were relevant to that analysis.

The decisions of the leaders, the worldviews of the elite and its hegemony were not challenged, but because Israel was a democratic state from start, some objections to the destruction of the Huleh nature and habitat were raised by scientists and nature lovers. But there were no real protest and oppositions to the project, even to think of such activity was considered "anti-Zionist", so even the muted criticism there was to the project, was expressed meekly and apologetically.

The Zionist movement considered the drainage project as accomplishing an old and almost forsaken dream as did early the entire population. The whole country took pride in the execution of the project. Those feelings were expressed clearly and openly in the many newspaper articles that dealt with the Huleh drainage, in movies, journals and professional magazines.

The discourse did not reach the public almost at all. Nevertheless, it is worth mentioning that some opposition was mounted or, at least some criticism of the project found its expression in a few articles and letters. It had one practical result - the creation of the Huleh reserve. On the other hand, civil society, in the modern sense of the concept, was undeveloped. In the interview with Azarya Alon about the Huleh drainage and the attitude to it of the scientists – botanists and zoologists – he was asked about the possibility of any kind of organizing against the project. His reaction was genuine surprise; according to him, it was unconceivable in those days – even in private meetings or discussions, to organize a protest against a project that symbolized the country's predominant ideology, a project supported by the country's elite. The environmental discourse in the 1950s focused on preservation of nature for the sake of nature.

The public discourse evolved mainly around national pride for the achievement of a large, technically complex national project and around the nostalgia caused by the "dying" of the lake and the swamp. It presented Israel as a progressive developing society in contrast to the Arab backward attitude. It helped also consolidate Israeli sovereignty over the frontier.

The study of the public discourse around the Trans-Israel Highway exemplifies the changes that Israeli society underwent between the 1950s and the 2000s. Civil society is in its third phase – passive exclusion. The state withdrew from many economic and social functions and the void was filled by various NGOs. So, by the 2000s, civil society was a well-developed sector, encompassing many voluntary organizations and covering a wide range of domains; awareness regarding public decisions and national projects was high which stimulated those organizations' activities.

Being so contested, the Trans-Israel stirred up controversy and caused intense activity of the "green" and social NGOs but also of other factors, such as politicians, scholars, etc.

Also significant and relevant were the modern means of communication; the media is no longer relegated to newspapers, the movies news journals and a few professional magazines. Nowadays, the electronic media, the web and all its ramifications – blogs, chats, private and public sites, make possible the spread of information in real-time, as well as contact with a very large number of citizens, and offering the possibility of organizing protests and demonstrations rapidly and easily.

Also, the liberal society of the 2000s is empowered to criticize decisions taken on almost every issue and aspect of life. A project is critiqued based on political, economic, transport, social, and environmental concerns, among others. Critics are loud and clear and no intimidation of a project's opponents is tolerated in any way. There is no automatic submission to the elite's worldview; no definite hegemony of the ruling elite; the many newspapers articles cited above explicitly demonstrate this. The NGOs and other organizations not only expressed clearly and openly their criticism, even opposition to the project, they mounted a spirited struggle for their beliefs and their cause – from public demonstrations to petitions to the High Court of Justice.

Framing of the public discourse existed in the 1950s as well as in the 2000s. In the fifties, it used the Zionist ideology and the hegemony of the ruling party to present the project's goals. It focused on the national aspect and on the economic-agricultural one. Making it easier than in the 2000s was the fact that the project was contested by no one and there were no public opponents to raise questions.

In the 2000s, the same tactics were used for framing the Trans-Israel Highway project. The project goals were presented to the public in a way meant to convince the people – especially those of the weaker strata – of the merits of the plan. But here, unlike with the Huleh drainage, the controversy was strong so a more expansive and emphasized framing was deployed. The framing in this case focused on a wide range of aspects, including social, economic and environmental issues.

Despite the obvious difference between the mobilized Israeli society of the 1950s and the strong and developed liberal civil society of the 2000s, there is a very important similarity to be remarked upon: for both projects, the decisions of the country's leaders in the 1950's and the coalition of capitalists and government agents in the 2000's were implemented in the end, in spite of any resistance and public opposition shown to the project. In both cases, public opinion played a role in those decisions – although to different degrees; in the 1950s, the Huleh reserve was created in part as a result of public pressure and in the 2000s, the intense activity of the "green" NGOs made the Trans-Israel reasonably considerate of environmental protection and the "greenest" infrastructure project.

The Environmental Effects of the Project

The debates over environmental issues can be subdivided into two:

- ◆ anthropocentric in character, referring to the sustainability of resources such as the soils, the peat and the water quality for human use.

◆   Natural in character, referring to considerations for unique and rare natural ecosystems.

While the anthropocentric considerations were the more critical for the success of the project, most of the public debate focused on the care for the natural ecosystems of the Huleh valley.

The Anthropocentric Issue

Consequences of the Swamps Drainage on the Peat and the Peat Soils

Concerning the anthropocentric issues most of the debate focused on the economic value of the peat and the ways to benefit from it. Surprisingly enough, the consequences of the drainage on water quality in the Sea of Galilee (the Kineret), the national water reservoir, were hardly discussed. Soon after the Huleh drainage plant completion, the project looked like a great success as it allowed cultivation of new fertile land and helped the economy in the region to flourish. However, during the following two decades, it became evident that there was an ever-widening gap between the project expectations and its consequences. A few researchers explained the process as follows:

> The interference in the natural system of the Huleh valley caused a series of physical and biogeochemical irreversible problems: the peat soils decomposed and settled, leading to deterioration of the soil quality and narrowing by 10-20 % the land suitable for cultivation; peat fires accelerated, causing dust and storms; poisonous weeds spread out; field mice multiplied; indigenous fauna and flora disappeared; water bird population declined; and the quality of the water in the Sea of Galilee (Lake Kinneret) became impaired.[309]

Dried peat soil from the bottom of the marsh decomposed, burned and released pollutants once filtered by the swamp, leaving a wasteland unfit for farming.

The Huleh drainage was expected to reclaim expanses of peat soil under the marsh that were considered to be both highly fertile and a source of fuel. But these results were not realized. Soon it became obvious that the peat was a problem. Although thousands of acres were brought under cultivation by neighboring settlements, problems emerged in large tracts of land with high concentrations of peat soil. The drainage led to the exposure of the peat to the atmosphere, rapid oxidation and, as a result, the drying out and disintegration of the peat, decomposition of the organic matter and rapid subsidence of the peat land. Underground fires erupted often, caused by spontaneous combustion following the exothermic oxidation reaction and fueled by the organic matter. Sometimes, the fires continued for months.

The underground conflagrations accelerated the disintegration of the soil and, because of strong winds, especially the hot, dry, desert winds (hamsin), flyaway peat dust spread around and covered nearby farm areas, rendering them unsuitable for cultivation. Declining soil fertility and productivity led to abandonment of agricultural land and to severe damage to the ecosystem.

As farmers stopped cultivating large areas, the land was overrun by mice and weeds. Peat dust, whipped up by winds, covered the region. The soil subsidence kept on, caused by the fires and the drying out of the peat which then spread out as dust or shrank. The average subsidence was of 10 centimeter per year. The valley center subsided 6-7 meter from its original level.

In parallel, exposure of the organic soils to oxygen accelerated the formation of nitrates which then leached into the Kinneret (the Sea of Galilee). The dried swamp soil became the main source of pollution for the Kinneret water. The nitrate compounds accumulating in the Kinneret were nutrients for algae. They sped up algae growth and the growth of other creatures feeding on algae. As water quality in the Kinneret deteriorated, scientific research indicated that Huleh peat lands contributed nearly 50% of the nitrates entering Israel's only freshwater surface reservoir.[310]

In the 1980s, the difficult problems regarding soil fertility in the Huleh Valley became obvious. The oxidized soil lost most of its nutrients (especially micro-nutrients) and the need for fertilizers increased. In addition to the other problems, the low hydraulic conductivity of the soil made farming very difficult. With time, some 500 hectares were abandoned and this brought on further oxidation and leaching of nutrients into the Kinneret.

Looking back to the Huleh drainage project, some of the objectives were attained – most of the area is still cultivated by the surrounding settlements. But the ongoing disintegration processes resulted in some second thoughts and the launch of research work. In the 1970s, hydrological, agricultural and ecological research began, intensifying over time, regarding the peat soil problems and how to deal with them. The conclusion was that it was necessary to rehabilitate the Huleh valley and some plans were proposed.

The research brought out some important facts about the peat:

◆ The peat hydraulic properties were determined in 1977 in the laboratory and the underground flow regime was studied in the field.[311] The main finding was that the groundwater in the Huleh valley created an artesian system. That meant that the pressure on the groundwater increased with depth, thereby tending to flow upwards to the surface. So, the disintegrated peat particles rose to the surface and during winter floods, they were washed into the Kinneret.

◆ The nitrification-denitrification processes were studied quantitatively in order to identify the factors that influence their rate. The results showed that sprinkling on dry soils slowed down nitrate rate formation.[312] Also, it was found that some kinds of fodder were intensive consumers of nitrates and therefore, prevented their leaching into the Kinneret.

◆ It was found that the best way to stop the disintegration process was to keep the groundwater level under control. The recommendation was to maintain the groundwater level at a depth of 120 centimeter in the summer and to allow up to a 60 centimeter rise after the rains in the winter. In this way, it was possible to maintain the humidity of the soil and to reduce to a minimum the organic matter decomposition.

◆ Other studies, not necessarily related to water resources, suggested ways to improve cultivation, to improve irrigation, how to use fertilizers and so on.[313]

It seems that much of the information about the peat and its problems was already known by the end of the 1950s and the beginning of the 1960s.

> ...These were not the only problems. All of a sudden it turned out that the peat soil shrank, the lake subsides and the groundwater level rises, so that in 25 years the Huleh may go back to being a lake...
>
> The peat was not used for industrial purposes...
>
> The possibility of the Huleh soil subsidence was known to the drainage project people from the professional literature and also from the experience with regular soils. Every kind of soil shrinks when its water is drained out of it. The peat, a soil rich in organic matter (because of plants decomposition while the Huleh was a swamp), in addition to the natural shrinkage, went through the natural process of organic matter weathering, mostly because of oxidation, area exposure to air and fires (the soil itself tends somewhat to ignite). At the Scranton farm, in California, the peat soil subsided 12-13 meter in 80 years, meaning an average of 15 centimeter per year. In the Huleh, the peat soil sank by 85 centimeter in the first 8 years of the

drainage project and in some places, even by 1.25 meter in the same period of time, meaning the same average of about 15 centimeter per year. The Tahal experts calculated and found that in 20-25 years the Huleh soil level will decrease, 2.5 meter and then, the Jordan water level will be higher than the surface level in the Huleh so that flooding of the lake will be inevitable unless very expensive engineering devices will be built. And more: the subsidence can cause the surface level to reach groundwater level and then the flood will be twofold – from the Jordan and from the groundwater at once…

The Huleh was drained so as to obtain great quantities of soil and water but the peat requires great quantities of water and is not fit as a cultivation soil…

It seems, according to Tahal experts, that the peat sensitivity requires a very careful treatment: the vegetation burn has to be minimal in order to prevent a too rapid oxidation of the organic matter; it is preferable to plan for crops that will cover the area all year long so the surface will not be exposed to oxidation and dust spread will be prevented; the mechanical equipment used for cultivation must not be too heavy; groundwater level must be kept high at all times but not too high so as it will not damage the crops; irrigation must be continuous, even beyond farming season; and so on. In Tahal's engineers opinion, the method enabling the exploitation of the peat properties for cultivation without the damages of subsidence and weathering, has yet to be found….

The industrial exploitation of the peat, that was estimated to be equivalent to 3 million tons of refined oil (from 26,000 dunam of 2.0 meter depth), remained the private dream of the Zionist American millionaire Zanzibar; The Huleh Development Authority agricultural exploitation became fruitful and profitable only for the last three years (10 years after the drainage), following almost 15 million IL in investment.[314]

Nature Conservation and Protection of the Environment

Before the establishment of the State of Israel, there was little consideration for nature conservation. During the period of time Palestine was under Ottoman rule, the only relevant issues were economic ones – how best to exploit nature in order to obtain the most material profits. Land was cultivated for agricultural products without concern for what was destroyed on the way, be they plants, animals, or entire habitats.

During the British mandate the foundations for nature conservation were laid. The Mandate government was concerned with flora preservation, especially forests, and for this reason it enacted "The Forests Ordinance" in 1926. Some species of trees were deemed "protected trees" and were not to be cut down at all. As much as 450 "forest reserves" were set aside from the public domain during the time of the British Mandate. Afforestation was also initiated over more than 5,300 hectares. The British did not, however, make any effort to preserve wildlife. The "rule of hunting", in 1924, although trying to regulate the hunt, even allowed the killing of rare and special animals, those in danger of extinction.

During the Mandate, the British enacted a number of ordinances that formed the groundwork for Israel's eventual oversight of the natural habitat. Before the establishment of the State, the Jewish community in Palestine did not much trouble itself with nature protection. Singular efforts were carried out by the botanist Alexander Ayg, but without significant results. During the pre-State era, it was common to promote geographical education and 'learning the land' through intensive walking. These efforts led to widespread knowledge of the flora and fauna native to the region, but did not translate into any specific activities to protect them. In fact, during those walks, collection of plants and even animals was encouraged by the guides. The Jewish community was not preoccupied with issues of nature conservation at this time.

With the founding of the State of Israel, the government established the Planning Administration, which began operations in the summer of 1948. From its inception, the scope of this office included the protection of nature and landscape as part of the Jewish people's historic birthright. This attitude was influenced and emphasized by the people that were entrusted with the management of the Planning Administration – architect Arieh Sharon, the Administration Head and architect Eliezer Brutzkus , Head of the Research and Survey Department. Both of them were passionate about nature and about the land as patrimony.

Materialistic and economic motives were the basis for some of the preservation efforts. These motives included tourism and establishment of recreation sites, among others. Nevertheless, there was also an appreciation for the value of nature and the importance of conservation in support of this valuable resource.

The Planning Administration looked to the nature conservation work carried out by other developed countries. The vast natural reserves of the United States, Canada and other large countries were not directly applicable to Israel because of its small size. The British and other European countries' models of pastoral landscapes, cultivated land and small towns and villages were also not entirely applicable because of the intense and rapid pace of development in Israel. The pioneer mentality of dedication to "development" and "the conquest of the desert" conflicted with the notion of nature conservation. Israel's decision was to adopt a compromise between the two models.[315]

A variety of organizations arose before The Society for the Protection of Nature came to be. For example, "The Circle for Landscape

Preservation" - created in 1944 by Brutzkus, "the Gardeners Organization", "The Consulting Committee for Gardening and Landscape," established in 1949 were but a few of these.

As early as 1948-1949, a survey of nature, landscape and historic places was prepared by the Planning Administration, with the contribution of the Zoological and Botanical Companies members. For the first time, a proposal was presented for the creation of nature reserves.

An outgrowth of this survey was the list prepared by the Department of Research and Survey delineating proposed national parks, with protected areas among them. Included in this list were also the Huleh Wetlands.[316] In Israel's first Master Plan, prepared and presented in 1950 by the Planning Administration, a portion of the Huleh Wetlands was included as part of a proposal for a nature reserve.[317]

But, although nature conservation was taken into consideration and even planned for, with some action taken by the Israeli Parliament (Knesset) as early as the 1950s, the emphasis always remained on development, economics and the conquest of the wilderness. Even the most enthusiastic of nature lovers and science researchers would not have given priority to nature conservation over development. This attitude was consistent with a mobilized society, a population that often subsumed its personal opinions to the will of the ruling elite.

According to Arieh Sharon – Head of the Planning Administration – in his speech from August 1949:

> Obviously, most of these areas (for parks and recreation) will
> be mountainous, without value to the economy and agriculture,
> but with great value for their nature beauty and for the needs
> of the soul.[318]

One of the basic considerations in deciding on where to locate a National Park was whether or not the area in question was found to be without any economic value – for agriculture, settlements, or any other type of development including job creation.[319]

The Planning Administration and the volunteer nature-related organizations pressed for the Knesset to enact special laws for the declaration of National Parks and Nature Reserves so that those areas would be protected under the law and thereby not subject to any development efforts (settlements, agriculture, industry and so on).

The committee appointed by the Prime Minister to recommend areas for National Parks, advocated for the creation of an agency responsible for the protection of nature.

But the Government and the Knesset were busy with legislation on subjects considered much more important and urgent than nature protection.[320] And, at times, many of the government ministries had interests that were in direct opposition to nature protection, with development being their overarching goal.[321]

The Huleh Reserve

Until approximately the middle of the 20th century, the Western world disliked and feared swamps. Their special fauna and flora was not appreciated and the preference was to drain swamps indiscriminately and use the land for cultivation. In Palestine/Israel, the attitude of the Zionist pioneers toward swamps was similar or even more so, as explained in chapter 3. Therefore, the Huleh drainage project was opposed by almost no one and embraced by nearly all, even by those who had some doubts about the project, as a necessary, important, even heroic Zionist action.

Nevertheless, the parties in charge of nature preservation did spare some thought for the Huleh swamps. The first attempt to preserve the Huleh ecosystem was made by the Planning Administration, specifically by the Department of Research and Survey, under Brutzkus' leadership.

During the years 1948-1949, that department prepared a countrywide survey regarding nature preservation and historical heritage. In that survey, the department involved participants from among academic zoologists, botanists, archeologists as well as nature enthusiasts. An important component of the survey was the proposal of the Commission for Nature Protection (formed of representatives of the Zoological Society and the Botanical Society) for scientific natural preserves. Based on the survey's results, a "Program for National Parks" was proposed in March 1950, with the intention of including in those parks nature, landscape and historic heritage preservation.

This was not, however, nature preservation circa 2000s. The mobilized Israeli society of the time was one that accepted and embraced the ideology of the elites, almost without any dissent; the priorities in choosing the National Parks were dictated by economic reasons and based on the ethos of development; a distant third consideration was of the value of nature itself.

The program was based on the assumption that within a short period of time, Israel would have to absorb, into its small area, a great number of immigrants and that this increase in population would lead to destruction of most of the country's natural and original landscape. It was expected that the country would become rich in a concrete landscape and intensively cultivated land. In order to mitigate, somewhat, this forecast, parks were needed, but they were to be chosen based only on the fact that the areas were otherwise lacking all economic value.[322]

The parks themselves were proposed to serve first and foremost as recreation areas for the whole country, then as touristic attractions and for educational purposes. Some sites inside the parks that contained special landscapes or valuable natural elements, were to be designated as nature reserves.

Based on this program and other information gathered by Brutzkus' department, a list of 40 National Parks was proposed, including the Huleh swamps.

Concomitantly with the Department of Research and Survey's work, a commission appointed directly by Prime Minister David Ben-Gurion, began its activity by assessing and proposing six locations for National Parks. The proposal was addressed to the Prime Minister himself. The commission included representatives of the Zoological Society and the Botanical Society. Under their influence, the commission's recommendations emphasized the issue of nature reserves.[323] That list of national parks and nature reserves did not include the Huleh swamps.

The commission's recommendations were not implemented. Implementation would have required the passage of special laws for the designation of parks and nature reserves, the existing laws being insufficient for this purpose. But the Knesset was busy with more important and urgent legislation so that subject was not addressed for a long time thereafter.

Nevertheless, there were scientists, researchers and nature enthusiasts that well understood and appreciated the value of the Huleh swamps ecosystem, realizing the damage and the losses the drainage project would cause. Under the influence of Professor Heinrich Mendelssohn and according to his recommendation, Brutzkus included in the proposal of parks and natural preserves, an area of 400 hectares of the Huleh swamp to be maintained as a nature reserve.[324]

In 1951, Arieh Sharon, the Head of the Planning Administration, published the book "Israel's Physical Planning", based on the recommendations of the National Parks Commission. The book included a map featuring sites proposed for national parks and for nature reserves. On this map, the Huleh swamps were marked as a proposed nature reserve. The book did mention the Huleh drainage project, but also the existences of a plan for the creation of a small nature preserve in the Huleh swamps for the conservation of the special fauna and flora of the place.[325]

The actions mentioned above regarding the creation of a nature reserve in the Huleh swamps were formal and put forth by official institutions or personalities, in the framework of their official roles. The lack of implementation of their proposal and the progress of the drainage project caused other individuals to take action and intervene in favor of the Huleh preserve. The actions were not coordinated among themselves and not organized as a protest. Nevertheless, they reflected the attitudes and feelings of both researchers and scientists toward the drainage project. Scientists intensified research relating to the Huleh's plants and animals. Among the researchers was Professor Mendelssohn's young assistant – Amotz Zahavi, one of the initiators of the Society for the Protection of Nature.[326]

On 3 August 1952, *Yediot Aharonot* published an article entitled, "Lights and Shadows" about the 42nd Botanical and Zoological Congress. At this Congress, scientists expressed their reservations regarding the Huleh drainage project and their concern about nature conservation in Israel. They suggested creating an official institution charged with nature and landscape preservation.

> The government's duty is to watch over and entrust a state-run institution to preserve the valuable plants and animals against destruction and extinction.[327]

In order to emphasize the ecological importance of the fauna and the flora of the Huleh, the Faculty of Natural Sciences of the Hebrew University in Jerusalem, commissioned a documentary about the Huleh Valley. In a letter to the Ministry of Interior, the representative of the Department of Zoology noted that the unique character of the Huleh Valley had not yet been sufficiently researched. Even scientists from abroad came to study the fauna and the flora of the Valley. Now, when the studies were at their most active, the Valley was about to be destroyed. The proposed documentary was intended to play a double role: one, as a first-class scientific document and two, to serve as an educational vehicle for future generations.[328]

The Commission for Nature Protection sent a letter on 28 January 1951, to the Minister of Education and Culture, the Minister of Agriculture and the Government Secretary regarding the Huleh reserve. Copies of the letter were sent to a long list of institutions, relevant to the issue and with some perceived ability to help.

The Commission was created by Professor Mendelssohn in 1951 and was composed of representatives from the Zoological Society and the Botanical Society.

The letter acknowledged the development of the drainage project and its importance for the country's economy and for agriculture. But it also emphasized the uniqueness of the swamp – the place farthest north of Africa where papyrus grew and with it, special plants and rare animals found in it their natural habitat. Total drainage of the swamp would destroy this special ecosystem – a great loss to nature, science and education. So, although the significance of the drainage project was not undeniable, the commission asked for a small area – 400 hectares – to be retained as a nature reserve (reservat).[329]

In September 1951, the Commission for Nature Protection submitted a proposal with details and maps of the nature reserve site in the Huleh. The proposal was based on scientific researches made on the Huleh swamps: "The Vegetation of the Huleh Plain" – on the plants of the Huleh Valley, prepared by M. Zohary and G. Orshansky and published in the Palestine Journal of Botany (1947-9), "1940-1944 Diary of the Hebrew University Expedition to Lake Huleh" prepared by H. Steinitz, K. Reich and H. Mendelssohn and containing among other topics, work on the hydrobiology of the Huleh.[330]

A further step in creating the reserve was made by Professor Mendelssohn who, with the help of his student Amotz Zahavi, organized a visit to the swamps for a few journalists. The visit, by boat and on foot, took place on 19 June 1952. Following that visit, an article was published in the newspaper *Davar*, claiming that *"reserves will be created in order to protect natural assets in the Huleh region"*.[331]

At the same time, an article was published in another newspaper, *Al Hamishmar*, in which the government and the JNF were encouraged to assist the Nature Protection Commission in their effort to conserve the fauna and the flora of the country, in general, and to create the Huleh reserve, in particular.[332]

The JNF, implementer of the drainage project, did not oppose the establishment of the reserve and it cooperated with the scientists and the researchers acting on behalf of the reserve's creation.

In June 1953, a new commission was nominated by the Minister of Agriculture Peretz Naftali, to examine the possibilities for the reserve creation. The commission was led by Dr. Peleg, head of the Plants Protection Department in the Ministry of Agriculture. The other participants were representatives of the Ministry of Health, JNF, Tahal (the Water Planning Company), the Commission for Nature Protection and the Hebrew University.[333] The commission was charged with bringing the reserve plans into being and for that to be achieved, the commission had to define the final size of the reserve and its exact location, decide on the technical methods of execution, and choose the responsible authority for the execution and, then, the maintenance and supervision of the reserve.[334] The commission did reach consensus regarding the size and the location of the reserve and also suggested the creation of a special authority empowered to *"survey, implement, maintain and protect the Huleh reserve and other reserves in the country"*.[335]

Concomitantly, in December 1953, the scientist members of the Commission for Nature Protection met to call for the creation of an authority to be in charge of the preservation of the country's fauna and flora. This authority was to be named "The Society for the Protection of Nature". Among the members of the commission were Azaria Alon and Amotz Zahavi, considered today the founding fathers of the SPN.[336]

There was some resistance to the reserve creation on the part of several Ministry of Agriculture employees. Abraham Hanochi was the head of the Agriculture Development Department. He was interested in a smaller area for the reserve in order to increase as much as possible the area earmarked for cultivation, after the drainage would be completed. He also opposed the involvement of the Ministry of Agriculture in the reserve survey and implementation process.[337]

Another ministry employee, who fiercely opposed the reserve plan, was Josef Reiskin, who wrote a letter to the General Manager of the Ministry of Agriculture – H. Gevati, explaining in detail his reasons for opposing the creation of the reserve. Those reasons were mainly economic: loss of land for cultivation and as a future means of livelihood for so many immigrant families; expenses for maintenance of the reserve; damages to crops from animals living in the reserve (hogs and such); and the dangers associated with resurgence of malaria. There was no reference at all in his letter to any of the nature-related values of the swamp.[338]

In answer to the above, Berchyau – the JNF drainage project manager – wrote a letter to the Minister of Agriculture and other individuals involved with the Huleh project, explaining the importance of the reserve.[339] Also, the Society for the Protection of Nature reacted to Reiskin's protests by sending a letter to the General Manager of the Ministry of Agriculture and emphasizing again the benefits of the reserve: the international scientific value of the reserve, its importance for education, tourism and nature walks.[340]

Apart from Reiskin, there were other protests against the reserve, such as the Local Council of *Isud Hama'ala* who complained to the JNF that their location close to the proposed reserve might again endanger them because of malaria.[341]

In 1954, another commission was nominated, in order to advance the Huleh reserve plan. The commission head was A. Hanochi, head of the Agriculture Development Department in the Ministry of Agriculture. The other members of the commission were representatives of the JNF, the Jewish Agency and the Society for the Protection of Nature. The commission was charged with deciding upon the proper site for the reserve, proposing an implementation plan and working out a financial plan for its execution and management.[342]

The commission accomplished its mission, and even tried to find a way to have the proposed reserve site legally declared a protected area, using the existing laws. The only thing the commission could not come to an agreement about was the authority in charge of supervision and management of the reserve.[343] The JNF took the final and official decision to create the reserve, on 20 April 1955, at the Board of Directors meeting.

The only circumstance in which anyone opposed openly the drainage project was on account of nature preservation, in a series of articles published in the newspaper *Haaretz* by a journalist, writing under the pseudonym of "Ron". The real person or persons behind that name remained unknown. In his column – "Observed, Heard," he claimed that the state was not doing enough and had not participated financially in the protection of the area chosen for the reserve.[344]

In the same column, he wrote about an open protest against the whole drainage project. In his opinion, the reason no one else had opposed the project could be attributed to the lack of interest in the country and in sports like fishing, hunting and sailing. That lack of interest resulted in a lack of knowledge and appreciation for the richness and beauty of the Huleh Valley nature. If the destruction of the Valley was to be inevitable, with only a portion being designated as a preserve, he noted that at least 1500 hectares would be required for this purpose.[345]

The only one to respond to Ron's articles was the JNF. Its project engineer – A. Berchyau – defended the goal and the design of the project, emphasizing its national importance.[346]

Huleh's Neighboring Inhabitants

The attitudes of the Jewish population living in settlements in the vicinity of the Huleh, were largely typical for the time and place.

Some Kibbutz Hulata inhabitants made their livelihood from fishing. Most of them were nature fans; they spent time watching and observing the plants and animal life in the swamp. They even wrote about it, took pictures and collected plants. The kibbutz invited a painter – Arieh Hatzor – from Givat Brener, to come and draw some of the birds and animals of the swamp.[347] At least some of Kibbutz Hulata people understood and appreciated the value of the nature and landscape in the Huleh swamps.

Nevertheless, none of them ever spoke up against the drainage project or even tried to bring up for discussion the damage the plan stood to do to nature in the Huleh valley. They also did not try to participate in the creation of the reserve. Their only reaction to the reserve was the problem of its boundaries which limited the available fishing area.

The Hulata kibbutz inhabitants did try to keep the reality of the Huleh swamp and landscape alive. Some of the Huleh nature fans – Gershoni, Glusman and Zigelman – prepared a book about the history, the climate, the population of the Huleh region and especially, about the fauna and flora living in the swamp. The book, to be entitled "The Huleh Book", was begun before the drainage project implementation, but was never published because during the time it was being prepared, the drainage project was accomplished. The draft manuscript still exists in the archives and is a testimony to the attitude of the Hulata inhabitants regarding the drainage project: appreciation and admiration for a mega-project designed to improve the country's economy and safety and to make possible a more intense settling of the country's north-eastern border. The purpose of "The Huleh Book" was to perpetuate the memory of the beautiful nature and the rich world of the swamp's animals and vegetation for the generations to come because, obviously, the swamp was to die and its nature world – to disappear.[348]

The same was the case with Peter Merom's book of photographs and text, "The Poem of the Dying Lake". The photographs were taken in 1954, during the implementation of the drainage project and were presented to the public in the Tel-Aviv Museum, in 1957, when the project had been completed. The book was published in 1960, so there was no opportunity for it to influence public opinion regarding the drainage, even if that had been at all possible. No criticism of the drainage project was voiced in the book, even though it deplored the disappearance of the rich wildlife of the Huleh. The practical importance of the drainage trumped all other concerns.[349]

The settlement that contributed the most to perpetuating the memory of the Huleh wildlife was Kibbutz Dan, situated farther north of the Huleh swamp.

The kibbutz inhabitants initiated the erection of a museum to commemorate "the redemption of the land." The JNF and Menahem Usishkin worked on this project. Their intent was to have in this museum a place to commemorate the nature of the Huleh Valley. The kibbutz asked for the JNF's help and cooperation to implement the museum project. The JNF board of directors agreed to cooperate and Josef Weitz and Shmuel Usishkin (Menahem's son) were nominated as JNF representatives for the museum project. Together with the kibbutz representatives, they chose a committee of specialists, including Prof. Mendelssohn and Prof. Zohari.[350]

At the Beth Usishkin cornerstone laying ceremony, on 25 October 1951, kibbutz member Elimelech Horvitz praised the conquest of the desolation that was Menahem Usishkin's life work and in this framework – the drainage project as a significant representative of that goal. His speech emphasized the national pride invested in the drainage project as a technical and economic accomplishment. The Huleh nature museum was mentioned as a tribute to the Huleh fauna and flora for the benefit of future generations to study and to know about, and as another aspect of the drainage project.[351]

On 13 January 1955, the Museum Beth Usishkin was inaugurated. Invitees to the ceremony included the State President, a few ministers, all the members of the JNF board of directors and members of the Society for the

Protection of Nature. One of the speakers was Prof. Bodenheimer, of the Hebrew University. Although he praised the drainage project and its benefits to agriculture, as did Elimelech Horvitz, his speech included references to the conflict between agricultural development and the need for ecological preservation. He mentioned the problem of planning for agricultural, industrial and urban development without concomitant consideration for environmental conservation and nature preservation. Moreover, he warned of possible ecological problems in the future, as a result of the Huleh swamp drainage.[352] The Usishkin museum represents the decision-making concerning the drainage and preservation of one corner of the swamp. The proponents and the opponents of the project, all members of one elite group, celebrated together the opening of the museum based on the agreement that the drainage contributed to the development of the country, with no mention of the criticism against the project.

Nature and Environment in a Mobilized Society

In the 1950s, the Israeli society was a mobilized, collectivist society, as detailed in chapter 3. The Zionist elite - the politicians that comprised the government as well as the public activists - embraced and spread their ideology and their vision of the new country and the requirements for nation-building.

The order of priorities was clear-cut; the ethos of development, of building a new modern country and of creating a unified nation from out of the immigrants arriving from all corners of the globe and from varying cultures, was the main and most important goal. The means to achieve that goal were also defined by the elite: development of rural life and of bonds to the land to be facilitated by building rural settlements, developing agriculture, draining the swamps and making the desert bloom. The spirit of the times conveyed that the good of the collective is primary, the individual wishes and interests must be subsumed to the interest of the collective. That ideology was accepted by the public wholeheartedly, without difference of opinions, debates or arguments. The hegemony of the elite was absolute.

The Huleh drainage project and the reserve represent a kind of test case to examine the events described as a paradigm of the 1950s. In February 2009, several conversations took place with individuals involved in the Huleh reserve project.

When asked about the issue, Amotz Zahavi – Prof. Mendelssohn's assistant and one of the pillars of the Society for the Protection of Nature, commented that no one, not even the most passionate of nature lovers or the scientists, dared speak against the drainage project or seek to forestall it. The most they dared hope for was the creation of the reserve. It went without saying and it was accepted by the whole population that the most important thing for the country was to drain the swamps and create more land for cultivation. No one was bothered by issues of environmental conservation, not even for the benefit of humankind. Some researches and scientists were of the opinion that drainage of the Huleh would precipitate an ecological disaster, but they were far from numerous and never considered speaking against the project. There was no mechanism in place to organize a protest and try to reverse the decision to drain the Huleh.[353]

An interview with Dr. Uzi Paz revealed that he held the same opinions as Prof. Amotz Zahavi and he told a very similar story. In the 1950s, no one was preoccupied by issues of environmental conservation and nature preservation. The first Jewish settlements in Eretz Israel were on drained swampland because that was the cheapest and the most available to be bought from the Arabs. So, draining swamps was taken for granted by the Jewish population as a normal activity. The general public was not concerned with ecology, neither for the sake of nature nor even for the sake of people. When anyone involved with the Huleh drainage project who had practical overseas experience working with peat warned about the problems to be expected from peat land, they were overruled and their warnings ignored. The oft-repeated phrase: "Zionist peat will not sink", ascribed to different people by different storytellers, is typical and perfectly reflects the spirit of the times – the Zionist ideology is stronger than everything, even than nature's elements.[354]

Azaria Alon, known for his devotion to nature preservation, wrote in his book "About Trees and Stones", as follows:

> If we were a larger and richer country, perhaps we could and even should have left the Huleh untouched, as a closed area for a National Park. Apparently, this was impossible; therefore we chose the lesser of two evils: an area of approximately 4000 dunams (400 hectares) in the north-eastern corner of the lake, on the river Malha and on part of the swamp to be left as a nature reserve.[355]

In a 1996 article, Azaria Alon wrote explicitly that some scientists and public personalities (especially Prof. Mendelssohn) were aware of the fact that the drainage would cause irreversible ecological damage, but even the request to leave a small area untouched for the nature reserve was considered at first an "anti-Zionist attitude".[356]

A February 2009 interview with Alon made clear the spirit of those times: there was no interest and no awareness regarding ecological problems that could damage people or the environment. Scientists were interested in nature for its own sake but that interest was considered relatively unimportant and at any rate, was secondary to the acute national problems of the time. The public was living the Zionist dream and ideology; the goals of the Huleh drainage project were intrinsically part of that dream. That was the decisive factor and the scientific data was not taken in consideration in that decision. Plans to drain the Huleh Valley existed from 1934. In 1950, reality changed in a way that enabled the independent state to fulfill the dreams with no burdens.

The implementation of the drainage project was obvious and undisputed. It was not only inconceivable for the scientists who might be worried about the consequences of the project, to act or organize meaningful opposition in any way; it was even considered unacceptable to discuss the matter between themselves in friendly meetings, which shows how strongly held were the prevailing attitudes of the hegemony of the elite and how definitively mobilized was the Israeli society in those days. These included the belief that even if problems were to arise during the implementation of the project, solutions would be found as needed and everything would work out (recall the famous "Zionist peat will not sink" motto).

The Huleh was a unique place – with the northern border featuring European fauna and flora and the southern border the African. Scientists were more sensitive to the damage the project would cause to that special region and not to the damage that could be caused to human beings. None thought or suspected that the Kinneret waters would become polluted because of the drainage project.[357]

In August 1952, during the 42nd congress of the Zoological Society and the Botanical Society, scientists brought up the subject of the Huleh drainage project and the ecological damage that would ensue. But nothing came out of the congress that would prevent the project's implementation. The congress and the reference to the Huleh project along with the issue of creating an authority in charge of nature preservation were mentioned in an article in the newspaper *Yediot Aharonot*.[358]

Thus, as is well known now, the Huleh drainage project was executed without any meaningful opposition or criticism and was, instead, regarded by the whole nation as a point of national pride and a manifestation of the Zionist dream come true.

Neo-Liberalism and Environment

Neo-liberalism is the most widespread ideological and political philosophy of global governance to follow Keynesianism. Yet, that philosophy is much criticized and has many flaws. Though it seemed to address a number of problems and difficulties in the political and economic arenas, it resulted in other issues, mostly social. There are some who consider it a total failure. One of the main issues of neo-liberalism is its attitude toward environment and conservation. The discourse develops around the neo-liberal reforms regarding the environment.

There is a strong connection between neo-liberalism, environmental reforms and environmental politics. Neo-liberalism has a significant impact on environment and it causes changes in social relations. Neo-liberalism and environmentalism are the ideologies that, in modern times deal the most with regulation of social relations. The strongest opponent to neo-liberalism nowadays is environmentalism.[359]

The neo-liberal attitude toward nature and environment is based on and influenced by the classical liberalism ideology regarding nature. It propagates managing nature by commodifying it. That includes the right to pollute for private property owners; the right to charge user fees from visitors of public nature reserves; the privatization of natural resources like forests, water, etc. Also, it is based on laissez-faire environmental praxis in various domains, especially agriculture.

The Keynesian regime brought a significant attribute to environmental protection by passing special rules and laws for that purpose. Those rules and laws restricted substantially the free movement of capitalist markets and investors in favor of public interests and so – restrained their benefits on behalf of public interests. One of the principal steps of the neo-liberal state was to abolish, or at least diminish those rules and regulations in order to give a free hand to the market and the investors to maximize their gains.

The struggle of the neo-liberal regime against environmental regulations was no less fierce than its struggle against labor protection and social welfare laws and regulations.[360] On one hand, the very core of the neo-liberal ideology – private ownership of natural resources, the tendency to maximize profit, the free market competition – brought on exploitation of natural resources without enough attention or consideration to damages caused to environment or to the legacy of future generations.[361]

On the other hand, neo-liberalism and environmentalism, in time, grew into each other, found common ground or at least common tangibles in order to act together instead of one against the other. Free market environmentalism has developed over the years in the form of exchangeable pollutants emission permits, fees for public goods, etc. Neo-liberal projects, in their turn, adopted environmental aspects like including "green" elements in their development projects, etc.[362]

As a matter of course, a society which on one hand conducts a liberal economy, but on the other hand is oriented toward environment protection, will suffer an intern conflict between the two. In a neo-liberal society, that conflict will be extreme because of the wish to maximize profits by saving investments required to preserve nature and environment, investments that do not bring back any direct profits to investors and constitute solely expanses.

That internal conflict is based on two structural aspects embedded in neo-liberalism and environmentalism. The first one is the neo-liberalism principle that individual benefit and interest are "sacred", one of the most important norms. So, common interest is reduced to a second place of creating a stable atmosphere in which private interests can thrive; the result being that resource management gave continuous priority to private rights over community interests. The second structural aspect is that a capitalist market functions in such a way that it has to expand incessantly so it constantly looks for more markets and for increasing efficiency and profit. The result of that economic system has been the exhaustion of natural resources and serious damages to nature and environment – sometimes irreversible.

> Liberal society is fundamentally organized around economic
> interaction….Liberal civic virtue remains privatized. There is
> no language of public interest apart from individual interest
> (or corporation), leaving the scope of public policy choices
> severely limited.[363]

In a liberal (and even more so – in a neo-liberal) society, the minimal interference of the government in the free-market and concerning the rights of the individual or the corporation to do as it pleases with its private property, the power of the state to control, regulate and monitor the treatment of the environment is reduced significantly. *"One of the processes associated with neo-liberalism is deregulation, the scaling back of states and their capacity to regulate."*[364]

On the other hand, the degradation of the environment quality and the spread of natural resources (air, water, land, etc.) pollution created the necessity to make changes in the attitude and conceptions of private good versus public good. A polluted environment can affect everyone, rich or poor, so environmental protection is to be considered a protection of private good as well as of communal good. *"Self-interest itself must include minimizing social bads, because anyone of us may, at some time, be exposed to those bads."*[365]

Public rights include the preservation of nature and natural resources for present and especially for future generations while the neo-liberal market focuses its interest in immediate benefits. That situation creates the conflict between the civil society, which represents the common good, against the alliance of political power and wealth, which represents private immediate interests. The tension between public rights and private rights is felt the strongest in the environmental policy because this policy is based on regulating the use and development of private property, with the tendency to give them a free hand as much as possible.

Despite the analysis detailed above, the last decades brought a change in attitude toward environmental protection, legally – by ruling new laws

– and also practically, by different actions of preventing pollution and of nature conservation.

That change in attitude is due to four factors:

First, as mentioned above, the pollution of natural resources can affect everyone so its prevention is a private, as well as public interest. Second, the progress of science and technology of the last decades, created a much better understanding of the dangers and problems resulting from the damages to the environment. Third, the understanding of the above-mentioned dangers, their exposure to the public and the creation of educational programs and other similar activities, increased considerably the awareness and the interest of the public in nature conservation and environment protection. Fourth, the development of the civil society created an ambiance for the birth of non-official, non-governmental organizations – NGOs – that deal constantly and intensely with issues regarding environment protection, nature conservation and other interrelated issues such as social/environmental justice, feminism and others. The activities and actions of the NGOs influenced and changed the way of the free market behavior. In the modern society, state, business, NGOs and communities are expected to share responsibility for the environment.

The attitude toward environment protection by all involved in the construction of the Trans-Israel Highway reflects clearly the tension between the wish to give a free hand to the project execution factors and the tendency of the institutions in charge with environment protection to curb and control that wish.

Trans-Israel Highway and Environmental Protection

The Trans-Israel Highway was a very controversial project in more than one way but none so much as on the issue of environment protection. The attitude toward that issue, connected with the planning and implementation of the highway is a strong and clear representative of the tension and the contradictory forces at work in a modern neo-liberal market.

The factors that presented the attitude toward that issue as a successful and efficient treatment of the environment were all of them the interested parties in implementing the project, the ones that had everything to gain from the highway. The means used by them to minimize the damages to air, water, landscape, land use, fauna and flora, were considered more than enough for what was necessary for the protection of the environment.

The factors in charge with environment protection, the "green" organizations fought for more action and more changes in the project in order to obtain their goal; they had much criticism of what was done about that issue, and that only after they gave up fighting for the complete annulment of the project. The result was the implement of a mega-engineering national project, more "green" than most others, nevertheless not "green" enough for some – the result of the opposite forces active in the country, concerning development on one side and environment protection on the other side.

The proponents of the project claimed as follows: **Care for environment protection started during the planning process** – According to the Cross-Israel Company, the issue of environment protection was included from the very first. Landscape consultants and environment planners were part of the planning team from the beginning; they guided the engineering planners and supervised their work on environment issues, every step of the way, all along the planning process. In many cases, changes were made in the highway routing in order to satisfy environmental demands. A complex body of research works and environmental studies were prepared for the project, some of them as part of the environmental impact studies required by the statutory commissions and others – initiated by the Cross-Israel Company.[366]

The Cross-Israel Company – the project initiator representing the government - and the Derech Eretz Consortium – the project entrepreneur – treated the project as a given fact and never questioned its necessity or its implementation. Their attitude toward the environmental issue was expressed in the means and steps they took in order to minimize the damages to the environment, with the understanding that some environmental damage will be inevitable.

Transparency toward the public and considerations for its reactions. According to the Derech Eretz Consortium, the environmental studies prepared in the framework of the project were accessible to the public at large. The consortium had intensive discussions with the representatives of the settlements close to the highway routing. Their remarks and suggestions were verified and taken into account by the professionals employed for the project planning and a few times - integrated in the agreed upon and accepted solutions.[367]

The construction of an ecological road. The Derech Eretz consortium and the Cross-Israel Company claimed that the Trans-Israel Highway would be the first "green" road of the country. The Derech Eretz Consortium claimed that it would be the first Israeli institution to adopt the Geneva Convention for plant conservation. The convention states that all countries have to avoid planting non-local flowers that can cause ecological damage. In the past, the use of non-indigenous plants in Israel caused local plants to be supplanted and disappear. Derech Eretz claimed that the Convention had not yet been applied anywhere in Israel but it committed itself to be the first to do it and use only local plants on the highway shoulders.

The Cross-Israel Company published a summary of its activities regarding ecological and environmental issues, in order to provide evidence of its efforts in matters of environmental protection and nature conservation.

The highway planners tried hard to demonstrate that the road would have no negative impact on the environment. The highway plans included some routing changes and other adjustments to prevent environmental nuisances or nature damages.[368]

For the construction of the Trans-Israel Highway, the Derech Eretz Consortium predicated its activities on three foundations:

First, the guidelines of the National Council for Planning and Construction, included in the plan instructions and the guidelines of the Israeli EPA.

Second, the planning perceptions of the Cross-Israel Company and the guidelines derived from those perceptions.

The third foundation was the attitude of the Cross-Israel Company to environment protection and its perception that it was its duty to apply maximum efforts to minimize environmental nuisances and damages caused by the highway implementation.[369]

Landscape restoration. On the issue of landscape restoration, significant efforts were made in order to minimize damages, by means of sustainable restoration of the landscape. Also, acoustic protection means, used in order to reduce noise disturbances, were integrated in the landscape design.[370]

> Every small detail was approved by a landscape architect, even the color of the infrastructure boxes, and that reduced significantly the environmental damages. Due to the intensive cooperation with the local authorities near the highway, even bicycle paths were created along it.[371]

The steps taken to diminish the powerful presence of the highway in the environment included the planting of local wildflowers along the road, replanting old trees that had been uprooted, planting cactuses between the asphalt loops as reminders of landscapes once typical of the country a few decades before (cactuses are the symbol of destroyed Arab villages from the 1948 war), etc.[372]

A special effort was invested in the restoration of the highway shoulders. Most of the highway surroundings were cultivated land, considered less sensitive, because the very fact of agricultural uses means changing the landscape appearance every season. Nevertheless, the agricultural landscape has a value of its own and is worth preserving. Restoration of the highway shoulders presented a real challenge because the agricultural landscape is a seasonal one and the restoration works tried to reflect that.[373]

Environment protection - Special, rare plants existing along the road were transplanted to other locations to prevent their disappearance.[374] Alongside the highway, special crossings for animals were built in order to facilitate their passage from one side of the road to the other and minimize the separation and isolation of segments of the animal population.[375]

Also special attention was given to nuisance noise, one of the most important problems created by the highway. Great pains were taken to minimize that disturbance, such as especially designed excavations, the use of acoustic barriers designed according to rigorous criteria, etc.[376]

The environment experts working on the highway project claimed that the road presented no danger to groundwater, viewing that the cultivated land around the road was covered with chemical fertilizers and was therefore much more polluting.[377]

Archeology - Substantial attention was accorded to archeology. In the framework of planning and construction of the Trans-Israel Highway, an entire archeological enterprise was executed along the route, on a strip of 100 meter width. It started first with a methodological study along the road and then, archeological excavations were performed on all relics, declared and undeclared. All archeological Israeli institutions that wished to, participated in that venture.[378]

According to Uzi Dahari – Deputy CEO of the Israel Antiquities Authority – the archeological enterprise was a big success due to the Cross-Israel Company attitude to the issue:

> The Cross-Israel Company was not a regular entrepreneur that considers the salvage excavations a necessity by law, their damage in money and wasted time only to be minimized, but a serious institution that looks from afar and understands the real importance of scientific research of what is going to be destroyed by the highway. The Company understood that from a historical point of view (and also financial), the time required for the excavations and the money invested for that purpose, are inconsequential in comparison with the scientific everlasting gain for all Israel's population and for the scientific community.[379]

In the framework of the archeological enterprise, when problems arose, great efforts were made by the highway planners to find engineering solutions approved and accepted by all parties involved, such as the highway route diversion, transfer of archeological relics to other sites without any damage to the relics themselves, etc.[380]

Prevention of environmental nuisances - The Derech Eretz Consortium took numerous measures to prevent, or at least minimize, environmental nuisances, during the project execution and also, for the operating stage of the highway. Those measures, during the implementation stage, included the reduction of dust nuisances from excavation works, equipment movement and quarrying and crunching activities, saving water and energy by using modern technologies, oil collection for recycling and others.

As early as the planning phase of the project, measures to protect the environment were taken, such as attaching to the planning staff and involving in the planning process landscape architects, environmental consultants and bridges architects, equilibrating planning of filling and excavation in order to minimize the need for quarrying, planning of tunnels in places of great landscape sensitivity, considering reduction of environment damages in the route selection, etc.

The preventing measures for the operation phase included noise levels monitoring, follow up of the acoustic protection efficiency, monitoring of landscape restoration, of animal crossings, etc.[381]

The "green" opponents of the highway were of a different opinion. Most of them completely opposed the project such that any amount of environment protection measures taken would not be enough to satisfy them – at best, those measures could reduce or minimize the environmental nuisances and damages but not avoid them completely. In any case, they were not convinced of the necessity of the project or that the Trans-Israel Highway was the best solution for the Israeli transport problems.

Their claims against environmental damages caused by the highway were usually mixed with social issues, viewing that the social issues were embraced by the public at large easier than the environmental ones. Their claims included various aspects, as follows:

Waste of land resources – The highway was to extend to vast areas of land, most of it used for agriculture and so, creating open, green spaces. Some calculations showed that the road will consume up to 23,000 square kilometer, others went up to 55,000 square kilometer – by any reckoning, resulting in significant damage to agricultural settlements, open spaces and fauna and flora. Other side effects of the highway – construction of gas stations, restaurants, shopping malls, motels, etc. would consume much of the open space left in the country's center. All the associated construction projects would increase, even more, the already high real estate prices.[382]

Also the lateral roads and the huge interchanges connecting them to the highway were going to deplete more green space and transform it into black asphalt.[383]

Landscape damages – The highway was set to pass through areas of green and beautiful open spaces, called by some "The Israeli Tuscany".

Any kind or degree of preventive measure would still not be able to avoid damages to the landscape along with a complete change in appearance of the area surrounding the highway.[384]

Tunneling, as a solution to landscape preservation was expensive and as such, was used sparingly. The tunneling under the Carmel Mountain was the result of intense lobbying activity of the Israel Union for Environmental Defense – IUED[385] (Adam, Teva Ve'Din).[386]

The oak trees reserve near Kiryat Tivon was slated to be damaged by the highway despite the Cross-Israel Company promises not just to uproot the trees but to transfer them to a different site.[387] Other corners of beautiful nature and green landscape were going to be destroyed because of the highway construction, such as the Ramat-Menashe Park and the Daliah Rivers Reserve – that would result in economic damage as well because of the loss of the area's tourism potential;[388] the Modyin-Afek Park and the Ben-Shemen Forest that will be damaged by the Ben-Shemen interchange. Those landscapes and tourism areas could be saved only by tunneling the highway there.[389]

Despite the preventive measures taken in the planning and the execution of the project, the green organizations considered the solutions adopted as to be far from enough.[390]

Elimination of green areas - The damage to nature and landscape caused by the construction of the highway was going to be compounded by the elimination of green open spaces, the few left in the country's center. The highway itself and in addition its large interchanges, were "land devourers", so a significant amount of open area was going to be lost to asphalt cover. Considering that the existence of green open spaces is a necessary condition to a high quality of life, that damage caused by the highway was one of the most disturbing for humans, more than for nature and a damage that was almost impossible to reduce.[391]

Disappearance of open spaces was known to affect tourism – local and foreign; parks, forests and green landscapes were to be destroyed by the deep excavations and the filling over hills, necessary to the construction of the highway.[392]

In addition to land consumed by the highway itself and its interchanges, more open areas were to be lost to real estate development along the sides of the highway – suburbs, industrial and commercial zones, impelled by the accessibility provided by the new road.[393]

The "green" organizations fought the highway construction in every possible way, including not only environmental protection but also and even more so, social arguments.

> In a letter sent by Amit Shapirah, the Head of the Environment Conservation Department of the Society for the Protection of Nature, to Miron Homesh, the Israel Land Authority Head, he claims that the change of land use from leisure and recreation designation to transport designation for the construction of the highway, will cause significant reduction in open spaces supply that are too scarce already in the country center. Josef Shak, the representative of the Society for the Protection of Nature in the struggle against the Trans-Israel Highway, says that we deal here with a process that increases even more the damage caused by the highway to the environment. 'The highway itself passes through open spaces and damages them and now more open spaces will be damaged, by the sides of the route, to enable the highway construction.'[394]

Air Pollution - One of the worst environmental nuisances for man, constituting a risk to health more than damage to nature, is air pollution, and that occurs significantly near highways crammed with traffic. Air pollution increases with the increase in the numbers of vehicles traveling on the country's roads.

The problem of air pollution in Israel is created first and foremost by private vehicle traffic. The Trans-Israel Highway would increase significantly the number of private cars and the traffic load and decrease the use of public transport. That will contribute immediately and directly to the increase in air pollution all along the highway, in a region where the air was still relatively clean.[395]

Air pollution also increases the global greenhouse effect.[396]

The viability studies performed on the highway did not take into account the potential damage to air quality and the increase in air pollution caused by the Trans-Israel and they should have done that.[397]

Groundwater pollution - Generally, any kind of pavement over natural ground reduces infiltration and the little water that infiltrates to the aquifer is polluted by oils and fuels. In addition, flooding is caused by water that cannot infiltrate and flows slowly to the sea. When main roads pass near water sources, the risk of polluting those sources by runoff infiltrating into the aquifer is significantly increased. That runoff carries with it all the pollutants of the road.

The "green" organizations claimed that no steps were taken to prevent pollution of the aquifer or other damages that the aquifer could suffer because of the Trans-Israel Highway, especially near water sources such as Rosh Ha'ayin.[398]

Mainly, there are two kinds of problems for the aquifer caused by the highway: pollution and diminishing of its refill. Ground water pollution can result from two factors: First factor is the rain that becomes runoff and infiltrates into the aquifer carrying with it the pollutants of the road – oils, fuels and such. Second factor is spill-off from tankers that carry hazardous material or fuels and turn over on the road; the aquifer is then infiltrated with those pollutants.

The other problem, as mentioned above, were the paving of natural ground that would prevent rainwater to infiltrate into the aquifer, reduce its refill and diminish the groundwater potential.[399]

Noise nuisance - Bustling, large highways are the source of noise at levels that create a real disturbance and nuisance for the population living or working close to them. The Trans-Israel Highway was going to be a multi-lane, speed road and as such, was going to create noise on a level that would be a health and environmental nuisance for people living or working in its vicinity, specifically – for the settlements close to the road.[400]

In some cases, when a dilemma arose between constructing the road closer to settlements or in open, green spaces, nature and landscape were sacrificed so that the settlements population will not be disturbed by the road's noise. Still, people complained about noise nuisances and asked for better acoustic protection.[401] Others claimed that the noise created by the highway caused a decline of value of their homes.[402]

Fauna and flora - A highway of the magnitude of Road 6 has a powerful negative impact on the fauna and the flora of the region it passes through. According to the Israeli Zoological Society, that impact covers three aspects: First – destruction of habitats. Second – splitting of open spaces to smaller, separate units that limit the animals' movement (fragmentation). Third — massive slaughter caused by cars running over wildlife.

The damage to animals and plants may be very severe. The highway was to cross between breeding and feeding areas of many kinds of animals and that can create a critical environmental nuisance. It can cause serious damage to animal population and even bring the extinction of some of them.[403] In some places along the Trans-Israel Highway, measures have been taken to enable animal-crossing, but there was no evidence to prove that those measures were enough to prevent destruction and extinction.[404] The highway could also cause damage to some habitats because of the introduction of certain plants that were not indigenous to those regions. Plants along the highway would also be damaged by air pollution.

The highway would block ecological continuity that enabled normal fauna and flora development and would rob people of the options of recreation and leisure.[405] The blocking of ecological continuity means the division of large open spaces into small parcels by the barrier of strips of asphalt, non-continuous, separated and segmented. It is a known phenomenon today, by nature preservation experts and considered by them the cause of great damage to ecological systems. It separates animal and plant habitats and prevents access to feeding sources. The underground crossings designed along the Trans-Israel Highway were supposed to enable animal passage, nevertheless they were only a partial solution.[406]

Some of the criticism was directed to a few of the "green" institutions that were not strict enough in their environmental requirements from the Cross-Israel Company. The Israel Nature and Parks Authority allowed the highway crossings for animals to be built without any environmental impact statement or professional examination. There was no way to know beforehand if those crossings would be sufficient or effective for the animals' passage.[407]

According to the Israeli Zoological Society, the construction of the highway itself, the covering with asphalt of thousands of hectares of natural ground, will be the cause of great damage to the fauna, because of the destruction of a large part of its habitat.[408]

Conclusions

The ideology and the worldviews of the 1950s and those of the 2000s have in common a lack of interest in environmental protection for different reasons but with the same result. Israel's leaders both during the state establishment period and present-day, tend to view nature as a resource to be exploited for economic benefits — collective benefits in the 1950s and individual (upper class) or large corporate in the 2000s— exploitation for human needs, without consideration for the needs of future generations or for nature itself.

The main difference between these eras is in the public reaction. In the 1950s, the reaction of mobilized Israeli society to the proposed destruction of the Huleh ecosystem was shy, barely audible and reserved. The response was modest – no real opposition to the drainage, no request to relinquish the project completely; just the comments from some scientists and the demand for creation of the reserve.

In the 2000s, Israeli civil society is well developed and has a voice. Yet, its opposition to the Trans-Israel Highway construction was not successful - the project was executed anyway; but the public opinion opposing the project was expressed loud and clear, in every possible way: newspapers, congresses, the web, demonstrations, even legal actions such as petitions to the High Court of Justice. Though they did not achieve their goal of aborting the project, they did make a substantial impact on the means applied in the project for environmental protection and preservation.

However, the failure was not total and in both projects some measures to protect the environments were taken. In the Huleh project, the "Greens" convinced the projects' managers to preserve 400 hectares of the swamp and in the case of cross-Israel, the "Greens" influenced the consortium to plan a relatively environmentally friendly road. The two periods differ also in the environmental concerns raised. While in the fifties the concern was mainly about nature, conservation in the 2000s is about the care for human well-being, social equity and preservation of natural ecosystems.

Social Justice/Injustice

Huleh Project and the Local Arab Population

Referring to the Huleh valley, its land was considered by the Zionists *"a wilderness in need of taming"*, but none took into consideration that a significant part of it was already cultivated by the locals.[409] The local inhabitants of the Huleh valley, the Ghawarna, lived in papyrus huts, raised water buffalos, wove mats and baskets and grew crops irrigated by hand-dug canals.

The Ghawarna tribe consisted of a blend of people – Bedouins and peasants from different parts of the Middle East. For instance, one of the villages in the valley was Salihiya, established by Algerian refugees in the late 1800s. Later on, the town of Khalisa, established by Bedouin tribes as a summer settlement, became the commercial center of the region.[410] In 1931 the town had 1,369 inhabitants. At that time, there were about 21 to 23 villages in the valley, most of them counted less than 200 people; only 2 villages had more than 1000 inhabitants.[411]

Nathan Shalem portrayed the local inhabitants of the Huleh valley as individuals with their own tradition, culture and habits. Some of them were simple but hardworking peasants who made their livelihood by fishing the lake and cultivating the land. Some were educated and their occupations were teaching or healing. In Shalem's opinion, those local occupations had a potential contribution to the weaving and fishing industries and had a possible market for medicinal plants.[412]

Others, like Yehuda Karmon, were influenced by the Zionist narrative of national development. They referred to the Huleh valley as inhabitable. The swamps were unhealthy environment. The river had to be changed in order to be useful to people and the destruction of local lives and ecological damage were not taken in consideration at all. The Arab population was considered primitive and insignificant because they did not use advanced technological means and showed no special interest in progress.[413] The aspiration to modernization and advanced technology was an important part of the Zionist ideology and discourse.

The local population's attitude toward the Huleh swamp differed completely from the Jewish settlers'. The Zionists considered the swamp as a nuisance to get rid of as quickly as possible: *"the worst and the most extensive in Palestine and it could only be eliminated by radical drainage"*. The local population instead regarded the swamp as a place which offered possibilities of making a livelihood, a place with potential for a habitat for plants, animals and birds. They named the swamp *al-Sheriat al-Kebira,* which means large watering place.

These two distinct Zionist/Arab visions about the same place – the Huleh swamp – reflect the difference in attitude and conceptions of each group toward nature and environment. The local inhabitants' attitude to nature – developing a personal relationship with nature, for instance nicknaming the swamp – was regarded by the Zionist settlers as a weakness, handicapping the locals and preventing them from changing nature and transforming it to their advantage. The Zionist way to approach nature was to separate it from culture, preventing feelings to take over and control their acts regarding the environment. Their view was that the right way to treat nature and environment is to use technological means and obtain maximum economic benefits from the surroundings. That difference in attitude was what Kavita Philip called as *"differential rational system of knowledge about nature, under-girded by unequal structures of economic, political and social practice"*.[414]

The Huleh swamp case is a good example of Philip's observations. In fact, the Zionist movement had a dichotomist attitude toward nature. On one hand, the Zionists strived to treat nature objectively and exploit it to their material interest and needs. On the other hand they mixed nature and culture by developing ideologies regarding environment, like conquest of land (*kibush hakarka*) and conquest of labor (*kibush ha'avoda*).

The Zionist settlers believed that their work of transforming nature by scientific means like the drainage work in the Huleh, helped establish their bonding to the land. They also considered that draining the Huleh would yield economic benefits.

The Zionists believed the Arab population did not hold a strong attachment to the land; they considered that for the Arabs to live by the swamp without trying to change it was a sign of carelessness toward land. According to Zionists worldviews, Arab attitude to nature in general and to the swamp in particular emanated from ignorance, laziness and lack of resourcefulness.[415]

The Arab population of the Huleh valley, the Bedouins of the Ghawarna tribe, occupied two villages, in the aftermath of the 1948 war: Kirad Ghannama and Kirad Baqqara. The villages contained approximately 350 people each. Those people were originally from Kurdistan and they made their living by raising cattle and sheep. Most of them had commercial and family relationships with Syria. They avoided relations with the Jews.

No record of a direct act of expulsion or occupation on the part of the Jewish settlers against the villages has been recorded. Nevertheless, the villagers left their dwellings and fled eastward, taking shelter in and around Arab villages, in the south of the Golan Heights. It is assumed that their departure was caused either by fear of a Jewish attack or apprehension of being caught in the middle, if the Syrians were to attack.

After the 1948 war, according to the General Armistice Agreement regarding the Demilitarized Zone and the authorization of the Chairman of the Mixed Armistice Commission, some of the villagers that fled the DZ before the war, could come back to their homes. Among those allowed to return were the Kirad people. They came back to their villages in 1950, holding Syrian documents, enabling them to move among Syria, Israel and Lebanon.[416]

The presence of Arab population whom the Syrians considered Syrian citizens, living in the sensitive DZ, an area whose sovereignty was disputed by Israel and Syria alike, was viewed as a problem and a disadvantage by Israel. Also, the twin Kirad villages were next to the area due to be dug for the Huleh drainage project. In 1951, the works for the drainage project began. One of the first sites to be dug was on land owned by those Arabs, an act which was fateful for the Kirad Bedouins. In fact, the more relations between Syria and Israel deteriorated, the more the Kirad Bedouins were used as a bargaining chip by the two sides of the conflict.

The Syrians tried to attract the Kirad people to their side so Israel considered them a security risk, liable to damage the Huleh project. The Prime Minister, David Ben-Gurion, sent a letter to the Government members, on 5 March 1951:

> In the DZ area, at the Syrian border, a dangerous situation developed: the Arab settlement in this area does not need the Israeli rule, they turn to Syria although they have relations with the Israeli side also.[417]

Soon after this letter, the decision taken by Ben-Gurion was as follows:

> The Israeli authorities in the Demilitarized Zone will carry out actions whose purpose is to maintain our sovereignty in that zone. Among the actions mentioned: transfer of Arab civilians from the zone to Israeli territory, outside the boundaries of the Demilitarized Zone, distribution of Israeli ID cards to all residents of the zone, supervision of the border and prevention of crossovers from the Demilitarized Zone to Syria and vice versa and severing the general attachment of the zone's residents to Syria.[418]

That decision was taken in order to clear the DZ area of what was considered by Israel "*hostile elements*".

On 31 March, 785 residents of Kirad Baqqara and Kirad Ghannama were transferred by the Israeli forces to Sha'ab – an Arab village situated in the western Galilee. Once in Sha'ab, the Kirad Bedouins could choose between relocation in the village or moving permanently to Syria. Most chose Sha'ab, where a large number remained. Others moved to Syria and a few families were allowed to return to their village but during the 1956 war they were chased across the Syrian border into the Golan Heights. The Kirad Bedouins are now scattered across Israel, Syria, Jordan and Lebanon.[419]

Israel claimed that the transfer of the Kirad Bedouins to the village of Sha'ab was done as a result of their request to leave the DZ area because they feared the shooting between Syrians and Israelis in connection with the Huleh drainage.[420]

After the shooting incident at the Al-Hama, when 6 Israeli policemen (who were, in fact, soldiers) were killed, the abandoned houses of the Kirad Baqqara and Kirad Ghannama villages were demolished by Israeli forces. Also, the same fate awaited the villages of Al-Samara and Nuqeib, whose residents were transferred to Syria at the same time as the Kirad people.[421]

The demolition of the Arab villages was a further step in the process intended to ensure Israel's sovereignty over the DZ. The formal explanation offered for the demolition of the villages, was that the Huleh project was part of the restoration of civil life in the DZ, a condition specified and required by the Armistice Agreement, and any disturbance or interference to the project had to be removed.[422]

As detailed in chapter 3, the Israeli attitude toward the Arab villages in the Huleh area was not solely a pragmatic one, dictated by the wish to advance the Huleh drainage project. General political interests influenced largely the decisions regarding the Arab population, as demonstrated by some

Israeli correspondence from those times, such as Eytan's telegram to Israeli representatives in London, (see chapter 3 above – Frontier Considerations).[423]

Sometimes the treatment of the local population was dictated by political goals and they were used as a means in the struggle to achieve those goals – (see Ramati's letter to Deputy Chief of Staff Makleff in chapter 3 above – Frontier Considerations.)[424]

The Highway and the Israeli-Arab Minority

The planning and construction of the Trans-Israel Highway was controversial for Israel's citizens, on many levels. But some of the problems were not relevant for all citizens to the same degree; they were specific to the Israeli-Arab minority, as will be detailed below.

On the political level, the new highway raised significant difficulties for the Arab-Israeli minorities and for other Arab populations in the region. The highway's route was located very close to the "Green Line" between Israel and the West Bank.

This could serve to advance development on the Israeli side, widening the difference between the Israeli population and the Palestinians. It could also weaken economic ties between the West Bank and Israel, given that only a few lateral roads were going to be constructed eastward in the direction of Judea and Samaria. Not much attention has been given to the possibility of Route 6 being used as a connection between Israel and the Arab West Bank.[425]

In addition, the highway was going to traverse the middle of the Arab triangle, with most of the Arab localities to remain on the east side and a few – Tira and Kalansawa – on the west side. The question was raised as to whether that partition would bring the west side Arab settlements closer to the Israeli ones or just make it harder for those Arab settlements to connect with the Arab communities on the other side of the highway.[426]

On the planning level, the Arab localities and communities along the highway were in a worse position than their Jewish counterparts. They had no representatives in any of the forums dealing with decision-making about development, industrialization and infrastructure strategies. The Arab municipalities could not include or take in account the highway in their local master plans, either because of total lack of local plans or because they could not keep up with the pace of progress of the Trans-Israel. Thus, the Arab localities could not take advantage of the new highway and use it to leverage their own development. The few existing master plans of those localities assigned the land to dwellings and not to industry or commerce.[427]

In any case, those responsible for the construction of the highway were not interested in cooperating with the local authorities, especially those in the Arab sector.[428]

The most crucial problem of all was with respect to land ownership and expropriation of land. That was a major and sensitive issue for everyone but especially for the Arab population. Concerning that issue, we must first look at the specifics of the Arabs attitude toward land and possession of it. The Arab population accords a special place to possession of land; beyond its economic value – land means social status, symbolic and national importance.[429]

Most of the Arabs in Israel were farmers, so the land was their main source of livelihood and to exchange it for money did not solve the problem of employment.

Even though only a small part of the Arab population today is farming, by their peasant tradition, land ownership is the main component of their status and power in society. The community elders maintain their power over the younger generation by controlling lands that their children are in line to inherit.[430] Another factor was the tradition of the Arabs that land ownership kept the family together and was an asset to be bequeathed to next generations.[431]

Their attachment to the land is also connected to the events surrounding the establishment of the State of Israel when Arabs fled en masse or were being driven out and lost lands. Some lands were also later expropriated by the government for security reasons. Those events played a role in their attitude toward the highway even in the 2000s. Thus, one of the most crucial problems regarding the construction of the Trans-Israel Highway was the expropriation of land necessary to build the highway, its interchanges and the transversal roads connecting to it. Most of that land was cultivated, some of it privately owned and another part – public property, in fact – state property.

To facilitate the project, especially the land seizure, and to regulate the issue of compensation for land owners, the government passed the Israel National Highway Law – 1994, providing a legal framework for the expropriation of land and the calculation of due compensation.[432] That was a drastic law, contradicting private property rights. Most of the expropriated land was owned by Jewish population and only a small part was owned by Arab citizens.

The attitude of the Arab population on that issue differed according to the specifics of each case: The landowners for whom the highway was going to pass through their fields, felt threatened by the law and unsure of the justness of the compensation for their expropriated land, keeping in mind that in many cases that land was their source of livelihood. Those landowners comprised the vehemently-opposed segment of the Arab population. Those whose lands merely bordered the highway feared the nuisances of noise, air pollution and difficulties in accessing their fields. Nevertheless, they were more open to accept the reality of the highway in hopes that they would benefit from it by urban development and by increases in their land's value. Those that held no land close to the highway route were largely indifferent to its construction.

On the issue of land expropriation and its compensations there was a considerable difference between the Jewish and the Arab population of Israel.

In complete contrast to the attitude and situation of the Arab minorities, the Jewish communities along the highway and other stakeholders began to feverishly organize regarding their real estate anticipating that the highway construction would be used as an imminent springboard to yield development – industry, commerce, employment centers.[433]

According to the Israel National Highway Law – 1994, the compensation for expropriated land could be in the form of monetary recompense - based on the appraisal of the government assessor - or in the form of alternative land of equal value. The Arabs, for the reasons explained above, chose to receive their compensation for confiscated land in the form of alternative land and absolutely refused monetary recompense. That choice was very difficult to achieve and presented many complications in its implementation. First of all, the issue of inheritance or ownership was complicated and intricate. In many cases, those that actually owned the land were not registered formally and lawfully. Many of the parcels were small, fragmented and/or had more than one owner, so that the issue of compensation was even more complicated. The avoidance to register the lands on the names of real owners derived from internal socio-political reasons.[434]

The law was not explicit enough regarding the allocation of alternative land as recompense for land confiscation, so a special committee was assembled to deal with that issue. The committee recommended, among other things, that in special cases the alternative land would be such that was already assigned to industry, commerce or tourism. That would be much more profitable and valuable land but, in fact, there was no such land available for the Arab population. Also, another problem was the fact that the highway law enabled the Cross-Israel company to seize the land before the compensation process was completed (60 days from the time of the announcement) so the negotiation from the beginning were putting the Arab farmers in a disadvantaged position. The process of negotiation was long, tiresome and full of bureaucratic complications. The Cross-Israel Company was seizing the land but the Israel Land Authority was the one to find and allocate the alternative land.

The Israeli Land Authority added a few steps to the process of finding and allocating alternative land to the Arab residents. Its procrastination was significant and the Land Authority became the delaying link in the complicated chain of alternative land as compensation.[435]

That was the situation of the private land expropriation.

The municipalities associated with the public land expropriation were not in any better position. In Arab localities there was minimal land owned publicly. Most of it was privately owned. Such localities had little or no claim to compensation for the land seized for the benefit of the road. The municipalities saw no way to take advantage of the new highway as leverage for development of their territory.

As noted previously, there was no help to be gotten on the planning level and few other avenues were open to the Arab municipalities.[436] That brings us to the general attitude of the Arab population living along the highway's route. In general, the Arab population, including the official authorities, was reluctant regarding the highway; they did not believe that any advantage to them would be accrued from it and even thought that the whole project was meant to benefit the Jewish population at the expense of the Arabs of the region. They were convinced, for instance, that the highway's route was designed in such a way as to seize Jewish land as little as possible and dispossess Arabs of their land as much as possible.[437]

The situation of the Jewish localities was much better. First of all, most of the land seized for the highway was state property, leased to kibbutzim (agricultural collectives) and *moshavim* (agricultural cooperatives). Second, the task of compensating those settlements was much easier due to the large size of the plots, the methods of cultivation and the small number of owners. Third and most important, for the Jewish population there was a mechanism to obtain compensation, convenient for all involved parties – seizure of land in exchange for increasing rights of building on the remaining land and permit to raise employment and economic centers in areas that adjoined the settlements.[438]

In fact, the Jewish population preferred that last solution, being much more profitable and much less complicated than making a living from land cultivation (lack of water, climate problems, unstable market, etc.). Also, the highway interchanges were designed so that they created access to the surrounding Jewish settlements. This facilitated the location of industrial, commercial and services centers to be developed into employment centers as compensation for land seizure for those settlements.[439]

Another issue of social justice, relevant to the whole population, Arabs and Jews alike, was the fact that the highway boosted the use of private cars for those who could afford one, use it on a daily basis and pay for a toll road instead of public transport. It increased the gap between the "haves" and the "have-nots". The highway diminished the government incentive to develop further the public transport means in the detriment of the weaker population who could not afford to travel to work by private car or to have one at all.[440]

> Forecasts that were prepared for the Cross-Israel Company show that, in 2020, the number of private owned cars in the north of the Negev will stand on 345 thousand cars for 1000 persons opposite 656 thousand cars for 1000 persons in Ramat Hasharon and Herzliya. That datum answers to the question of the chances of an average unemployed person from Ofakim to use the highway in order to travel to Gush Dan for employment.[441]

An additional social injustice expected to be created by the highway, which was mentioned by all NGOs dealing with the social issues, was the development of employment centers along the Trans-Israel in the center of the country and not in the periphery. In that way, the already-developed center was going to benefit from the new highway and the periphery was going to lose momentum and continue suffering from underdevelopment and unemployment.[442]

> It seems that along the first tens of kilometers that will be constructed in the country's center already the consortium Derech Eretz plans to build large centers of productive real estate such as an industrial zone of half a million of square meters at the Qasem interchange, the Global Village in the Ben-Gurion Airport area, residential neighborhoods and commercial centers. The national road, whose main goal was to connect the periphery to the center, was born perhaps as a national transport solution but somewhere along the way mutated to a real estate project, a huge and multi tentacles project and, in fact, its execution preferences are based on economic considerations.[443]

Conclusions

Israel's mega-engineering projects of the 1950s (e.g. the Huleh drainage) were driven by the ethos of the modernist view of economic growth, achieved using advanced technologies, implemented with the collectivist belief of centrally planned large scale projects. Moreover, the young State used the Huleh drainage project to exercise sovereignty over disputed frontiers. The Kirad villagers were just additional victims in the conflict between the new State of Israel and the surrounding hostile Arabs. In the view of the State, the success of the entire Huleh project was a matter of survival, and of achieving victory over a foe; questions of ethics and/or justice were simply not taken into consideration.

The 2000s were a time of a completely different societal structure in Israel. The country was well developed, notions of ethics and social justice are an important issue on the public agenda of the active civil society. So, in the matter of the Trans-Israel Highway construction and the issue of land seizure, the state tried to take into account the special needs of the Arab minorities. The Israeli National Law provided alternative compensations for land expropriation that correspond to the way of life of the Arab population – equal value alternative land for the land seized to build the highway.

Other actions were neglected, such as the placement of interchanges which eased access for Jewish settlements, but neglected to do so for Arab localities alongside the highway. So, in the end, the Arab minorities were in a worse position than the Jewish population, regarding the compensation for land seizure. Perhaps not intentionally, but merely through negligence, the results insofar as social justice/injustice are concerned less discriminated Arabs relative to the 1950s, but still the compensations they have received were less effective in serving their interests.

⌘ **8** ⌘
Concluding Remarks

The Huleh drainage did not justify the expectations and hopes it inspired. The main and most significant benefit from the drainage was the additional land for agriculture. About 6,000 hectares of land became fit for intensive cultivation – most of them virgin land and a small part – cultivated before but only extensively. The new land was used for field crops, orchards and fish ponds.

Also, much work was required in order to overcome the problems caused by the drainage of the peat soil. That included the irrigation of the cultivated fields and the necessary coordination for that process. A more detailed assessment of that subject is brought in the chapter regarding the peat. The Authority for the Huleh Development employed many workers to deal with the peat soil problems and one of the benefits was the relief of the unemployment problem.

On one hand, the benefits of the drainage for agriculture were much above expectations. On the other hand, on other aspects, much less than expected was gained from the Huleh project. The reclaimed area fit for cultivation was used as additional land for existing settlements that had suffered from land shortages including Misgav-Am, Metula and Meayan-Harod in the north to Genosar in the south, Shamir and Gonen in the east and Sasa at the far west. No new settlement was established on the reclaimed land since the area had been dense with Jewish settlements even before the drainage was completed.

Concerning the other formal goals of the project, the malaria disease was abolished before the drainage implementation, thanks to the use of pesticides, namely DDT, as mentioned before,[444] energy was not produced from the peat, the transport problems were not solved or even alleviated, the addition to

Israel's water resources is doubtful because of lack of conclusive data before the drainage.[445]

With time, many environmental and other problems arose as a result of the drainage, the main and most serious of them being the peat problem.

In comparing the two mega-projects discussed in this book the following aspects are underlined:

Economic Impact – from an economic point of view, both projects, in the different periods of time they were executed, were treated and conducted similarly. No real feasibility studies were performed – in the case of the Huleh drainage – none at all, and no viability analysis were done in order to confirm the economic profitability of the projects. The main importance and meaning of mega-engineering projects is not their economic value but the symbol they represent and the message they deliver to the people. So, both cases affirm the above statement. The Huleh drainage was born from the Zionist ideology of building the country as an advanced modern state by, among other actions, draining swamps. No studies were performed on the amount of agricultural land required for the country's economy in order to confirm the necessity of the Huleh drainage. Another example of that attitude was the treatment of the peat. Researches and studies were conducted concomitantly with the drainage, without waiting for their results. There was total belief in the Zionist ideology or hegemonic attitude of the rulers that science and technology will solve every problem and that "Zionist peat will not sink". The mobilized Israeli society of the 1950s accepted and embraced their leaders' ideology, and by extension, the Huleh project unquestioningly.

In the 2000s, a different ideology was predominant, an ideology that glorified private property and personal material benefit and relied on the link between wealth and political power. In that atmosphere, the Trans-Israel was a project that secured the profit of the large powerful consortiums and the political powers connected to them. It was based on the tendency of the country's leaders to privatize as many functions and services as possible and so, the Trans-Israel was built as a BOT project and a toll road. The political message conveyed was not especially connected to transport – for some, the Highway meant a direct connection between Egypt and Syria, through Israel, when peace is achieved, for others – the reinforcement of Jewish settlements on the other side of the "green line". Even the benefits of the highway for traffic problems were not clear or definite. The highway could enforce the use of private cars and delay public transport development but those effects were disregarded.

Environmental Impact – in the 1950s, the Zionist ideology concerning nature and environment consisted mostly of a tendency to use nature for people's benefit and to accord minimum importance to environmental protection and nature conservation. At its roots, Zionism had an ambivalent relation to nature, on one hand wishing to subdue it and transform it to the benefit of the country's (Jewish) inhabitants, on the other hand – having a romantic view of nature. In the end, the practical necessities and the imperative needs of the times prevailed. So the Huleh drainage was executed without much thought for the damages it would bring to nature and environment, such as harm to the habitat of plants and animals, even extinction of some species. The only redeeming quality that can be accorded to that venture was the small reserve carved out of the swamp as a reminder of the original landscape of the Huleh Valley. Furthermore, despite the intensive investigation of the usefulness of the peat and the risks posed by it, works on the drainage were pushed forward with the blind belief that science will solve any problem arising along the way securing the effectiveness and efficiency of the project.

In the 2000s, things are different and the results are not identical but much alike. Four important changes occurred globally, in general and in Israel, in particular. First, the state is dominated by large corporations that gain the power to recruit support for their cause from the political elite. The neo-liberal ideology, which appraises the exclusion of governments from direct responsibility to public services created the ideal milieu for large corporations to use the system for their benefits. Second, the general awareness of the public concerning environmental sustainability and social justice, for the benefit of present people and future generations and for the benefit of nature itself as well, is much more developed than in the 1950s. Third, civil society is well developed and active. The civil sector can organize, unite around a common cause and act to influence the outcome. Forth, the development of technological means of the media (the web, TV shows and programs, etc.) changed the pace and the intensity of communication between people and so, the means for public reaction. Despite these changes and although civil society reacted strongly and forcefully to the construction of the Trans-Israel, the outcome was not much different from the Huleh drainage. The energetic opposition to Road 6 by almost all "green" and social NGOs did not prevent the execution of the highway, but improved considerably measures taken to protect nature and environment, for the benefit of the population and of nature itself.

Social (In)justice – manifestations of social injustice were displayed in both mega-projects. In connection with the Huleh project, the Arab population of the Huleh Valley – especially the Kirad people – were poorly treated, as we saw in chapter 7, and were used as a tool in the Israeli-Syrian conflict, while their personal interests and problems largely dismissed. Explanations, reasons and even justifications for that attitude exist, but the fact remains that there was a measure of social injustice in the way the Huleh project was conducted.

In connection with the Trans-Israel, on a formal basis there is more awareness and consideration for equality and human rights. The state tried to take in consideration particularities of the Arab population culture and practice and included in the Trans-Israel law the alternative of compensating expropriation of land by other, equivalent land. De facto, that did not work well and the Arab landowners whose land was expropriated for the benefit of the highway, felt cheated, exploited and not fairly compensated.

The project of the Trans-Israel also benefited the center of the country to the detriment of the periphery and the stronger population segment at the expense of the poorer and the less fortunate. The highway brought on real estate development in the center that did not help the peripheral areas' progress; it also eased traffic for private cars owners, but did not encourage the development of public transport for those who could not afford private vehicles.

The changes in the Israeli society structure, ideology, political regime and even social norms did not change the basic fact that the wealthy and politically powerful took advantage of their position at the expense of the poorer and weaker part of the population.

The Public Discourse – around the Huleh project reflected well the hegemonic state of the Israeli society of the 1950s. The leaders of the country, operating under the Zionist ideology of the time, considered the drainage of the swamps an obvious and necessary action in the context of nation-building. The public discourse, as carried out in the media – Geva news journals in cinemas, articles in newspapers and professional journals, etc., showed, first and foremost, national pride in the project and very little opposition from researchers and nature enthusiasts. Some articles referred to nature preservation and to the damage to the swamp ecosystem the drainage would cause, but they did not contribute to a strong and influential voice in the public discourse. The framing of the project reflected clearly the ideology and practice of the time. In the media, the project's goals were presented within the framework of the most popular causes of the time: malaria prevention, additional arable land, new settlements building, peat exploitation, etc. In fact, there were also other goals no less important, such as affirmation of Israel's sovereignty on the DZ, the struggle for water sources, etc.

There was a deep disparity between the environmental discourse and the development discourse; the first one referred solely to preservation of nature and habitat without any reference to human needs, the second referred solely to human needs and did not care about saving nature. The outcome was an acceptable compromise for the time – the small reserve along the large area of the drainage project.

The Israeli society of the 2000s enjoys a different public discourse, much more vivid, assertive, even violent - the highway being a very controversial project. Civil society is a well-developed sector and much of its energy was committed to the struggle to terminate the project. When it became clear that the highway implementation would go on as planned, that struggle was directed toward improving, as much as possible, the strategies to minimize environmental and other highway-related damages.

All media means were deployed – newspapers articles, the radio, the web, etc. The modern technology of the 2000s eased the path to communication, organization and cooperation among NGOs, other organizations and regular citizens, enabling them to act against the highway plan or to demand – and receive – special requirements concerning its execution.

The framing of the project was more elaborate than just the Huleh drainage. Discussing the goals of the project, the government included the most "attractive" issues, such as bringing the periphery closer to the country's center, developing employment centers on the periphery, solving traffic problems, sparing public finances by using the BOT system for execution of the project, etc. On the other hand, the same issues, only in the opposite direction were used by the opponents of the project in their framing of the subject in the public discourse.

The environmental aspect took on a different form than in the 1950s, it focused on nature and environment preservation for the sake of present and future generations.

The Process of Decision-Making – the players that took part in the process of decision-making regarding the Huleh project were mainly official bodies – the government and especially Prime Minister David Ben-Gurion, along with the relevant ministries and the JNF. Although there were not yet definite and clear rules for approval of engineering plans and technical projects, special committees were named to follow up and survey the project. But the real decision-makers and initiators of the project were the political entities, the leaders of the country. The different committees dealt with technical problems and decisions, but the substantial and fundamental aspects were decided by the political elite. Their hegemony was such that almost no comments or criticism of any kind were voiced regarding the drainage.

The Trans-Israel Highway was a mega-project of an entirely different caliber in Israel. The most important player in the process of decision-making was the entity that held the power – political or financial or both. However, in contrast to era of the Huleh project, another player was now very active in the process – the third sector – civil society. Though comments, opposition and criticism were expressed often and loudly, the outcome was still decided by the leaders. Civil society had influence, but could not effect drastic change in the results. The highway was to be executed, in spite of NGOs opposition. However, their demands were taken into consideration in the alignment of the road and in the measures taken to protect environment and preserve nature.

The Trans-Israel was obviously the product of a neo-liberal society, with a strong tendency to privatization in every sector, even the most basic of infrastructure.

Finally, comparing the Israeli society and its social structure in the two different eras discussed here, by studying the two mega-engineering projects – the Huleh drainage and the Trans-Israel Highway, we conclude that despite the deep difference between the Israeli society of the 1950s and that of the 2000s, despite the significant development of civil society and despite the change in ideology and all other changes, the outcome remains the same in both cases – the decisions of the leaders were implemented. A developed and active civil society reacted strongly and made its voice heard, not like in a hegemonic society, but it could only influence and not radically change the course of events.

From the present study, we concluded that each mega-project analyzed here was the product of the type of social structure existing in its epoch and each project shaped the cultural landscape of its surroundings according to the message the powers that executed it were willing to transmit; each project symbolized that power, its interests, points of view and aspirations.

If one had no prior understanding of the society in Israel and one was just to study these two projects one could gain a true and clear insight of the social structure, the ideology, norms and practices of the society of each epoch – the 1950s and the 2000s.

Studying each one of the two projects and even without knowing the society of its time and its characteristics, we could have learned to know that society and its structure.

Endnotes

1   M. E. Zimmerman, *Heidegger's Confrontation with Modernity – Technology, Politics, Art*, Indiana University Press, 1990, p. 205.

2   B.L. Turner, et al., *The Earth as Transformed by Human Action*, Cambridge, U.S.A.: Press Syndicate of the University of Cambridge, 1990, p.vii; I. Schnell & A. Rosenberg, "We Shall Dress You in a Robe of Cement and Concrete": How Discourse Concerning Mega-Engineering Projects Has Been Changing in Israel", in S. Brunn, (Editor), *Engineering Earth: The Impacts of Mega-Engineering Projects*, Springer, 2011, p. 663.

3   B. Marsh & J. Jones, "Building the Next Seven Wonders: the Landscape Rhetoric of Large Engineering Projects", in S. Brunn, (Editor), *Engineering Earth: The Impacts of Mega-Engineering Projects*, Springer, 2011, pp. 14-15.

4   A. R. H. Baker, "Introduction: On Ideology and Landscape", in A. R. H. Baker & G. Biger, (Eds.), *Ideology and Landscape in Historical Perspective: Essays on the Meanings of Some Places in the Past*, (pp. 1-15), Cambridge: Cambridge University Press, 1992, p. 5, in B. Marsh & J. Jones, "Building the Next Seven Wonders: the Landscape Rhetoric of Large Engineering Projects", in S. Brunn, (Editor), *Engineering Earth: The Impacts of Mega-Engineering Projects*, Springer, 2011, p. 15.

5   B. Marsh & J. Jones, "Building the Next Seven Wonders: the Landscape Rhetoric of Large Engineering Projects", in S. Brunn, (Editor), *Engineering Earth: The Impacts of Mega-Engineering Projects*, Springer, 2011, pp. 16-17.

6   Ibid., p. 32.

7   Jewish Agency for Israel, The National Water Carrier, http://www.Jewish.org/JewishAgency/English/Jewish+Education/Compelling+content/Jewish+History/Zionist+Alliot/1960s.htm; National Water Carrier of Israel, Wikipedia.

8   Rail Transport in Israel, Wikipedia.

9   The Port of Ashdod, Wikipedia; Ashdod Port Company Ltd., http://www.Ashdodport.co.il/port-library/port-guide/Pages/history-of-ashdod-port.aspx (in Hebrew).

10   E. Kowalski & Z. Efrat, "The Politics of New Towns in Israel", International New Towns Institute Conference, 2010, http://efrat-kowalski.co.il/files/zvi-efrat-text-for-new-towns-conf.pdf; J. Ash, "The Progress of New Towns in Israel", *Town Planning Review*, Vol. 45, No. 4, October 1974, p. 387.

11   E. Ya'ar & Z. Shavit, *Trends in Israeli Society*, Ramat Aviv: The Open University of Israel, 2001, (in Hebrew), p. 1.

12   Ibid., p. 4.

13   S. N. Eisenstadt, *Changes in the Israeli Society*, Ministry of Defense Press, 2004, (in Hebrew), p. 16.

14   E. Ya'ar and Z. Shavit, *Trends in Israeli Society*, Ramat Aviv: The Open University of Israel, 2001, (in Hebrew), pp. 5, 8.

15   Ibid., p. 8.

16   S. N. Eisenstadt, *Changes in the Israeli Society*, Ministry of Defense Press, 2004, (in Hebrew), pp. 27-34.

17   E. Ya'ar and Z. Shavit, *Trends in Israeli Society*, Ramat Aviv: The Open University of Israel, 2001, (in Hebrew), p. 189.

18   I. Schnell and D. Bar-Tal, "The Occupied Territories as Cornerstone in the Reconstruction of Israeli Society", in D. Bar-Tal and I. Schnell, (Eds.), *The Impact of Lasting Occupation – Lessons from Israeli Society*, Oxford University Press, 2012.

19   S. N. Eisenstadt, *Changes in the Israeli Society*, Ministry of Defense Press, 2004, (in Hebrew), p. 11.

20   Ibid., pp. 57-61.

21   Ibid., pp. 62-63.

22   B. Kipnis, "The Globalization Processes and their Impact on Space, Economy and Society: Israel – a Link in the Global Community", Haifa University, http://public-policy.huji.ac.il/upload/kipnis.doc, (in Hebrew), p. 2.

23   R. D. Keohane & J. S. Nye, "Globalization: What's New? What's Not? (And So What?)", *Foreign Policy*, 118, 2000, p. 105.

24   M. Kahler & D. A. Lake, "Globalization and Governance: Definition, Variation and Explanation", The Asrudian Center Wordpress, *International Politics, Irtheory, Economics, Philosophy*, 2003.

25   T. L. Friedman, *The Lexus and the Olive Tree*, New-York: Farrar Straus Giroux, 1999, pp.7-8.

26   J. A. Scholte, *Globalization: A Critical Introduction*, London: MacMillan Press Ltd., , 2000, pp. 46-48.

27   G.D. Randall, (Ed.), *Globalization and its Critics: Perspectives from Political Economy*, Great Britain: Palgrave MacMillan Press, 2000, pp. xv-xvi.

28   U. Ram, "Globalization", http//bgu.uniclass.co.il/psicho06/uploader php?file=סר_ירוא-היצזילבולג, (in Hebrew), p. 1.

29   Ibid., pp. 2-3.

30 R. Hirschl, "The Constitutional Revolution and the Emergence of a
    New Economic Order in Israel", *Israel Studies*, Vol. 2, No.1, Spring
    1997, pp. 139- 140.

31 Ibid., p. 146.

32 U. Ram, *The Globalization of Israel: McWorld in Tel-Aviv, Jihad in Jerusalem*,
    New-York and London: Routledge, 2008, p. 121, in E. Sheppard,
    "Review - The Globalization of Israel: McWorld in Tel-Aviv, Jihad in
    Jerusalem", *Israel Studies*, Vol. 15, No. 1, Spring 2010, pp. 184-185.

33 R. Hirschl, "The Constitutional Revolution and the Emergence of a
    New Economic Order in Israel", *Israel Studies*, Vol. 2, No.1, Spring
    1997, p. 138.

34 B. Kipnis, "The Globalization Processes and their Impact on Space,
    Economy and Society: Israel – a Link in the Global Community",
    Haifa University, http://public-policy.huji.ac.il/upload/kipnis.doc,
    (in Hebrew), p. 15.

35 Y. Karmon, "The Drainage of the Huleh Swamps", *Geographical Review*,
    Volume 50, No. 2, April 1960, p. 170.

36 M. Livne, "The Huleh Drainage – Advantages and Disadvantages",
    Ecology and Environment, 4, Vol. 1, 1994, (in Hebrew), p. 167;
    H. Gwirtzman, *Water Resources in Israel: Chapters in Hydrology and
    Environmental Sciences*, Jerusalem: Yad Yitzhak Ben-Zvi, 2002,
    (in Hebrew), pp. 55-57.

37 Ibid.

38 Ibid.

39 Y. Karmon, "The Drainage of the Huleh Swamps", *Geographical Review*,
    Volume 50, No. 2, April 1960, p. 170.

40 A. Freuindlich, "Eretz Israel Geography Summary: Water from the Aspect
    of Environment", 2006, http://www.broker.org.il/geography/info/israel/
    meida/environment/arielwateril2006.doc; (in Hebrew), e-green, JNF
    Friends Circlehttp://212.199.128/kkl/kklink.asp?Offer, (in Hebrew); JNF
    site, "JNF Contribution to the Huleh Development", http://www.kkl.org.il/
    kkl/hebrew/nosim_ikarim/kkl_eichut_hasviva/truma_lechut_hasviva/hula,
    (in Hebrew).

41 D. Shalev, The Huge Huleh Plant had been Completed, *Davar*, November 1ˢᵗ,
    1957, (in Hebrew).

42 A. Freuindlich, "Eretz Israel Geography Summary: Water from the Aspect
    of Environment", 2006, http://www.broker.org.il/geography/info/israel/
    meida/environment/arielwateril2006.doc, (in Hebrew) ;e-green, JNF
    Friends Circle, http://212.199.128/kkl/kklink.asp?Offer, (in Hebrew); JNF

site, "JNF Contribution to the Huleh Development", http://www.kkl.org.
il/kkl/hebrew/nosim_ikarim/kkl_eichut_hasviva/truma_lechut_hasviva/
hula, (in Hebrew).

43   A. Berchyau, "The Huleh Drainage at its End", *Karnenu*, Issue A, January,
      1958, (in Hebrew), pp. 2-5.

44   JNF website – "JNF Contribution to the Valley Development", http://www.
      kkl.org.il/kkl/hebrew/nosim_ikarym/kkl_eichut_hasviva/truma_lechut_
      hasviva_hula (in Hebrew); Gwirtzman H., *Water Resources in Israel: Chapters in
      Hydrology and Environmental Sciences*, Jerusalem: Yad Yitzhak Ben-Zvi, 2002,
      (in Hebrew), pp. 55-57.

45   M. Dar, "The Imaginary Huleh – the Story of the Huleh Lake", *The Nature of
      Things*, Issue 55, 2000, (in Hebrew), pp. 100-117.

46   Ibid.; M. Livne, "The Huleh Drainage – Advantages and Disadvantages",
      Ecology and Environment, 4, Vol. 1, 1994, (in Hebrew), p. 169; M. Yakobovitz,
      Water in Israel, Shikmona, 1971, (in Hebrew), pp. 73-76.

47   M. Dar, "The Imaginary Huleh – The Story of the Huleh Lake", *The
      Nature of Things*, Issue 55, 2000, (in Hebrew), pp. 100-117.

48   G. Shaham, "The Huleh Project – The Dynamics of Human Intervention in
      Nature", *Ecology and Environment* 4, Vol. 1, August 1994, (in Hebrew), p. 1.

49   H. Gwirtzman, *Water Resources in Israel: Chapters in Hydrology and Environmental
      Sciences*, Jerusalem: Yad Yitzhak Ben-Zvi, Jerusalem, 2002, (in Hebrew), pp. 55-57.

50   M. Dar, "The Imaginary Huleh – The Story of the Huleh Lake", *The Nature
      of Things*, Issue 55, 2000, (in Hebrew), pp. 100-117; M. Livne, The Huleh
      Drainage – Advantages and Disadvantages, *Ecology and Environment*, 4, Vol. 1,
      1994, (in Hebrew), pp. 171-174; H. Gwirtzman, *Water Resources in Israel:
      Chapters in Hydrology and Environmental Sciences*, Jerusalem: Yad Yitzhak Ben-Zvi,
      2002, (in Hebrew), pp. 55-57; Observed, Heard, *Ha'aretz*, The State Archive,
      P-1500/6, P-1501/18, 9/5/1954, (in Hebrew); "The Drainage Plant of the
      Huleh Swamps", The Zionist Archive, A246-438 (JNF files), 1995,(in Hebrew).

51   JNF website – "JNF Contribution to the Valley Development", http://www.
      kkl.org.il/kkl/hebrew/nosim_ikarym/kkl_eichut_hasviva/truma_lechut_
      hasviva_hula, (in Hebrew); M. Livne, "The Huleh Drainage – Advantages and
      Disadvantages", *Ecology and Environment*, 4, Vol. 1, 1994, (in Hebrew), p. 174;
      M. Yakobovitz, *Water in Israel*, Shikmona, 1971, (in Hebrew), pp. 73-76; T. Hatalgi,
      "About Damascus' Four Sins", *Yediot Aharonot*, 6/5/1951, (in Hebrew).

52   E-green – JNF Friends Circle – http://www212.199.160.128/kkl/
      kklink.asp?Offer, (in Hebrew).

53   M. Livne, "The Huleh Drainage – Advantages and Disadvantages",
      Ecology and Environment, 4, Vol. 1, 1994, (in Hebrew), pp. 174-175.

54 A. Goren, "The Huleh Lake will not be Peat", *Green, Blue, White*, 5 Sept.-Oct. 1955 (in Hebrew), pp. 22-24, http://www.amalnet.K12.il/meida/water/maamar_print.asp?code_name+A_maim0174.

55 "Peat Found in the Huleh Marshes", *Jerusalem Post*, January 21st, 1951.

56 Dr. B. Roth, "The Huleh Area Drainage", Letter to the Secretary of Industry and Commerce, May 1955, The State Archive, G-4532/12, (in Hebrew).

57 A. Alon, "The Huleh – Past and Present", *Country and Nature*, Issue 42, April 1996, (in Hebrew), p. 87.

58 A. Berchyau, "Facts and Numbers about the Huleh Drainage, Letter to G. Alkana", April 29th, 1951, The Ben-Gurion Archive, http://bgarchives.bgu.ac.il/bgarchive/img/13/94/0000142094001.gif, (in Hebrew).

59 S. Blass, A. Berchyau, K. Cohen, Y. Karmon, D. Koblanov, B. Roth, "The Huleh Drainage Committee Report", June 1st, 1949, The Zionist Archive, A 246-438, (in Hebrew).

60 "JNF on the Verge of its Jubilee", (in Hebrew), *Karnenu*, Issue A-B, December 1950.

61 "The Peat", *Karnenu*, Issue A, November, 1952, (in Hebrew).

62 Ibid.

63 D.A. Schmidt, Israel is Draining Swamps for Farms, *The New York Times*, August 18th, 1953.

64 Ibid.

65 Commercial Value of the Huleh Peat; Second Phase of Drainage Project Begun, Israel Digest, May 8th, 1953, The State Archive, P-1500/6.

66 S. Rabicovitz, "The Agricultural Research Station, Rehovoth, Report on the Study of Peat as a Fertilizer for the Period March 31st 1956 – May 1st 1957", Ministry of Agriculture, June 3rd, 1956, The State Archive, G-2434/4, (in Hebrew).

67 E. Berchyau, "Toward the Second Phase of the Huleh Drainage", *Karnenu*, Issue D-E, July 15th, 1953, (in Hebrew); Efraym A., "The Peat", *Karnenu*, Issue D, September, 1954, (in Hebrew).

68 E. Berchyau, The Peat Issue, *Davar*, September 30th, 1955, The State Archive, G-2434/4, (in Hebrew).

69   The Huleh Drainage Committee Report, The Zionist Archive, A246-438, 1949, p. 10.

70   Commercial Value of the Huleh Peat; Second Phase of Drainage Project Begun, *Israel Digest,* May 8th, 1953, The State Archive, P-1500/6.

71   Regional Counsel of Upper Galilee, Peat Production Plant In the Huleh, Letter to the Ministry of Agriculture, November 24th, 1954, The State Archive, G – 4532/12, (in Hebrew); Reyskin Y., The Huleh Development Authority, Letter to the Agricultural Research Station, November 20th, 1955, The State Archive, GL – 19781/8, (in Hebrew); S. Rabikovitz, 1957, The State Archive, G – 2434/4, (in Hebrew).

72   P. Sapir, Letter to Kabulan Ltd., November 6th, 1952, The State Archive, G – 4532/12, (in Hebrew); E. Berchyau, Peat-Production in Israel, Letter to Denmark, February 1st, 1954, The Zionist Archive, KKL5 – 23127; A. Bartal, Public Works Department Manager, The investigation on the Causes of the Peat Fires Burst and its Spread on the Peat Areas in the Huleh on September 28th, 1955, Final Report to the Minister of Agriculture, January 9th, 1956, The State Archive, G-2434/4 (in Hebrew); Report on Peat Development Areas, 1956-7, The State Archive, G – 4532/12, (in Hebrew).

73   The Huleh Drainage, Peat Research Summary Report, 1957, The State Archive, G-4532/12, (in Hebrew).

74   "The Huleh Drainage Plant", *Nature and Country,* October, 1952, (in Hebrew).

75   E. Berchyau, Peat Production in Israel, February 21st, 1954, The Zionist Archive, KKL-5-23127, (in Hebrew).

76   J. Zuckerman, Letter to the Huleh Authority Manager, February 18th, 1956, The State Archive, G-2434/4.

77   The Preparation of Peat Areas and their Irrigation, Tahal, Report to the Ministry of Agriculture, July 15th, 1955, The State Archive, G-19781/8, (in Hebrew).

78   The Investigation into the Fires in the Huleh is Continuing, *Yediot Aharonot,* December 27th, 1954, (in Hebrew).

79   P. Naphtali, Minister of Agriculture, Letter to A. Bartal, Public Works Department Manager, October 30th, 1955, The State Archive, G-2434/4, (in Hebrew).

80   K. Luz, Minister of Agriculture, Investigation of the Circumstances of the Peat Area Fires in the Huleh, Letter to A. Bartal, Public Works Department Manager, February 6th, 1956, The State Archive, G-2434/4, (in Hebrew).

81 A. Bartal, Public Works Department Manager, The Investigation on the Causes of the Peat Fire Burst and its Spread on the Peat Areas in the Huleh, on September 28th, 1955, Final Report to the Minister of Agriculture, January 9th, 1956, The State Archive, G-2434/4, (in Hebrew).

82 Ibid.

83 Ibid.

84 A. Berchyau, Prevention of Fire Bursts in Peat Soils in the Huleh, Letter to the Huleh Development Authority, July 5th, 1956, The State Archive, G-2434/4, (in Hebrew).

85 I. Nahmani, JNF, Letter to Reyskin I., The Huleh Development Authority Manager, September 4th, 1956, The State Archive, G-2434/4, (in Hebrew).

86 The Peat Areas Irrigation in the Huleh Drainage Plant, Water Works and Civil Engineering Corporation, Letter to H. Givati, Ministry of Agriculture General Manager, August 22nd, 1955, The State Archive, GL-19781/8, (in Hebrew).

87 A. Ben-Moshe, "The Huleh Valley – A Continuous Block of Fertile Soil", *Karnenu*, Issue A, February 1957, (in Hebrew).

88 A. Boico, Dr., The Huleh, Letter to Hanochi, Development Department Manager, Ministry of Agriculture, July 14th, 1955, The State Archive, GL-19781/8, (in Hebrew).

89 E. Berchyau, Irrigation of the Peat Areas in the Huleh, Ministry of Agriculture General Manager, July 19th, 1955, The State Archive, GL-19781/8, (in Hebrew).

90 The Preparation of Peat Areas and their Irrigation, Tahal, Report to the Ministry of Agriculture, July 15th, 1955, The State Archive, G-19781/8, (in Hebrew).

91 Ibid.

92 Ibid.

93 Z. Rinat, The More is Black, the More is Green, *Ha'aretz*, November 30th, 1999, (in Hebrew).

94 R. Khamaisi & D. Shmueli, "Shaping a Culturally Sensitive Planning Strategy – Mitigating the Impact of Israel's Proposed Transnational Highway on Arab Communities", *Journal of Planning Education and Research*, 21, 2001, p. 127.

95 Z. Rinat, A Green Blurred Line, *Ha'aretz*, May 2nd, 1997, (in Hebrew).

96 Road 6 - The Israeli EPA Stance, *Biosphere*, October–November 1994, (in Hebrew); R. Shir, A Dead-End Road, *Green, Blue, White* (The

Israeli Economy and Environment Protection Forum Journal),
Issue 1, October-November 1994, (in Hebrew).

97   Z. Zarhya, The Knesset Approved the Trans-Israel Law on First Call,
Ha'aretz, December 14th, 1994, (in Hebrew).

98   G. Alon & Z. Zarhya, The Trans-Israel Highway Proposed Law will be
Brought before the Knesset Plenum for Approval in the Next Few Days,
Ha'aretz, July 25th, 1995, (in Hebrew).

99   Road 6 – The Israeli EPA Stance, *Biosphere*, October-November 1994,
(in Hebrew); R. Shir, "A Dead-End Road", *Green, Blue, White* (The Israeli
Economy and Environment Protection Forum Journal), Issue 1, October-
November 1994, (in Hebrew).

100   Ibid.

101   Road 6 – The Israeli EPA Stand, *Biosphere*, October-November 1994,
(in Hebrew).

102   I. Schnell, "Nature and Environment in the Socialist-Zionist Pioneers'
Perceptions: A Sense of Desolation", *Ecumene*, 4 (1), 1997, p. 73.

103   A. De-Shalit, "From the Political to the Objective: The Dialectics of Zionism
and the Environment", *Environmental Politics*, Vol. 4, No.1, Spring 1995, p. 71;
A. De- Shalit, *The Environment between Theory and Practice*, New York: Oxford
University Press, 2000, p. 40.

104   I. Schnell, "Nature and Environment in the Socialist-Zionist Pioneers'
Perceptions: A *Sense* of Desolation", *Ecumene*, 4 (1), 1997, p. 80.

105   S. Schoenfeld, *Types of Environmental Narratives and their Utility in Understating
Israeli and Palestinian Environmentalism*, Glendon College, York University,
November 2004, p. 6.

106   E. Chowers, "The End of Building: Zionism and the Politics of the Concrete",
The Review of Politics, Vol. 64, No. 4, Autumn 2002, p. 600.

107   A. De-Shalit, A., *The Environment between Theory and Practice*, New-York: Oxford
University Press, 2000, p. 40.

108   W. Cronon, *The Trouble with Wilderness in Uncommon Ground – Rethinking the
Human Place in Nature*, New York: W. W. Norton & Company, 1996, p. 73.

109   M. Heidegger, *Building, Dwelling, Thinking, in Basic Writings*, ed. D. F. Krell,
New York: Harper and Row, 1977, p. 339, in E. Chowers, "The End of
Building: Zionism and the Politics of the Concrete", *The Review of Politics*,
Vol. 64, No. 4, Autumn 2002, p. 600.

110 D. Vogel, "Israeli Environmental Policy in Comparative Perspective", *Israel Affairs*, 1999, p. 247.

111 M. Gerstenfeld, "Zionism and the Environment", *Midstream*, December 2001, p. 16.

112 I. Schnell, "Nature and Environment in the Socialist-Zionist Pioneers' Perceptions: A Sense of Desolation", *Ecumene*, 4 (1), 1997, p. 82.

113 A. D. Gordon, *Letters and Notes*, (Tel-Aviv, 1917), in I. Schnell, "Nature and Environment in the Socialist-Zionist Pioneers' Perceptions: A Sense of Desolation", *Ecumene*, 4 (1), 1997, p. 82.

114 N. Greenwood, The Redeemers of the Land, Israel Ministry of Foreign Affairs, The American-Israeli Cooperative Enterprise, 1998.

115 Y. Wilkansky, *On the Road*, Jaffa 1918, (in Hebrew), p. 129, in R. Kark, "Land-God-Man: Concepts of Land Ownership in Traditional Cultures in Eretz-Israel", p. 73 in *Ideology and Landscape in Historical Perspective*, (Ed.) A. H. Baker & G. Biger, Cambridge, U.K.: Cambridge University Press, 1992; A. Kellerman, *Society and Settlement – Jewish Land of Israel in the 20ᵗʰ Century*, Albany: State Univ. of New-York Press, 1993, p. 40.

116 R. Kark, "Land-God-Man: Concepts of Land Ownership in Traditional Cultures in Eretz-Israel", p. 69 in *Ideology and Landscape in Historical Perspective*, (Ed.) A. H. Baker & G. Biger, Cambridge, U. K.: Cambridge University Press, 1992.

117 S. Almog, "The Redemption in the Zionist Rhetoric", in *Redemption of the Land*, edited by R. Kark, Jerusalem: Yad Yitzhak Ben-Zvi, 1990, (in Hebrew), p. 13; J. Weitz, *Megamda Lerevaha – the History of Soil Preparation in Israel*, Ramat-Gan: Masada, 1972, (in Hebrew), p. 35.

118 S. Almog, "The Redemption in the Zionist Rhetoric", in *Redemption of the Land*, edited by R. Kark, Jerusalem: Yad Yitzhak Ben-Zvi, 1990, (in Hebrew), p. 18.

119 Kark R., "Land-God-Man: Concepts of Land Ownership in Traditional Cultures in Eretz-Israel", p. 71 in *Ideology and Landscape in Historical Perspective*, (Ed.) A. H. Baker & G. Biger, Cambridge, U.K.: Cambridge University Press, 1992.

120 H. Near, "Land Redemption, Man Redemption and Pioneering in the Minds of the Zionist Labor Movement-from the Second to the Fifth Wave of Immigrants (1904-1935)", in *Redemption of the Land*, edited by R. Kark, Jerusalem: Yad Yitzhak Ben-Zvi, 1990, p. 33.

121 A. De-Shalit, "From the Political to the Objective: The Dialectics of Zionism and the Environment", *Environmental Politics*, Vol. 4, No.1, Spring 1995, p. 70.

122 H. Near, "Land Redemption, Man Redemption and Pioneering in the Minds of the Zionist Labor Movement-from the Second to the Fifth Wave of Immigrants (1904-1935)", in *Redemption of the Land,* edited by R. Kark, Jerusalem: Yad Yitzhak Ben-Zvi, 1990, p. 37.

123 Hebrew expression meaning treatment of the soil in order to make it usable for cultivation (e.g. swamps draining, rocks removal, etc.) – became a Zionist slogan.

124 H. Near, "Land Redemption, Man Redemption and Pioneering in the Minds of the Zionist Labor Movement – from the Second to the Fifth Wave of Immigrants (1904-1935)", in *Redemption of the Land,* edited by R. Kark, Jerusalem: Yad Yitzhak Ben-Zvi, 1990, pp. 41-44.

125 A. De-Shalit, "From the Political to the Objective: The Dialectics of Zionism and the Environment", *Environmental Politics*, Vol. 4, No.1, Spring 1995, p. 74.

126 Hebrew expressions meaning "Conquest of the Land" and "Conquest of Labor" respectively; became Zionist slogans.

127 S. Sufian, *Healing the Land and the Nation – Malaria and the Zionist Project in Palestine, 1920-1947*, Chicago: The University of Chicago Press, 2007, p. 161.

128 A. De Shalit, "From the Political to the Objective: The Dialectics of Zionism and the Environment", *Environmental Politics*, Vol. 4, No.1, Spring 1995, p. 76.

129 Ibid., p. 77.

130 S. Schoenfeld, *Types of Environmental Narratives and their Utility in Understating Israeli and Palestinian Environmentalism*, Glendon College, York University, November 2004, p. 6.

131 A. De-Shalit, "From the Political to the Objective: The Dialectics of Zionism and the Environment", *Environmental Politics*, Vol.4, No.1, Spring, 1995, p. 78.

132 J. Weitz, *Megamda Lerevaha – The History of Land Preparation in Israel*, Ramat-Gan: Masada, 1972, (in Hebrew), p. 63.

133 A. De-Shalit & M. Talias, "Green or Blue and White? Environmental Controversies in Israel", *Environmental Politics*, Vol. 3, No. 2, Summer 1994, p. 289.

134 Ibid., p. 290.

135 A. Kellerman, *Society and Settlement – Jewish Land of Israel in the 20th Century*, Albany: State University of New-York Press, 1993, p. 44.

136 D. Horovitz & M. Lisak, *Hardships in Utopia: Israel-A Society under Pressure*, Tel-Aviv: Am Oved, , 1990, (in Hebrew), pp. 153, 193.

137 A. Kellerman, *Society and Settlement – Jewish Land of Israel in the 20th Century*, Albany: State University of New-York Press, 1993, p. 45.

138 A. De Shalit, "From the Political to the Objective: The Dialectics of Zionism and the Environment", *Environmental Politics*, Vol. 4, No.1, Spring 1995, p. 79.

139 A. De Shalit & M. Talias, "Green or Blue and White? Environmental Controversies in Israel", *Environmental Politics*, Vol. 3, No. 2, Summer 1994, p. 289.

140 A. Shalev, *Israel-Syria Armistice Regime*, pp. 51-52, in D. Rabinovitz and S. Khawalde, "Demilitarized, then Dispossessed: The Kirad Bedouins of the Huleh Valley in the Context of Syrian–Israeli Relations", *International Journal of Middle East Studies*, 32, 2000, p. 522; L. M. Alexander, "The Arab-Israeli Boundary Problem", *World Politics*, Vol. 6 No. 3, April 1954, p. 329; G. Anton, "Blind Modernism and Zionist Waterscape", *Jerusalem Quarterly*, Issue 35, Autumn 2008, p. 87.

141 M. Muslih, "The Golan: Israel, Syria, and Strategic Calculations", *Middle East Journal*, 47, No. 4, Autumn 1993, p. 615.

142 Government Session Protocol, The State Archive, The First Government Meetings Records, Vol. 22, March 29th, 1950, (in Hebrew).

143 R. Kark, "Land-God-Man: Concepts of Land Ownership in Traditional Cultures in Eretz-Israel", p. 71 in *Ideology and Landscape in Historical Perspective*, (Ed.) A. H. Baker & G. Biger, Cambridge, U. K.: Cambridge University Press, 1992, p. 78.

144 JNF Board of Directors Session Protocol, The Zionist Archive, September 24th, 1950, (in Hebrew).

145 A. Granot, *Toward the Second Jubilee*, "*Kama*", Vol. D, The JNF Year Book, Jerusalem, 1951, (in Hebrew), p. 3.

146 Ibid., p. 15.

147 J. Weitz, *In My Path – To Settle the Country*, Jerusalem: Nir, 1960, (in Hebrew), pp. 378-380.

148 J. Weitz, *Land for the Nation, in In my Path – To Settle the Country*, Jerusalem: Nir, 1960, (in Hebrew), p. 379.

149 A. Granot, *Settling the Nation*, Jerusalem – Tel-Aviv: D'vir, 1950, p. 220.

150 D. Ben-Gurion, *Vision and Path*, Tel-Aviv: Am Oved, 1951, (in Hebrew), p. 136, in A. Kartin, "A Geographical Review of the Influence of Hostile Neighborly Relations on the Settlement of the Frontier Zone in Israel", (Ph.D. Dissertation), Tel-Aviv University, 1995, p. 125.

151 A. Oren & R. Regev, *Land in Uniform – Territory and Defense in Israel*, Jerusalem: Carmel Press, 2008, (in Hebrew), pp. 50-52.

152 A. Reynitz, The Huleh Drainage Works in the Central DZ, The Zionist Archive, 708/68/100, October 6th, 1950, (in Hebrew).

153 M. Duani, From Drainage to Conservation of the Huleh Wetlands: Tracing the Dynamics of Nature Intervention, (Ph. D. Dissertation), Haifa University, March 2010, p. 85.

154 J. Tekoa, The Huleh Concession, Letter to Dr. Eytan W., The State Archive, Ministry of Foreign Affairs, HZ-2440/10, November 3rd, 1950, (in Hebrew).

155 The Huleh Conflict (Summary), Information for Israeli Representatives Abroad, No. 256,The State Archive, Ministry of Foreign Affairs, HZ-2452/8, April 6th, 1951, (in Hebrew).

156 F. Khouri, "Friction and Conflict on the Israeli-Syrian Front", *The Middle East Journal*, No. 1 & 2, Vol. 17, Winter-Spring 1963, p. 15.

157 A. Kaufman, "Let Sleeping Dogs Lie': On Ghajar and Other Anomalies in the Syrian-Lebanon-Israel Tri-Border Region", *Middle East Journal*, Volume 63, No. 4, Autumn 2009, p.546.

158 F. Khouri, "Friction and Conflict on the Israeli-Syrian Front", *The Middle East Journal*, No. 1 & 2, Vol. 17, Winter-Spring 1963, pp.15-19; M. Muslih, "The Golan: Israel, Syria, and Strategic Calculations", *The Middle East Journal*, 47, no. 4, Autumn 1993, pp. 613-616.

159 The Huleh Conflict (Summary), Information for Israeli Representatives Abroad, No. 256, The State Archive, Ministry of Foreign Affairs, HZ-2452/8, April 6th, 1951, (in Hebrew).

160 Ibid.

161 Ibid.

162 Israel's Reservations to the U.N. Chief of Staff Report Regarding our Position in the Huleh Matter, Information for our Representatives Abroad, No. 270, The State Archive, Ministry of Foreign Affairs, P-2440/10, May 2nd, 1951, (in Hebrew).

163 The Failure of the Armistice, Israel Ministry of Foreign Affairs, Foreign Relations, Historical Documents vol. 1-2, 1947-1974, August 13th, 2000 http://www.mfa.gov.il/MFA/Foreign+Relations/Israel+Foreign+Relations+since+1947.

164 Col. D. Jeremiah, Declaration, The Zionist Archive, 447/53/13 in M. Duani, "From Drainage to Conservation of the Huleh Wetlands: Tracing the Dynamics of Nature Intervention" (Ph. D. Dissertation), Haifa University, March 2010, (in Hebrew), p. 91.

165 A. Shalev, *Cooperation under Conflict – The Syria-Israel Armistice Regime 1949-1955*, Ministry of Defense, Tel-Aviv, 1989, pp. 167-173, in M. Duani, From

Drainage to Conservation of the Huleh Wetlands: Tracing the Dynamics of Nature Intervention, (Ph. D. Dissertation), Haifa University, March 2010, (in Hebrew), p. 91.

166 I. Yadin, Foreign Affairs and Defense Committee Meeting KZ/3, The State Archive, A-7562/9, 8/4/1951, pp. 12-13, in M. Duani, From Drainage Conservation of the Huleh Wetlands: Tracing the Dynamics of Nature Intervention (Ph. D. Dissertation), Haifa University, March 2010, (in Hebrew), p. 91.

167 M. Sharet, Memorandum 3/8 from the 7th of June Regarding the Huleh Problem, The Zionist Archive, 1559/52/30, June 11th, 1951, (in Hebrew), p. 1.

168 M. Duani, From Drainage to Conservation of the Huleh Wetlands: Tracing the Dynamics of Nature Intervention (Ph. D. Dissertation), Haifa University, March 2010, (in Hebrew), p. 96.

169 The Huleh Conflict (Summary), Information for Israeli Representatives Abroad, No. 256, The State Archive, Ministry of Foreign Affairs, HZ-2452/8, April 6th, 1951, (in Hebrew).

170 J. Tekoa, Summary and Conclusions of the Meeting with the Prime Minister about the Huleh, (March 3rd, 1951), The State Archive, Ministry of Foreign Affairs, HZ-2440/10, April 1st, 1951, (in Hebrew); J. Tekoa, Transfer of Arab Citizens from the Demilitarized Zone, Letter to the Manager of the Middle East Sector - Legal Department, Ministry of Foreign Affairs, The State Archive, HZ-2440/10, April 2nd, 1951, (in Hebrew).

171 Ibid., Tekoa, 2/4/1951, (in Hebrew).

172 The Huleh Conflict (Summary), Information for Israeli Representatives Abroad, No. 256, The State Archive, Ministry of Foreign Affairs, HZ-2452/8, April 6th, 1951, (in Hebrew).

173 A. Galin, "The Decline of a Strong Union – What Can be Learnt from the Israeli Experience", in R. Blanpain & R. Ben Israel, *Labour Law, Human Rights and Social Justice*, The Hague, Netherlands: Kluwer Law International, 2001, p. 209; R. Hirschl, "Israel's Constitutional Revolution: The Legal Interpretation of Entrenched Civil Liberties in an Emerging Neo-liberal Economic Order", *The American Journal of Comparative Law*, Vol. 46, No. 3, Summer 1998, p. 427.

174 A. Shapira, "Central Privatization Processes in Israel", Israel Democracy Institute,15, College, May 6th, 2007; F. Salmon, "In Praise of Infrastructure Privatization", Portfolio. Com. – A Bizjournal Property, May 3rd, 2007.

175 Standpoint on Privatization in the Public Sector, Netanya Academic College, May 6th, 2007. Salmon F., "In Praise of Infrastructure Privatizaton", Portfolio. Com. – A Bizjournal Property, May 3rd, 2007.

176   Ibid.

177   D. Goutwin, "The Changes in the Economic Policy of the Israeli Right, 1977-2003: from Nationalized Privatization to Oligarchic Privatization", *Labor, Society and Law*, 10, 2004, pp. 221-239.

178   The Privatization of Infrastructure and Social Services, The Forum for Unemployment Struggle, http://www.knesset.gov. il/LegalDept/privatization/heb/privatization14.pdf, (in Hebrew).

179   E. Ben-Yemini, "Between British Rail and Trans-Israel Highway", *Another Country*, October 31st, 2002, http://acheret.co.il/?cmd=articles.169&act=read&id=859&print=1, (in Hebrew).

180   S. Kadmi, The Technion Report: The Economic Benefit of the Trans-Israel Highway is Lower by Tens of Billions of Shekels than the Evaluations, *Ha'aretz*, January 1st, 2007, (in Hebrew).

181   The Cross-Israel Company, Home-Web, http://www.hozeisrael.co.il, (in Hebrew).

182   N. Strassler, The Swamp Dragonfly, *Ha'aretz*, November 11th, 1999, (in Hebrew).

183   Rinat Z., The Hierarchy on the Roads, *Ha'aretz*, September 20th, 1996, (in Hebrew).

184   Ibid.; The Cross-Israel Highway Company, *Information Bulletin*, 2000, (in Hebrew).

185   The Highway – Part of the Solution, *Ha'aretz*, December 3rd, 1996, (in Hebrew).

186   H. Schwartzman, To Cross the Country, *Ha'aretz*, July 11th, 1999, (in Hebrew).

187   N. Strassler, The Swamp Dragonfly, *Ha'aretz*, November 11th, 1999, (in Hebrew).

188   Z. Rinat, The New Society for the Protection of Nature, *Ha'aretz*, February 25th, 2000, (in Hebrew).

189   D. Rabinowitz, "The Road that Yields Real Estate", *The Internal Journal of the Teachers Federation*, Issue 21, Summer 2002, (in Hebrew).

190   R. Shir, "A Dead-End Road", *Green, Blue, White* (The Israeli Economy and Environment Protection Forum Journal), Issue 1, October-November 1994, (in Hebrew).

191   D. Rabinovitz, "The Road that Yields Real Estate", *The Internal Journal of the Teachers' Federation*, Issue 21, Summer 2002, (in Hebrew).

192   Ibid.

193 Ibid.

194 Ibid.

195 Ibid.; Trans-Israel – Transport and Social Damage, The Green Course, www.
greencourse.org.il, (in Hebrew); Urel, Road 6, The Trans-Israel Highway,
The Green Course, www.greencourse.org.il, (in Hebrew); E. Ben-Ari,
(attorney for Israel Union For Environmental Defense – IUED – Adam,
Teva V'Din), They Hide their Heads under the Road, *Ha'aretz*, December
5th, 1999, (in Hebrew); Questions and Answers Regarding the Highway, The
Movement for Social Change From Below's website, http://www.bdidut.
com, (in Hebrew); Why Are We Against the Trans-Israel Highway, The
Movement for Social Change From Below's website, http://www.bdidut.
com, (in Hebrew).

196 Y. Asidon, The Price of the Trans-Israel Highway, *Ha'aretz*, December 12th,
1999, (in Hebrew).

197 R. Gabay, The Road that Rips the Country Apart, *Ha'aretz*, November 8th,
1999, (in Hebrew).

198 B. Rosen, The Transport was Meant for People, not for Vehicles, *Ha'aretz*,
April 25th, 2000, (in Hebrew); Z. Rinat, The Trans-Israel Highway Received
the Final Approval and Now the Experts Have Doubts, *Ha'aretz*, April 13th,
2000, (in Hebrew); U. Sheiness, Who Wants the Road, Columbia University,
New York, *Ha'aretz*, February 8th, 1998, (in Hebrew); R. Shir, "A Dead-End
Road", *Green, Blue, White* (The Israeli Economy and Environment Protection
Forum Journal), Issue 1, October-November 1994, (in Hebrew).

199 *The Ombudsman Report* 47-48, Segments, 1997-8, (in Hebrew)

200 *The Ombudsman Report* 47-48, Segments, 1997-8, (in Hebrew); Z. Rinat,
The Short Way to the Next Traffic Jam, *Ha'aretz*, January 11th, 1996, (in
Hebrew); E. Ben Ari, (attorney for Israel Union For Environmental Defense
– IUED – Adam, Teva V'Din), They Hide their Heads under the Road,
Ha'aretz, December 5th, 1999, (in Hebrew); A. Samuel, Trans-Israel or
Trans Gush Dan, *Ha'aretz*, July 13th, 1997, (in Hebrew); A. Zigelman, The
Social Lobby: The Trans-Israel will Cross between the Periphery and
the Center, *Ha'aretz*, September 19th, 2000, (in Hebrew); Z. Rinat, The
Suburbs Generator, *Ha'aretz*, January 27th, 1998, (in Hebrew).

201 Z. Rinat, Fast Path to Nowhere, *Ha'aretz*, October 13th, 1998, (in Hebrew);
Z. Rinat, The Trans-Israel Highway Received the Final Approval and Now
the Experts Have Doubts, *Ha'aretz*, April 13th, 2000, (in Hebrew); The
Trans-Israel Highway – Facts List, The Movement for Social Change from
the website, http://www.bdidut.com, (in Hebrew).

202 Z. Rinat, The Trans-Israel Highway Received the Final Approval and Now
the Experts Have Doubts, *Ha'aretz*, April 13th, 2000, (in Hebrew); Y. Asidon,
Route 6 – The Difference between Reality and Fantasy (in answer to
N. Strassler N. article), *The Green Wave*, November 13th, 2004, (in Hebrew);

Z. Rinat, Why Do We Have to Pay, *Ha'aretz*, December 27th, 1998, (in Hebrew); The Trans-Israel Highway – Facts List, The Movement for Social Change from the website, http://www.bdidut.com, (in Hebrew).

203   Z. Rinat, A Green Blurry Line, *Ha'aretz*, May 2nd, 1997, (in Hebrew); Urel, 6, The Trans-Israel Highway, The Green Course, www.greencourse.org. il, (in Hebrew); Questions and Answers regarding the Highway, The Movement for Social Change From Below's website, http://www. bdidut.com, (in Hebrew); Y. Asidon, "The Road that will Cross Israel Socially and Economically", *Green, Blue, White* (The Israeli Economy and Environment Protection Forum Journal), Issue 31, April-May 2000, (in Hebrew); The Trans-Israel Highway – Facts List, The Movement for Social Change From Below's website, http:// www.bdidut.com, (in Hebrew).

204   Z. Rinart, Fast Path to Nowhere, *Ha'aretz*, October 13th, 1998, (in Hebrew); Y. Asidon, "The Road that will Cross Israel Socially and Economically", *Green, Blue, White* (The Israeli Economy and Environment Protection Forum Journal), Issue 31, April-May, 2000, (in Hebrew).

205   M. Kaplan, On a Clear Day you can See Tel-Aviv, *Ha'aretz*, November 22nd, 1999, (in Hebrew).

206   Y. Asidon, The Price of the Trans-Israel Highway, *Ha'aretz*, December 12th, 1999, (in Hebrew); Questions and Answers Regarding the Highway, The Movement for Social Change From Below's website, http://www.bdidut. com, (in Hebrew); Why Are We Against the Trans-Israel Highway, The Movement for Social Change From Below's website, http://www.bdidut. com, (in Hebrew); Z. Rinat, Why Do We Have to Pay, *Ha'aretz*, December 27th, 1998, (in Hebrew); The Trans-Israel Highway – Facts List, The Movement for Social Change From Below's website, http://www.bdidut.com, (in Hebrew); B. Sagiv, Who Wants the Highway, *Ha'aretz*, February 8th, 1998, (in Hebrew); U. Sheiness, Who Wants the Road, Columbia University, New York, *Ha'aretz*, February 8th, 1998, (in Hebrew).

207   Y. Ringwartz, The Transport was Meant for People, not for Vehicles, *Ha'aretz*, April 25th, 2000, (in Hebrew); U. Sheiness, Who Wants the Road, Columbia University, New York, *Ha'aretz*, February 8th, 1998, (in Hebrew); B. Tirosh, The Price of the Trans-Israel Highway, *Ha'aretz*, December 5th, 1998, (in Hebrew); U. Sheiness, Haifa University – Oranim, "Amateur Planning Bordering on Criminal Negligence", *Green, Blue, White* (The Israeli Economy and Environment Protection Forum Journal), April-May, 2000, (in Hebrew).

208   The Trans-Israel Highway – Facts List, The Movement for Social Change from the website, http://www.bdidut.com, (in Hebrew).

209   M. Kaplan, The Transport was Meant for People, not for Vehicles, *Ha'aretz*, April 25th, 2000, (in Hebrew).

210   U. Sheiness, "Who Wants the Road", Columbia University, New York, *Ha'aretz*, February 8th, 1998, (in Hebrew).

211 Z. Rinat, "The Short Way to the Next Traffic Jam", *Ha'aretz*, January 11th, 1996, (in Hebrew).

212 "The Trans-Israel Highway", The Green Course, www.greencourse.org.il, (in Hebrew).

213 H. Sagy, "The Trans-Israel Highway – The Society for the Protection of Nature Renews its Struggle", *Ha'aretz*, December 8th, 2996, (in Hebrew).

214 Ibid.

215 L. Hagar, "Everyone Talks, Maa'tz Paves", *Ha'aretz*, May 20th, 1997, (in Hebrew); M. Raily & Z. Rinat, "5 Ministers Opposed the Construction of Another Section of the Trans-Israel", *Ha'aretz*, August 21st, 2000, (in Hebrew); Z. Rinat, "The New Society for the Protection of Nature", *Ha'aretz*, February 25th, 2000, (in Hebrew).

216 Z. Rinat, 'Fast Path to Nowhere", *Ha'aretz*, October 13th, 1998, (in Hebrew); E. Ben Ari, "They Hide their Heads under the Road", *Ha'aretz*, December 5th, 1999, (in Hebrew); Z. Rinat, "Why Do We Have to Pay", *Ha'aretz*, December 27th, 1998, (in Hebrew); L. Hagar, "Everyone Talks, Maa'tz Paves", *Ha'aretz*, May 20th, 1997, (in Hebrew); D. Itzic – "The Minister for Environment, The Sole Solution of the Trans-Israel is not Enough", *Ha'aretz*, May 7th, 2000, (in Hebrew); H. Sagy, L. Hagar, & N. Craw, "The Ben-Shemen Interchange of the Trans-Israel was Inaugurated", *Ha'aretz*, April 14th, 1997, (in Hebrew).

217 R. Gabay, "The Road that Rips the Country Apart", *Ha'aretz*, November 8th, 1999, (in Hebrew).

218 R. Shir, "A Dead-End Road", *Green, Blue, White* (The Israeli Economy and Environment Protection Forum Journal), Issue 1, October-November 1994, (in Hebrew).

219 R. Shir, "A Dead-End Road", *Green, Blue, White* (The Israeli Economy and Environment Protection Forum Journal), Issue 1, October-November 1994, (in Hebrew); The Ombudsman Report 47-48, Segments, 1997-8, (in Hebrew); Z. Rinat, "The Trans-Israel Highway Received the Final Approval and Now the Experts Have Doubts", *Ha'aretz*, April 13th, 2000, (in Hebrew).

220 Z. Rinat, "A Green Blurry Line", *Ha'aretz*, May 2nd, 1997, (in Hebrew).

221 Y. Asidon, Route 6 – The Difference between Reality and Fantasy (in answer to N. Strassler article), *The Green Wave*, November 13th, 2004, (in Hebrew).

222 M. Kaplan, "On a Clear Day you can See Tel-Aviv," *Ha'aretz*, November 22nd, 1999, (in Hebrew); A. Samuel, "Trans-Israel or Trans-Gush Dan", *Ha'aretz*, July 13th, 1997, (in Hebrew); M. Kaplan, "The Transport was Meant for People, not for Vehicles", *Ha'aretz*, April 25th, 2000, (in Hebrew).

223 A. Zigelman, The Social Lobby: "The Trans-Israel will Cross between the Periphery and the Center", *Ha'aretz*, September 19th, 2000, (in Hebrew);

D. Rabinovitz, "The Road that Yields Real Estate", *The Internal Journal of the Teachers Federation,* Issue 21, Summer 2002, (in Hebrew).

224 D. Rabinovitz, "The Road that Yields Real Estate", *The Internal Journal of the Teachers Federation,* Issue 21, Summer 2002, (in Hebrew); Z. Rinat, "A Worthy Environmental Fight – That is Something Too", *Ha'aretz,* July 5th, 2000, (in Hebrew); Z. Rinat, "The More is Black, the More is Green", *Ha'aretz,* November 30th, 1999, (in Hebrew).

225 Why Are We Against the Trans-Israel Highway, The Movement for Social Change from the website, http://www.bdidut.com, (in Hebrew); Z. Rinat, "The Hierarchy on the Roads", *Ha'aretz,* September 20th, 1996, (in Hebrew).

226 Questions and Answers regarding the Highway, The Movement for Social Change from the website, http://www.bdidut.com, (in Hebrew).

227 R. Shir, "A Dead-End Road", *Green, Blue, White* (The Israeli Economy and Environment Protection Forum Journal), Issue 1, October-November 1994, (in Hebrew); Z. Rinat, "The Hierarchy on the Road", *Ha'aretz,* September 20th, 1996, (in Hebrew); A. Ydov (Head of "Transport – Today and Tomorrow" NGO – The Israeli Organization for Sustainable Transport), The Price of the Trans-Israel, *Ha'aretz,* December 5th, 1999, (in Hebrew); D. Morgenstern, "Don't Want the Trans-Israel", *Green, Blue, White* (The Israeli Economy and Environment Protection Forum Journal), Issue 27, August-September 1999, (in Hebrew).

228 R. Gabay, "The Road that Rips the Country Apart", *Ha'aretz,* November 8th, 1999, (in Hebrew).

229 Z. Rinat, "The New Society for the Protection of Nature", *Ha'aretz,* February 25th, 2000, (in Hebrew); Y. Asidon, "The Road that will Cross Israel Socially and Economically", *Green, Blue, White* (The Israeli Economy and Environment Protection Forum Journal), Issue 31, April-May 2000, (in Hebrew); The Trans-Israel Highway, The Green Course, www.greencourse. org.il, (in Hebrew).

230 U. Ben-Eliezer, *The Making of the Israeli Militarism,* Bloomington and Indianapolis: Indiana University Press, 1998.

231 S. Blas, The Huleh Drainage Plan – General Scheme, The State Archive, the Ministry of Agriculture, The Huleh Drainage File, GL – 19781/8, November 12th, 1950, (in Hebrew).

232 Appointment and Instructions for the Committee, The Zionist Archive, A 246/438, June 1st, 1949, (in Hebrew), p. 1.

233 M. Livne, "The Huleh Drainage – Advantages and Disadvantages", *Ecology and Environment,* 4, Vol. 1, 1994, (in Hebrew), pp. 169-170

234 S. Blas, The Huleh Concession, Ministry of Agriculture, Letter to J. Govrin from the Ministry of Commerce and Industry, The State Archive, G-2179/33, July 24[th,] 1949, (in Hebrew).

235 R. Weitz, *The Huleh Region Planning Committee,* The Jewish Agency, The State Archive, G-2179/33, September 18th, 1949, (in Hebrew).

236 S. Blas, "The Letter of the Minister of Finance from the 4th of June 1950, Ministry of Agriculture", The State Archive, G-2179/33, Jun3 14th ,1950, (in Hebrew).

237 "The JNF Meeting Protocol", *The JNF Protocols Books,* The Zionist Archive, November 15th, 1950, (in Hebrew).

238 A. Brutzkus, Ministry of Interior, "In Charge with National Planning", "Letter to A. Horn" from the Society for the Protection of Nature, The State Archive, G-2736, February 2nd, 1955, (in Hebrew).

239 "The Huleh Drainage Plant and its Maintenance", The Zionist Archive, A246-439, 1965, (in Hebrew).

240 Government Session Protocol, The State Archive, The First Government Meetings Records, Vol. 22, March 29th, 1950, (in Hebrew).

241 "The Trans-Israel Along and Across the Country", *Ha'aretz,* April 2nd, 2000, (in Hebrew).

242 N. Strassler, "The Road that Crosses Populism", *Ha'aretz,* February 15th, 2000, (in Hebrew).

243 The Congress on Economic and Environmental Aspects of the Trans-Israel Highway, January 22nd, 2001, http://ichut.macam.ac.il/ecokenes.html, (in Hebrew).

244 D. Danieli, D. Shmueli, "Conflicts Assessment: The Trans-Israel Highway, Haifa University", The Israeli EPA, 2002, (in Hebrew), pp. 181, 185.

245 Ibid., p. 183.

246 Ibid., p. 187.

247 P. Gazit, A. Sofer, *The In-Between Zone between the Sharon and Samaria,* Haifa University, August 2005, (in Hebrew), p. 96.

248 D. Rabinowitz, I. Vardi, *Driving Forces: Trans-Israel Highway and the Privatization of Civil Infrastructures in Israel,* Jerusalem: The Van Leer Jerusalem Institute, Hakibbutz Hameuhad Publishing House, 2010, (in Hebrew), pp. 55-57.

249 D. Horowitz & M. Lisak, *Hardships in Utopia: Israel –A Besieged Society,* Tel-Aviv: Am Oved, 1990, (in Hebrew), p. 142.

250 Ibid., pp. 192-193.

251 *Geva News Journal,* No. 140, G-16, November 7th, 1957, (in Hebrew); *Geva News Journal,* No. Y-13,C-55, November 7th, 1957, (in Hebrew); *Geva News Journal,* No. 263, C-64, September 26th, 1958, (in Hebrew).

252 *Geva News Journal,* No. 140, G-16, November 7th, 1957, (in Hebrew).

253 *Geva News Journal,* No. Y-13,C-55, November 7th, (in Hebrew).

254 *Geva News Journal,* No. 263, C-64, September 26th, 1958, (in Hebrew).

255 A. Berchyau, "The Disposal of the Swamp", *Karnenu,* January 1953, (in Hebrew), p. 3.

256 Ibid.

257 Y. Zilbersheid, "In a Little While the Huleh Lake will Disapear from the Country's Map", *Lamerhav,* May 2nd, 1955, in "The Completion of the Huleh Drainage Plant", A. Berchyau, *Karnenu,* January 1958, (in Hebrew), pp. 2-3.

258 Al Hamishmar, in "The Country's Newspapers on the Drainage Plant Completion", *Karnenu,* Issue A, January 1958, (in Hebrew).

259 K. Shabtay, Nothing is Done, *Davar,* January 29th, 1954, (in Hebrew).

260 "Israel and Syria Representatives Met at Rosh-Pina", *Yediot Aharonot,* May 28th, 1951, (in Hebrew); "The Syrian Provocative Demand", *Yediot Aharonot,* May 25th, 1951, (in Hebrew); "The Syrian Complaint Regarding the Huleh Drainage", *Ha'aretz,* Mars 9th, 1951, (in Hebrew); "The Work on the Huleh Drainage Will Continue", *Ha'aretz,* Mars 21st, 1951, (in Hebrew); "The Huleh Problem was Discussed", *Ha'aretz,* April 2nd, 1951, (in Hebrew); B. Welles, "Issues in Huleh Dispute", *The New York Times,* June 11th, 1951; A.E. Barrekette, "Jordan's Valley Project", *The New York Times,* July 4th, 1951.

261 T. Hatalgi, "About Damascus' Four Sins", *Yediot Aharonot,* May 6th, 1951, (in Hebrew).

262 H. Levin, "The Huleh Marshes", *The Christian Science Monitor,* Boston, June 11th, 1951.

263 T. Hatalgi, "About Damascus' Four Sins", *Yediot Aharonot,* May 6th, 1951, (in Hebrew).

264 "The Riotous Villages were Destroyed – Reveals the Prime Minister", *Davar,* April 8th, 1951, (in Hebrew).

265 "Thunder Shots Echo on the Jordan Border", *Yediot Aharonot,* March 26th, 1951, (in Hebrew).

266 "No Progress was Made on the Negotiations on the 28 Dunams", *Ha'aretz,* June 7th, 1951, (in Hebrew).

267 "The Arab Owners of the 28 Dunams in the Huleh are under Syrian Government Pressure", *Davar,* June 1ˢᵗ, 1951, (in Hebrew).

268 J. Greenberg, "Israel Restoring Drained Wetland, Reversing Pioneers' Feat", *The New-York Times,* December 5ᵗʰ, 1993.

269 "The Song of the Dying Lake", *Davar,* September 9ᵗʰ, 1960, (in Hebrew).

270 E. Talmi E, "That is the Zatia, She is Laughing", *Davar,* August 1ˢᵗ, 1952, (in Hebrew).

271 A. H. Elhanani, "What Caused the Drying of the Natural Huleh Reserve", *Davar,* July 6ᵗʰ, 1958, (in Hebrew).

272 R. Grinker, "Memorial to Disappearing Beauty", *Davar,* October 4ᵗʰ, 1957, (in Hebrew).

273 "Lights and Shadows", *Yediot Aharonot,* August 3ʳᵈ, 1952, (in Hebrew).

274 Ibid.

275 E. Talmi, "Last Sail on the Huleh Lake", *Davar,* November 10ᵗʰ, 1957, (in Hebrew).

276 E. Talmi, "Nature Reserves will be Created to Protect Nature Assets in the Huleh Region", *Davar,* June 20ᵗʰ, 1952, (in Hebrew).

277 "Ben-Gurion Visits Site", *New-York Times,* August 18ᵗʰ, 1953.

278 D. A. Schmidt, "Israel is Draining Swamps for Farms", *New-York Times,* August 18ᵗʰ, 1953.

279 Y. Nir, "The Huleh – The Destiny of a Pioneering Plant", *Ha'aretz,* July 4ᵗʰ, 1965, (in Hebrew); "The Investigation of the Fire in the Huleh Continues", *Yediot Aharonot,* December 27ᵗʰ, 1954, (in Hebrew).

280 "The JNF Plan for the Development of the Galilee", *Davar,* September 7ᵗʰ, 1954, (in Hebrew); "The Huleh Drainage Approaches its End", *Lamerhav,* January 14ᵗʰ, 1955, (in Hebrew).

281 A. Granot, "The Jubilee of the J.N.F.," *Davar,* December 28ᵗʰ, 1950, (in Hebrew).

282 "The J.N.F. Strengthens Israel's Economy", *Davar,* June 3ʳᵈ, 1955, (in Hebrew); Z. Rotem, "The Continuation of the Glorious Tradition of the JNF will be Guaranteed", *Davar,* August 7ᵗʰ, 1951, (in Hebrew).

283 "The Huleh Drainage and the Planting of 'The Saints Forest' – the Core of the JNF Tasks", *Davar,* January 18ᵗʰ, 1952, (in Hebrew).

284 "The Huleh Drainage – The Highlight of the JNF Plants", *Davar*, February 2nd, 1951, (in Hebrew).

285 S. Dayan, "The Huleh Land – for Settlement", *Davar*, November 9th, 1962, (in Hebrew).

286 A. H. Elhanani, "We Have to Change our Attitude toward the Water System", *Davar*, January 31st, 1969, (in Hebrew).

287 "The Price of the Huleh Drainage", *Davar*, October 26th, 1950, (in Hebrew).

288 D. Shalev, "The Huleh Drainage – Reality and Planning", *Davar*, September 9th, 1955, (in Hebrew).

289 Protocol of the JNF Board of Directors, Jerusalem, September 24th, 1950, (in Hebrew).

290 M. Dar, "The Imaginary Huleh – the Story of the Huleh Lake", *The Nature of Things*, Issue 55, 2000, (in Hebrew), pp. 100-117; M. Livne, "The Huleh Drainage – Advantages and Disadvantages", *Ecology and Environment*, 4, Vol. 1, 1994, (in Hebrew), pp. 171-174; H. Gwirtzman, *Water Resources in Israel: Chapters in Hydrology and Environmental Sciences*, Jerusalem: Yad Yitzhak Ben-Zvi, , 2002, (in Hebrew), pp. 55-57; "Observed, Heard", *Ha'aretz*, The State Archive, P-1500/6, P-1501/18, 9/5/1954, (in Hebrew); The Drainage Plant of the Huleh Swamps, The Zionist Archive, A246-438 (JNF files), 1995, (in Hebrew).

291 The Committee for Nature Protection, The Execution of a Scientific and Cultural Plan, The State Archive, File 5495/6-G, January 28th, 1951, (in Hebrew).

292 E. Berachyau, "The Huleh Reserve", The State Archive, File 19781/8-GL, December 11th, 1955, (in Hebrew).

293 The Green Club (Moadon Yarok) - Discussion Group – The Trans-Israel Highway – http://science.cet.ac.il/science/ecology/forums/forum.asp?Asp=401&nSubProjectID=0&bFillMsgFields..., (in Hebrew).

294 D. Rabinowitz, "The Road that Yields Real Estate", *The Internal Journal of the Teachers Federation*, Issue 21, Summer 2002, (in Hebrew), p. 1.

295 Ibid., p. 2

296 Y. Asidon, *Road 6 – The Difference between Reality and Fantasy*, The Green Wave, November 13th, 2004, (in Hebrew), p. 1; Richter E., "The Road 6 Myth", The Movement for Social Change From Below's website, http://www.bdidut.com/transp/road6-a7.htm, (in Hebrew); Gabai R., "The Road that Rips the Country Apart", The Movement for Social Change From Below's website: http://www.bdidut.com/transp/road6-a6.htm, (in Hebrew); The Trans-Israel – Transport and Social Damage, The Green Course, http://www.greencourse.

org.il, (in Hebrew); E. Ben-Ari, "They Hide their Heads under the Road", *Ha'aretz*, December 5th, 1999, (in Hebrew).

297 R. Shir, "A Dead-End Road", *Green, Blue, White* (The Israeli Economy and Environment Protection Forum Journal), Issue 1, October-November 1994, (in Hebrew), pp. 2-3.

298 Z. Zarhia, "The Trans-Israel Highway Law was Approved by the Knesset on the Second and Third Call", *Ha'aretz*, December 14th, 1994, (in Hebrew); G. Alon & Z. Zarhia, "The Trans-Israel Highway Bill will be Brought before the Knesset Plenum in the Next Few Days", *Ha'aretz*, July 25th, 1995, (in Hebrew).

299 Y. Asidon, The Price of the Trans-Israel, The Movement for Social Change from the website, http://www.bdidut.com/transp/road6-a2.htm, (in Hebrew); Y. Asidon, "The Road that will Cross Israel Socially and Economically", *Green, Blue, White* (The Israeli Economy and Environment Protection Forum Journal), Issue 31, April-May, 2000, (in Hebrew); Z. Rinat, "The More is Black, the More is Green", *Ha'aretz*, November, 30th, 1999, (in Hebrew); Z. Rinat, "The New Society for the Protection of Nature", *Ha'aretz*, February 25th, 2000, (in Hebrew); Z. Rinat, "Hierarchy on the Roads", *Ha'aretz*, September 20th, 1996, (in Hebrew).

300 The Cross-Israel Company, Home-Web, http://www.hozeisrael.co.il, (in Hebrew).

301 Z. Rinat, "The New Society for the Protection of Nature", *Ha'aretz*, February 25th, 2000, (in Hebrew).

302 Ibid.

303 T. Darel-Fosfeld & A. Prujinin, "Driving Politely (Derech Eretz) on the Road", *Green, Blue, White*, The Israeli Economy and Environment Protection Forum Journal), Issue 31, April-May, 2000, (in Hebrew).

304 U. Dahari, The Archeological Plant along the Trans-Israel Highway, The Israel Antiquities Authority, 2003, (in Hebrew).

305 Z. Rinat, "Drawings Instead of Signs", *Ha'aretz*, June 18th, 1998, (in Hebrew); Z. Rinat, "The Trans-Israel Highway will be Partially Tunneled", *Ha'aretz*, August 8th, 2001, (in Hebrew); Z. Rinat, "The Final Fight over a Tunnel on the Trans-Israel", *Ha'aretz*, December 26th, 2004, (in Hebrew); Z. Asir-Itzik, The Highway in the Center, Logic Aside, Adam, Teva Ve'Din, November 10th, 2004, (in Hebrew).

306 The Trans-Israel Highway Facts List, The Movement for Social Change from the website, http://www.bdidut.com, (in Hebrew).

307 Y. Asidon, "The Price of the Trans-Israel Highway", *Ha'aretz*, December 12th, 1999, (in Hebrew); Questions and Answers Regarding the Highway,

The Movement for Social Change from Below website, http://www.
bdidut.com, (in Hebrew); Why Are We Against the Trans-Israel Highway,
The Movement for Social Change from Below website, http://www.bdidut.
com, (in Hebrew); Z. Rinat, "Why Do We Have to Pay", *Ha'aretz*, December
27th, 1998, (in Hebrew); The Trans-Israel Highway – Facts List, The
Movement for Social Change from Below website, http://www.bdidut.com,
(in Hebrew); B. Sagiv, "Who Wants the Highway", *Ha'aretz*, February 8th,
1998, (in Hebrew); U. Sheiness, "Who Wants the Road", Columbia University,
New York, *Ha'aretz*, February 8th, 1998, (in Hebrew).

308 A. Ostfeld, K. E. Lansey, Y. Salingar, T. Maddock, On Development of a
Decision Support System for the Lake Hula Project, ESRI User Conference,
1997, http://gis.esri.com/library/userconf/proc97/proc97/to600/pap596/
p596.htm.

309 The Huleh: A Dream Reborn – May 95, Israel Environment Bulletin, Israel
Ministry of Foreign Affairs, May 1st, 1995, http://www.israel-mfa.gov.
il/MFA/Archive/Communiques/1995/THE%20HULA-%20A%20DR...,
(in Hebrew); J. Greenberg, "Israel Restoring Drained Wetland, Reversing
Pioneer's Feat", *The New York Times*, Dec. 5th, 1993, http://query.nytimes.
com/gst/fullpage.html?res=9F0Ce7D6143F936A965958260&sec=&spo...;
H. Gvirtzman, *Water Resources in Israel*, Jerusalem: Yad Yitzhak Ben-Zvi, 2002,
(in Hebrew), pp. 56-57.

310 H. Gvirtzman, *Water Resources in Israel*, Jerusalem: Yad Yitzhak Ben-Zvi,
2002, (in Hebrew), p. 57.

311 Ibid., p. 57.

312 Ibid., pp. 56-57.

313 J. Nir, "The Huleh – The Fate of a Zionist Project", *Ha'aretz*, August 24th,
1965, (in Hebrew).

314 J. Katz, *To Stop the Bulldozer*, Ramat-Gan: Bar Ilan University Press, , 2004,
p. 13-15.

315 Ibid., p. 20.

316 Ibid., p. 30.

317 Ibid., p. 14.

318 Ibid., pp. 17,19, 33, 42.

319 Ibid., p. 26.

320 Ibid., pp. 36, 39.

321 Ibid., pp. 16-17.

322 Ibid., p. 24.

323 E. Brutzkus, Proposal for National Parks, The Zionist Archive, A246/166, March 3rd, 1950, (in Hebrew).

324 A. Sharon, *Israel's Physical Planning*, Jerusalem: The Government Press, 1951, (in Hebrew), p. 7.

325 O. Regev, *40 Years of Blooming – The Society for the Protection of Nature, 1953-1993*, SNP Press,1993, (in Hebrew), p. 18.

326 "Lights and Shadows", *Yediot Aharonot*, August 3rd, 1952, (in Hebrew).

327 H. Steinitz, (The Zoological Department of The Hebrew University), Letter to the Ministry of Interior (Press And Film Department), The State Archive, G-716/55, January 7th, 1951, (in Hebrew).

328 J. Glimtzer & J. Hofeyin, (The Commission for Nature Protection, The Botanical Society & The Zoological Society), Implementation of a Scientific and Cultural Plan, Letter to the Minister of Education and Culture, the Minister of Agriculture and the Government Secretary, The State Archive, G-5495/6, January 28th, 1951, (in Hebrew).

329 H. Mendelssohn, (the Commission for Nature Protection), Letter to E. Brutzkus, The State Archive, G-2736/6, September 30th, 1951, (in Hebrew).

330 E. Talmi, "Reserves will be Created in Order to Protect Natural Assets in the Huleh Region", *Davar*, June 20th, 1952, (in Hebrew).

331 D. Spector, "Nature Protection in the Huleh", *Al Hamishmar*, June 27th, 1952, (in Hebrew).

332 N. Peretz, The Commission for Examination of the Possibilities to Create a Reserve for Wild Plants and Animals in the Huleh, The State Archive, G-4475/1, June 12th, 1953, (in Hebrew).

333 The Commission for the Huleh Nature Preservation Meeting Report, The State Archive, G-4475/1, July 22nd, 1953, (in Hebrew).

334 I. Peleg, The Commission for Examination of Possibilities to Create the Huleh Reserve,The State Archive, G-4475/1, July 23rd, 1953, (in Hebrew).

335 "In the Society for the Protection of Nature", *Nature and Country*, 8-10, 1953, (in Hebrew), p. 457.

336 A. Hanochi, The Establishment of a Reserve in the Huleh, The State Archive, G-4475/1, November 23rd, 1953, (in Hebrew).

337 J. Reiskin, The Decision to Leave 5000 Dunam of the Huleh Land and Lake as a Nature Reserve, The State Archive, GL-19781/8, November 28th, 1955, (in Hebrew).

338 Berchyau A., The Huleh Reserve, Letter to the Minister of Agriculture et al., The State Archive, GL-19781/8, December 11th, 1955, (in Hebrew).

339 Zahavi A., Mr. Reiskin's Memorandum of the 28th of November 1955, Letter to the General Manager of the Ministry of Agriculture, The State Archive, GL-19781/8, January 7th, 1956, (in Hebrew).

340 Lubovski D., The Nature Reserve in the Huleh Region, Letter to Weitz J. of the JNF, The State Archive, GL-19781/8, December 19th, 1954, (in Hebrew).

341 Naftali P., Regarding the Creation of a Reserve in the Huleh Valley, The State Archive, G-4471/5, February 23rd, 1954, (in Hebrew).

342 Hanochi A., The Huleh Reserve, The State Archive, G-4471/5, November 16th, 1954, (in Hebrew).

343 Ro'n, The Reserve in the Huleh, Ha'aretz, December 14th, 1953, in M. Duani, From Drainage to Conservation of the Huleh Wetlands: Tracing the Dynamics of Nature Intervention (Ph. D. Dissertation), Haifa University, March 2010, (in Hebrew), pp. 140-141.

344 "Ro'n, Observed, Heard", *Ha'aretz,* April 30th, 1954, in M. Duani, *From Drainage to Conservation of the Huleh Wetlands: Tracing the Dynamics of Nature Intervention* (Ph. D. Dissertation), Haifa University, March 2010, (in Hebrew), p. 145.

345 A. Berchyau, The Drainage of the Huleh Swamps and the Creation of the Reserve, The Zionist Archive, KKL5/21512, December 14th, 1953, (in Hebrew); A. Berchyau, "Nature Protection in the Huleh", *Ha'aretz,* May 31st, 1954, in M. Duani, *From Drainage to Conservation of the Huleh Wetlands: Tracing the Dynamics of Nature Intervention* (Ph. D. Dissertation), Haifa University, March 2010, (in Hebrew), p. 145.

346 Y. Braslavski, *Hayadata et Ha'aretz,* Hakibbutz Hameuhad, 1960, vol. 5, (in Hebrew), pp. 237, 261.

347 M. Duani, *From Drainage to Conservation of the Huleh Wetlands: Tracing the Dynamics of Nature Intervention,* (Ph. D. Dissertation), Haifa University, March 2010, (in Hebrew), p. 158.

348 Ibid., pp. 159-160.

349 The JNF Board of Directors Meeting Protocol, The Zionist Archive, KKL10/21 and KKL10/22, January 2nd, 1951, (in Hebrew).

350 M. Duani, *From Drainage to Conservation of the Huleh Wetlands: Tracing the Dynamics of Nature Intervention,* (Ph. D. Dissertation), Haifa University, March 2010, (in Hebrew), p. 157.

351 Prof. Bodenheimer's Speech at the Beth Usishkin Inauguration, January 13th, 1955, in M. Duani, *From Drainage to Conservation of the Huleh Wetlands: Tracing*

the Dynamics of Nature Intervention, (Ph. D. Dissertation), Haifa University, March 2010, (in Hebrew), p. 162.

352   Interview with Prof. Amotz Zahavi, Tel-Aviv University, February 12th, 2009, (in Hebrew).

353   Interview with Dr. Uzi Paz at his home – Ramat Efal, February 6th, 2009, (in Hebrew).

354   A. Alon, *About Trees and Stones,* Hakibbutz Hameuhad, 1956, in "In the Huleh, Before its Disappearance", *Karnenu,* Issue 3-4, August 1956, (in Hebrew).

355   A. Alon, "The Huleh – Past and Present", *Country and Nature,* Issue 42, April 1996, (in Hebrew), pp. 87, 90.

356   Interview with Azaria Alon at his home, in Kibbutz Beth Hashita, February 14th, 2009, (in Hebrew).

357   "Lights and Shadows", *Yediot Aharonot,* August 3rd, 1952, (in Hebrew).

358   J. McCarthy & S. Prudham, "Neo-liberal Nature and the Nature of Neo-liberalism", *Geoforum* 35, 2004, p. 275.

359   Ibid., pp. 277-278.

360   J.A. Elliot, *An Introduction to Sustainable Development,* New York: Rutledge, 1994, p. 28.

361   J. McCarthy & S. Prudham, "Neo-liberal Nature and the Nature of Neo-liberalism", *Geoforum* 35, 2004, p. 279.

362   M. A. Cahn, *Environmental Deceptions: The Tension between Liberalism and Environmental Policymaking in the United States,* Albany: State University of New York Press, 1995, p. 120.

363   J. Igoe & D. Brockington, "Neoliberal Conservation: A Brief Introduction", *Conservation & Society,* Vol. 5, Issue 4, 2007, p. 433.

364   M. A. Cahn, *Environmental Deceptions: The Tension between Liberalism and Environmental Policymaking in the United States,* Albany: State University of New York Press, 1995, p. 124.

365   The Cross-Israel Company, Home-web, http://www.hozeisrael.co.il, (in Hebrew).

366   T. Darel-Fosfeld & A. Prujinin, "Driving Politely (Derech Eretz) on the Road", *Green, Blue, White,* The Israeli Economy and Environment Protection Forum Journal), Issue 31, April-May, 2000, (in Hebrew).

367 Z. Rinat, "The New Society for the Protection of Nature", *Ha'aretz*, February 25th, 2000, (in Hebrew).

368 T. Darel-Fosfeld & A. Prujinin, "Driving Politely (Derech Eretz) on the Road", *Green, Blue, White*, The Israeli Economy and Environment Protection Forum Journal), Issue 31, April-May, 2000, (in Hebrew).

369 Ibid.

370 B. Frankel, "There is Such a Thing as a Beautiful Road", *Ma'ariv* –Biting Green, November 14th, 2007, (in Hebrew).

371 E. Zandberg, "The Interchanges Country", *Ha'aretz*, August 15th, 2002, (in Hebrew).

372 T. Darel-Fosfeld & A. Prujinin, "Driving Politely (Derech Eretz) on the Road", *Green, Blue, White*, The Israeli Economy and Environment Protection Forum Journal), Issue 31, April-May, 2000, (in Hebrew).

373 "Along the Trans-Israel Rout Every Flower is Taken Care Of", *Ha'aretz*, April 26th, 2005, (in Hebrew).

374 T. Darel-Fosfeld & A. Prujinin, "Driving Politely (Derech Eretz) on the Road", *Green, Blue, White*, The Israeli Economy and Environment Protection Forum Journal), Issue 31, April-May, 2000, (in Hebrew).

375 Ibid.

376 Ibid.

377 U. Dahari, "The Archeological Plant along the Trans-Israel Highway, The Israel Antiquities Authority", 2003, (in Hebrew); S. Hametz, "The Cross-Israel Company Spent 8 Mil. Shekel on Archeological Salvage Excavations", *Ha'aretz*, August 11th, 1996, (in Hebrew).

378 U. Dahari, The Archeological Plant along the Trans-Israel Highway, The Israel Antiquities Authority, 2003, (in Hebrew).

379 E. Zandberg, The Interchanges Country, *Ha'aretz*, August 15th, 2002, (in Hebrew); A. George, "A Tomb was Uncovered? Let's Divert the Road", *Ha'aretz*, October 23rd, 2003, (in Hebrew).

380 T. Darel-Fosfeld & A. Prujinin, "Driving Politely (Derech Eretz) on the Road", *Green, Blue, White*, The Israeli Economy and Environment Protection Forum Journal), Issue 31, April-May, 2000, (in Hebrew).

381 R. Shir, "A Dead End Road", *Green, Blue, White* (The Israeli Economy and Environment Protection Forum Journal), Issue 1, October-November 1994, (in Hebrew); Why Are We Against the Trans-Israel Highway, The Movement for Social Change From Below website, http://www.bdidut.com, (in Hebrew).

382 A. Mendelssohn, "The Trans-Israel Highway – A New Phase in the Struggle", *The Moose (Ha'Ayal Hakore)*, (Journal of Cultural and Current Events), July 13th, 2000, (in Hebrew); Z. Rinat, "Why Do We Have to Pay", *Ha'aretz*, December 27th, 1998, (in Hebrew).

383 The Ombudsman Report 47-48, 1977-8, (in Hebrew); Z. Rinat, "Segment 13 South – An Exquisitely Designed Nuisance", *Ha'aretz*, January 26th, 2000, (in Hebrew).

384 IUED - The Israel Union for Environmental Defense– Adam, Teva Ve'Din – an Israeli NGO, prominent in the struggle for nature protection.

385 The accomplishment of Adam, Teva Ve'Din – The Alternative of Tunneling of the Road 6 under the Carmel will be Examined, The IUED Website, May 7th, 2007, http://www.yarok.org.il/text_item.aspx?tid=915&menu=15, (in Hebrew).

386 A. Raba'd, "We Protest: Route 6 Is Going to Destroy the Oak Reserve", *Yediot Aharonot*, April 9th, 2006, (in Hebrew); G. Sofer, "The Purely Paved Mountain Air", *Yediot Aharonot*, January 12th, 2006, (in Hebrew).

387 M. Reily & Z. Rinat, "5 Ministers Opposed the Construction of Another Segment of the Trans-Israel", *Ha'aretz*, August 21st, 2000, (in Hebrew); Z. Asir-Ytzik, "The Trans-Israel Highway – the Highway - in the Center, the Logic – Pushed Aside", *IUED*, November 11th, 2004, (in Hebrew); Z. Rinat, "Drawings Instead of Signs", *Ha'aretz*, June 18th, 1998, (in Hebrew); Z. Rinat, "A Proposal: the Trans-Israel Highway will be Partially Tunneled", *Ha'aretz*, August 8th, 2001, (in Hebrew); "Adam, Teva Ve'Din: the Continuation of the Trans-Israel to the North will Damage Badly the Environment", *Ha'aretz*, December 12th, 2006, (in Hebrew); A. George, "The Periphery is Still Cut off of the Center", *Ha'aretz*, September 21st, 2003, (in Hebrew); D. Morgenstern, "The Erase-Israel Highway", *Yediot Aharonot*, February 20th, 2006, (in Hebrew).

388 Z. Rinat, "Deep Wounds of the Area", *Ha'aretz*, June 19th, 1996, (in Hebrew); Z. Rinat, "Little Parcels of Green", *Ha'aretz*, December 8th, 1994, (in Hebrew); Z. Rinat, "Today – The "Green Day" Events, Against the Trans-Israel Highway Construction", *Ha'aretz*, November 30th, 1994, (in Hebrew).

389 A. Mendelssohn, "The Trans-Israel Highway – A New Phase in the Struggle", *The Moose (Haayal Hakore)*, (Journal of Cultural and Current Events), July 13th, 2000, (in Hebrew).

390 Y. Asidon, "Route 6 – The Difference Between Reality and Fantasy", *The Green Wave*, November 13th, 2004, (in Hebrew); Z. Rinat, "Why Do We Have to Pay", *Ha'aretz*, December 27th, 1998, (in Hebrew); D. Shehory, "The High Court of Justice Rejected the Petition to Delay the Trans-Israel Highway Construction until the Examination of its Environmental Impact", *Ha'aretz*, July 24th, 1995, (in Hebrew).

391 Z. Rinat, "The Asphalt Crawls Latitudinally", *Ha'aretz*, March 29th, 1998, (in Hebrew); Z. Rinat, "Segment 13 South: An Exquisitely Designed Nuisance", *Ha'aretz*, January 26th, 2000, (in Hebrew); Z. Rinat, "Without the Statement's Impact", *Ha'aretz*, July 31st, 1995, (in Hebrew).

392 Z. Rinat, "The More is Black, the More is Green", *Ha'aretz*, November 30th, 1999, (in Hebrew); Z. Rinat, "The Asphalt Crawls Laterally", *Ha'aretz*, March 29th, 1998, (in Hebrew); The Trans-Israel- An Environmental Damage, The Movement for Social Change From Below website, http://www.bdidut.com, (in Hebrew); also Z. Rinat, "One Step Forward, One Step Backward", *Ha'aretz*, February 14th, 1995, (in Hebrew); "The Trans-Israel Highway", The Green Course, www.greencourse.org.il, (in Hebrew).

393 Z. Rinat, "The Recompense Forest will Become Perhaps a Construction Site", *Ha'aretz*, January 31st, 2001, (in Hebrew).

394 R. Shir, "A Dead-End Road", *Green, Blue, White* (The Israeli Economy and Environment Protection Forum Journal), Issue 1, October-November 1994, (in Hebrew); Questions and Answers Regarding the Highway, The Movement for Social Change From Below website, http://www.bdidut.com, (in Hebrew); U. Sheiness, "Who Wants the Road", Columbia University, New York, *Ha'aretz*, February 8th, 1998, (in Hebrew); Z. Rinat, "The Asphalt Crawls Laterally", *Ha'aretz*, March 29th, 1998, (in Hebrew); A. Mendelssohn, "The Trans-Israel Highway – A New Phase in the Struggle", *The Moose (Haayal Hakore)*, (Journal of Cultural and Current Events), July 13th, 2000, (in Hebrew); The Trans-Israel – An Environmental Damage, The Movement for Social Change From Below website, http://www.bdidut.com, (in Hebrew); Z. Rinat, "Without the Statement's Impact", *Ha'aretz*, July 31st, 1995, (in Hebrew).

395 Why Are We Against the Trans-Israel Highway, The Movement for Social Change from Below website, http://www.bdidut.com, (in Hebrew).

396 U. Sheiness, "Amateur Planning Bordering on Criminal Negligence", *Green, Blue, White* (The Israeli Economy and Environment Protection Forum Journal), Issue 31, April-May 2000, (in Hebrew).

397 Z. Rinat, "The Connection Between the Car and the Well", *Ha'aretz*, August 9th, 2000, (in Hebrew); The Convention Regarding Economic and Environmental Aspects of The Trans-Israel Highway, January 21st, 2001, (in Hebrew).

398 R. Shir, "A Dead-End Road", *Green, Blue, White* (The Israeli Economy and Environment Protection Forum Journal), Issue 1, October-November 1994, (in Hebrew); U. Sheiness, "Amateur Planning Bordering on Criminal Negligence", *Green, Blue, White* (The Israeli Economy and Environment Protection Forum Journal), Issue 31, April-May 2000, (in Hebrew); Z. Rinat, "One Step Forward, One Step Backward", *Ha'aretz*, February 14th, 1995, (in Hebrew); Z. Rinat, "Experts: The Trans-Israel will Put in Danger the

Yarkon Water Sources", *Ha'aretz*, February 4th, 2000, (in Hebrew); Z. Rinat, "The Final Fight on Tunneling Parts of the Trans-Israel", *Ha'aretz*, December 26th, 2004, (in Hebrew).

399 Questions and Answers Regarding the Highway, The Movement for Social Change from Below website, http://www.bdidut.com, (in Hebrew); Z. Rinat, "Segment 13 South: An Exquisitely Designed Nuisance", *Ha'aretz*, January 26th, 2000, (in Hebrew); The Trans-Israel – An Environmental Damage, The Movement for Social Change from Bellow Website, http://www.bdidut.com, (in Hebrew).

400 Z. Rinat, "The Asphalt Crawls Laterally", *Ha'aretz*, March 29th, 1998, (in Hebrew); also Z. Rinat, "Drawings Instead of Signs", *Ha'aretz*, June 18th, 1998, (in Hebrew).

401 Z. Rinat, "The Asphalt Crawls Laterally", *Ha'aretz*, March 29th, 1998, (in Hebrew).

402 The Trans-Israel – An Environmental Damage, The Movement for Social Change from the website, http://www.bdidut.com, (in Hebrew); A. Mendelssohn, "The Trans-Israel Highway – A New Phase in the Struggle", *The Moose (Ha'ayal Hakore)*, (Journal of Cultural and Current Events), July 13th, 2000, (in Hebrew); also Z. Rinat, "Without the Statement's Impact", *Ha'aretz*, July 31st, 1995, (in Hebrew).

403 Z. Rinat, "Segment 13 South: An Exquisitely Designed Nuisance", *Ha'aretz*, January 26th, 2000, (in Hebrew).

404 Z. Rinat, "Little Parcels of Green", *Ha'aretz*, December 8th, 1994, (in Hebrew); U. Sheiness, "Amateur Planning Bordering on Criminal Negligence", *Green, Blue, White* (The Israeli Economy and Environment Protection Forum Journal), Issue 31, April-May 2000, (in Hebrew).

405 Z. Rinat, "The More is Black, the More is Green", *Ha'aretz*, November 30th, 1999, (in Hebrew); Why Are We Against the Trans-Israel Highway, The Movement for Social Change From Below website, http://www.bdidut.com, (in Hebrew); The Convention Regarding Economic and Environmental Aspects of The Trans-Israel Highway, January 21st, 2001, (in Hebrew).

406 U. Sheiness, "Amateur Planning Bordering on Criminal Negligence", *Green, Blue, White* (The Israeli Economy and Environment Protection Forum Journal), Issue 31, April-May 2000, (in Hebrew).

407 U. Sheiness, "Amateur Planning Bordering on Criminal Negligence", *Green, Blue, White* (The Israeli Economy and Environment Protection Forum Journal), Issue 31, April-May 2000, (in Hebrew); The Convention Regarding Economic and Environmental Aspects of The Trans-Israel Highway, January 21st, 2001, (in Hebrew).

408 E. Gorney, "The Drainage of Huleh Wetlands, an Eco-feminist Reading",
International Feminist Journal of Politics, 9:4 December 2007, p. 467.

409 G. Anton, "Blind Modernism and Zionist Waterscape", *Jerusalem Quarterly*,
Issue 35, Autumn 2008, p. 84.

410 Y. Karmon, "The Huleh Valley and its Surroundings", *Ariel*, August 1990,
(in Hebrew), p. 57.

411 E. Gorney, "The Drainage of Huleh Wetlands, an Eco-feminist Reading",
International Feminist Journal of Politics, 9:4, December 2007, p. 470.

412 V. Shiva, "Development as a New Project of Western Patriarchy", in
I. Diamond and G. F. Orenstein (eds), *Reweaving the World: The Emergence of
Eco-feminism*, San-Francisco: Sierra Club Books, CA, 1990, pp. 189-200, in
E. Gorney, "The Drainage of Huleh Wetlands, an Eco-feminist Reading",
International Feminist Journal of Politics, 9:4, December 2007, p. 470.

413 K. Philip, *Civilizing Natures: Race, Resources and Modernity in Colonial South India*,
Hyderabad, India: Orient Longman Private Ltd., 2003, p. 98, in S. Sufian,
Healing the Land and the Nation – Malaria and the Zionist Project in Palestine, 1920-
1947, Chicago: University of Chicago Press, 2007, p. 161.

414 S. Sufian, *Healing the Land and the Nation – Malaria and the Zionist Project in
Palestine, 1920-1947*, Chicago: University of Chicago Press, 2007, p. 161.

415 D. Rabinowitz & S. Khawalde, "Demilitarized, then Dispossessed: The Kirad
Bedouins of the Huleh Valley in the Context of Syrian-Israeli Relation",
International Journal of Middle East Studies, vol. 32, 2000, pp. 520-521.

416 D. Ben-Gurion, The Zionist Archives, 1559/52/56, March 9th, 1951, (in
Hebrew), p. 1.

417 A. Shalev, *The Israel-Syria Armistice Regime - 1949-1955*, JCSS Study no. 21,
Boulder, Colorado: Westview Press, 1993, p. 70, (The Commission of
Foreign Affairs and Defense Meeting, KH/3 The Israeli State Archive
– (104.51) 7562/9 A) in D. Rabinowitz & S. Khawalde, "Demilitarized, then
Dispossessed: The Kirad Bedouins of the Huleh Valley in the Context of
Syrian-Israeli Relation", *International Journal of Middle East Studies*, vol. 32,
2000, p. 523.

418 D. Rabinowitz & S. Khawalde, "Demilitarized, then Dispossessed: The Kirad
Bedouins of the Huleh Valley in the Context of Syrian-Israeli Relation",
International Journal of Middle East Studies, vol. 32, 2000, pp. 523-524.

419 A. Shalev, *The Israel-Syria Armistice Regime –1949-1955*, JCSS study no. 21,
Boulder, Colorado: Westview Press, 1993, pp. 166-167.

420 The Commission of Foreign Affairs and Defense Meeting, KZ/3, The State
Archive, 7562/9, pp. 12-13, April 8th, 1951, (in Hebrew).

421 D. Ben-Gurion, "Ben-Gurion Reports on the Demolition of Two Villages", *Al Hamishmar,* April 8th, 1951, (in Hebrew).

422 W. Eytan, Telegram to Israeli Representatives in London, Washington, New-York and Paris, The State Archive, Ministry of Foreign Affairs, HZ-2440/10, April 6th, 1951, (in Hebrew).

423 S. Ramati, G.S.O. i/c Mixed Armistice Commission, Policy on Syrian MAC, Letter to Deputy Chief of Staff M. Makleff, The State Archive, Ministry of Foreign Affairs, HZ-2440/10, March 8th, 1951, (in Hebrew).

424 E. Efrat, "Israel's Planned New 'Crossing Highway'", *Journal of Transport Geography,* 2(4), 1994, p. 276; R. Khamaisi, D. Shmueli, "Shaping a Culturally Sensitive Planning Strategy – Mitigating the Impact of Israel's Proposed Transnational Highway on Arab Communities", *Journal of Planning Education and Research,* 21, 2001, p. 128.

425 P. Gazit, A. Sofer, *The Border Zone between the Sharon and Samaria,* Haifa University, August 2005, (in Hebrew), p. 103.

426 D. Rabinowitz, I. Vardi, *Driving Forces: Trans-Israel Highway and the Privatization of Civil Infrastructures in Israel,* Jerusalem: Van Leer Jerusalem Institute, Hakibbutz Hameuchad Publishing House, 2010, (in Hebrew), p. 111.

427 R. Khamaisi, D. Shmueli, "Shaping a Culturally Sensitive Planning Strategy – Mitigating the Impact of Israel's Proposed Transnational Highway on Arab Communities", *Journal of Planning Education and Research,* 21, 2001, p. 132.

428 Ibid., p. 133.

429 S. Suleiman, *The Structure of Housing Decision-making in Arab Towns in Israel,* (Ph.D. Dissertation), Tel-Aviv University, 2010, (in Hebrew).

430 R. Khamaisi, "The Impact of Trans-Israel Highway on Arab Localities: Threat or Promoter of Development", *The Floersheimer Institute for Policy Studies,* 1999, (in Hebrew), p. 39, also D. Rabinowitz, I. Vardi, *Driving Forces: Trans-Israel Highway and the Privatization of Civil Infrastructures in Israel,* Jerusalem: Van Leer Jerusalem Institute, Hakibbutz Hameuchad Publishing House, 2010, (in Hebrew), p.123; S. Suleiman, "The Structure of Housing Decision-making in Arab Towns in Israel", (Ph. D. Dissertation), Tel-Aviv University, 2010, (in Hebrew).

431 R. Khamaisi, D. Shmueli, "Shaping a Culturally Sensitive Planning Strategy – Mitigating the Impact of Israel's Proposed Transnational Highway on Arab Communities", *Journal of Planning Education and Research,* 21, 2001, p. 131.

432 D. Rabinowitz, I. Vardi, *Driving Forces: Trans-Israel Highway and the Privatization of Civil Infrastructures in Israel,* Jerusalem: Van Leer Jerusalem Institute, Hakibbutz Hameuchad Publishing House, 2010, (in Hebrew), p. 112.

433 R. Khamaisi, D. Shmueli, "Shaping a Culturally Sensitive Planning Strategy –
Mitigating the Impact of Israel's Proposed Trans-national Highway on Arab
Communities", *Journal of Planning Education and Research*, 21, 2001, p. 133;
D. Rabinowitz, I. Vardi, *Driving Forces: Trans-Israel Highway and the Privatization
of Civil Infrastructures in Israel*, Jerusalem: Van Leer Jerusalem Institute,
Hakibbutz Hameuchad Publishing House, 2010, (in Hebrew), p. 124;
S. Suleiman, The Structure of Housing Decision-making in Arab Towns in
Israel, (Ph.D. Dissertation), Tel-Aviv University, 2010, (in Hebrew).

434 D. Rabinowitz, I. Vardi, *Driving Forces: Trans-Israel Highway and the Privatization
of Civil Infrastructures in Israel*, Jerusalem: Van Leer Jerusalem Institute,
Hakibbutz Hameuchad Publishing House, 2010, (in Hebrew), pp. 124-128.

435 R. Khamaisi, D. Shmueli, "Shaping a Culturally Sensitive Planning Strategy –
Mitigating the Impact of Israel's Proposed Trans-national Highway on
Arab Communities", *Journal of Planning Education and Research*, 21, 2001, p. 134.

436 D. Rabinowitz, I. Vardi, *Driving Forces: Trans-Israel Highway and the Privatization
of Civil Infrastructures in Israel*, Jerusalem: Van Leer Jerusalem Institute,
Hakibbutz Hameuchad Publishing House, 2010, (in Hebrew), p. 112.

437 R. Khamaisi, D. Shmueli, "Shaping a Culturally Sensitive Planning Strategy –
Mitigating the Impact of Israel's Proposed Transnational Highway on Arab
Communities", *Journal of Planning Education and Research*, 21, 2001, p. 133.

438 D. Rabinowitz, I. Vardi, *Driving Forces: Trans-Israel Highway and the Privatization
of Civil Infrastructures in Israel*, Jerusalem: Van Leer Jerusalem Institute,
Hakibbutz Hameuchad Publishing House, 2010, (in Hebrew), pp. 110-111,
115, 117-118.

439 Z. Rinat, "The New Society for the Protection of Nature", *Ha'aretz*,
February 25th, 2000, (in Hebrew), The Green Course, www.greencourse.org.il,
(in Hebrew).

440 Y. Asydon, "The Road that will Cross Israel Socially and Economically",
Green, Blue, White (The Israeli Economy and Environment Protection Forum
Journal), Issue 31, April-May 2000, (in Hebrew).

441 The Trans-Israel Highway – Facts List, The Movement for Social Change
from Below website, http://www.bdidut.com, (in Hebrew); Trans-Israel –
Transport and Social Damage, The Green Course, www.greencourse.org.il,
(in Hebrew).

442 D. Rabinowitz, "The Road that Yields Real Estate", *The Internal Journal of the
Teachers Federation*, Issue 21, Summer 2002, (in Hebrew).

443 G. Kent, "That is the Way to Fight the Malaria Evil", *Yediot Aharonot*, March 28th 1951, (in Hebrew).

444 JNF website – JNF Contribution to the Valley Development, http:// www.kkl.org.il/kkl/hebrew/nosim_ikarym/kkl_eichut_hasviva/truma_ lechut_hasviva_hula, (in Hebrew); M. Livne, "The Huleh Drainage – Advantages and Disadvantages", *Ecology and Environment*, 4, Vol. 1, 1994, (in Hebrew), pp. 184-185; A. Alon, "The Huleh – Past and Present", *Country and Nature*, Issue 24, April 1996, (in Hebrew), p. 90.

445 JNF website – JNF Contribution to the Valley Development, http://www. kkl.org.il/kkl/hebrew/nosim_ikarym/kkl_eichut_hasviva/truma_lechut_ hasviva_hula, (in Hebrew); Livne M., "The Huleh Drainage – Advantages and Disadvantages", Ecology and Environment, 4, Vol. 1, 1994, (in Hebrew), pp.184-185; Alon A., "The Huleh – Past and Present", Country and Nature, Issue 24, April 1996, (in Hebrew), p. 90.

Bibliography

Archives

Ben-Gurion Archive

State Archive

Zionist Archive

Newspapers & Periodicals

Al Hamishmar

Conference proceedings

Christian Science Monitor

Davar

Eretz Acheret

Geva Newsjournal (Film)

Ha'aretz

Jerusalem Post

Karnenu (JNF monthly Hebrew Magazine)

Lamerhav

Ma'ariv

New York Times

Yarok, Kahol, Lavan (*Green, Blue, White* - The Israeli Economy & Environment
Protection Forum virtual magazine)

Yediot Aharonot

Books and Journals

Alexander, L. M., "The Arab-Israeli Boundary Problem", World Politics, vol. 6 no. 3, April 1954, pp. 322-337.

Almog, S., "The Redemption in the Zionist Rhetoric", in Redemption of the Land, edited by Kark, R., Jerusalem: Yad Itzhak Ben-Zvi, 1990 (in Hebrew), pp. 13-32.

Alon, A, "The Huleh – Past and Present", Country and Nature, 42, April 1996 (in Hebrew), pp. 87- 90.

Anton, G., "Blind Modernism and Zionist Waterscape", Jerusalem Quarterly, 35, autumn 2008, pp. 87-92.

Ash, J., "The Progress of New Towns in Israel", Town Planning Review, vol. 45, no. 4, 1974, pp. 387-400.

Ben-Eliezer, U., The Making of the Israeli Militarism, Bloomington and Indianapolis: Indiana University Press, 1998.

Ben-Gurion, D., Vision and Path, Tel-Aviv: Am Oved, 1951, (in Hebrew), in Kartin A., A Geographical Review of the Influence of Hostile Neighborly Relations on the Settlement of the Frontier Zone in Israel, (Ph. D. Dissertation), University of Tel-Aviv, 1995.

Braslavski,Y., Hayadata et Ha'aretz, Hakibbutz Hameuhad, 1960, vol. 5 (in Hebrew).

Cahn, M. A., Environmental Deceptions: The Tension between Liberalism and Environmental Policymaking in the United States, Albany: State University of New York Press, 1995.

Chowers, E., "The End of Building: Zionism and the Politics of the Concrete", The Review of Politics, vol. 64, no. 4, 2002, pp. 599-626.

Cronon, W., The Trouble with Wilderness in Uncommon Ground – Rethinking the Human Place in Nature, New York: W. W. Norton & Company, 1996.

Dar, M., "The Imaginary Huleh – the Story of the Huleh Lake, The Nature of Things, Issue 55, 2000", (in Hebrew), pp. 100-117.

Darel-Fosfeld, T. & Prujinin, A., "Driving Politely (Derech Eretz) on the Road", Yarok, Kahol, Lavan, 31, April-May, 2000, (in Hebrew).

De-Shalit, A., "From the Political to the Objective: The Dialectics of Zionism and the Environment", Environmental Politics, vol. 4, no.1, 1995, pp. 70-87.

De- Shalit, A., The Environment between Theory and Practice, New York: Oxford University Press, 2000.

De-Shalit, A. & Talias, M., "Green or Blue and White? Environmental Controversies in Israel", Environmental Politics, vol. 3, no. 2, 1994, pp. 273-294 (in Hebrew).

Efrat, E., "Israel's Planned New "Crossing Highway"", Journal of Transport Geography, 2(4), 1994, pp. 274-277.

Eisenstadt, S. N., Changes in the Israeli Society, Ministry of Defense Press, 2004 (in Hebrew).

Elliot, J.A., An Introduction to Sustainable Development, New York: Rutledge, 1994.

Friedman, T. L., The Lexus and the Olive Tree, New York: Farrar Straus Giroux, 1999.

Galin, A., "The Decline of a Strong Union – What Can be Learnt from the Israeli Experience", in Blanpain, R. & Ben Israel, R., Labour Law, Human Rights and Social Justice, The Hague: Kluwer Law International, 2001, pp. 203-214.

Gerstenfeld, M., "Zionism and the Environment", Midstream, December 2001, pp. 16-19.

Goren, A., "The Huleh Lake will not be Peat", Yarok, Kahol, Lavan, 5, Sept.-Oct. 1955 (in Hebrew).

Gorney, E., "The Drainage of Huleh Wetlands, an Eco-feminist Reading", International Feminist Journal of Politics, 9:4, 2007, pp. 465-474.

Goutwin, D., "The Changes in the Economic Policy of the Israeli Right, 1977-2003: from Nationalized Privatization to Oligarchic Privatization", Labor, Society and Law, 10, 2004, pp. 221-239.

Granot, A., Settling the Nation, Jerusalem – Tel-Aviv: D'vir, 1950.

Granot, A., Toward the Second Jubilee, "Kama", The JNF Year Book, Jerusalem, 1951 (in Hebrew).

Gwirtzman, H., Water Resources in Israel: Chapters in Hydrology and Environmental Sciences, Jerusalem: Yad Yitzhak Ben-Zvi, 2002, (in Hebrew).

Hirschl, R., "The Constitutional Revolution and the Emergence of a New Economic Order in Israel", vol. 2, no.1, 1997, pp. 136-155.

Hirschl, R., "Israel's Constitutional Revolution: The Legal Interpretation of Entrenched Civil Liberties in an Emerging Neo-liberal Economic Order", The American Journal of Comparative Law, vol. 46, no. 3, 1998, pp. 427-452.

Horovitz, D. & Lisak, M., Hardships in Utopia: Israel-A Society under Pressure, Tel-Aviv: Am Oved, 1990 (in Hebrew).

"The Huleh Drainage Plant", Nature and Country, October, 1952 (in Hebrew), pp. 42-43.

Igoe, J. & Brockington, D., "Neoliberal Conservation: A Brief Introduction", Conservation & Society, vol. 5, no. 4, 2007, pp. 432-449.

Kahler, M. & Lake, D. A., "Globalization and Governance: Definition, Variation and Explanation", The Asrudian Center Wordpress, International Politics, Irtheory, Economics, Philosophy, 2003, pp. 1-26.

Kark, R., "Land-God-Man: Concepts of Land Ownership in Traditional Cultures in Eretz-Israel", in Ideology and Landscape in Historical Perspective, ed. Baker, A. H. & Biger, G., Cambridge, U. K.: Cambridge University Press, 1992, pp. 63-82.

Karmon, Y., "The Drainage of the Huleh Swamps", Geographical Review, vol. 50, no. 2, April 1960, pp. 169-193.

Karmon, Y., "The Huleh Valley and its Surroundings", Ariel, August 1990, (in Hebrew), pp. 37-63.

Katz, J., To Stop the Bulldozer, Ramat-Gan: Bar-Ilan University Press, 2004, (in Hebrew).

Kaufman, A., "'Let Sleeping Dogs Lie': On Ghajar and Other Anomalies in the Syrian-Lebanon-Israel Tri-Border Region", Middle East Journal, vol. 63, no. 4, Autumn 2009, pp. 539-560.

Kellerman, A., Society and Settlement – Jewish Land of Israel in the 20th Century, Albany: State Univ. of New-York Press, 1993.

Keohane, R. D. & Nye J.S., "Globalization: What's New? What's Not? (And So What?)", Foreign Policy, 118, 2000, pp. 104-119.

Khamaisi, R., "The Impact of Trans-Israel Highway on Arab Localities: Threat or Promoter of Development", The Floersheimer Institute for Policy Studies, 1999, (in Hebrew), pp. 31-59.

Khamaisi, R. & Shmueli, D., "Shaping a Culturally Sensitive Planning Strategy – Mitigating the Impact of Israel's Proposed Transnational Highway on Arab Communities", Journal of Planning Education and Research, 21, 2001, pp. 127-140.

Khouri, F., "Friction and Conflict on the Israeli-Syrian Front", Middle East Journal, vol. 17, no. 1 & 2, Winter-Spring 1963, pp. 14-34.

Livne, M., "The Huleh Drainage – Advantages and Disadvantages", Ecology and Environment, 4, vol. 1, 1994, (in Hebrew), pp. 165-188.

Marsh, B. & Jones, J., "Building the Next Seven Wonders: the Landscape Rhetoric of Large Engineering Projects", in Brunn, S., (ed.), Engineering Earth: The Impacts of Mega-Engineering Projects, Springer, 2011, pp. 13-33.

McCarthy, J.& Prudham, S., "Neo liberal Nature and the Nature of Neo-liberalism", Geoforum 35, 2004, pp. 275-283.

Morgenstern, D., "Don't Want the Trans-Israel", Yarok, Kahol, Lavan 27, August-September 1999, (in Hebrew).

Muslih, M., "The Golan: Israel, Syria, and Strategic Calculations", Middle East Journal, 47, No. 4, 1993, pp. 611-632.

Near, H., "Land Redemption, Man Redemption and Pioneering in the Minds of the Zionist Labor Movement-from the Second to the Fifth Wave of Immigrants (1904-1935)", in Redemption of the Land, ed. Kark, R., Jerusalem: Yad Yitzhak Ben-Zvi, 1990, pp. 33-47.

Oren, A. & Regev, R., Land in Uniform – Territory and Defense in Israel, Jerusalem: Carmel, 2008, (in Hebrew).

Rabinowitz, D., "The Road that Yields Real Estate", Hed Hachinuch 21, Summer 2002, (in Hebrew).

Rabinowitz, D., Khawalde, S., "Demilitarized, than Dispossessed: The Kirad Bedouins of the Huleh Valley in the Context of Syrian-Israeli Relation", International Journal of Middle East Studies, vol. 32, 2000, pp. 511-530.

Rabinowitz, D., Vardi I., Driving Forces: Trans-Israel Highway and the Privatization of Civil Infrastructures in Israel, Jerusalem: The Van Leer Jerusalem Institute, Hakibbutz Hameuhad Publishing House, 2010, (in Hebrew).

Randall, G.D., (ed.), Globalization and its Critics: Perspectives from Political Economy, London: Palgrave MacMillan.

Regev, O., 40 Years of Blooming – The Society for the Protection of Nature, 1953-1993, SNP Press, 1993, (in Hebrew), pp. 18-19.

"Road 6 - The Israeli EPA Stance", Biosphere, October-November 1994, (in Hebrew), pp. 27-35.

Schnell, I., "Nature and Environment in the Socialist-Zionist Pioneers' Perceptions: A Sense of Desolation", Ecumene, 4 (1), 1997, pp. 69-85.

Schnell, I., Bar-Tal, D., "The Occupied Territories as a Cornerstone in the Reconstruction of Israeli Society", in Bar-Tal, D., Schnell, I.(eds.), The Impact of Lasting Occupation – Lessons from Israeli Society, Oxford University Press, 2012, pp. 507-540.

Schnell, I. & Rosenberg, A., "'We Shall Dress You in a Robe of Cement and Concrete': How Discourse Concerning Mega-Engineering Projects Has Been Changing in Israel", in Brunn S., (ed.), Engineering Earth: The Impacts of Mega-Engineering Projects, Springer, 2011, pp. 663-681.

Schoenfeld, S., Types of Environmental Narratives and their Utility in Understating Israeli and Palestinian Environmentalism, Glendon College, York University, November 2004.

Scholte, J. A., Globalization: A Critical Introduction, London: MacMillan, 2000.

Shaham, G., "The Huleh Project – The Dynamics of Human Intervention in Nature", Ecology and Environment 4, vol. 1, August 1994, (in Hebrew), pp. 1-5.

Shapira, A., "Central Privatization Processes in Israel", Parliament, Journal of the Israel Democracy Institute, 64, 2010, (in Hebrew).

Sharon, A., Israel's Physical Planning, Jerusalem: The Government Press, 1951 (in Hebrew).

Sheppard, E., "Review - The Globalization of Israel: McWorld in Tel-Aviv, Jihad in Jerusalem", Israel Studies, vol. 15, no. 1, 2010, pp. 183-187.

Sufian, S., Healing the Land and the Nation – Malaria and the Zionist Project in Palestine, 1920-1947, Chicago: The University of Chicago Press, 2007.

Turner, B. L. et al., The Earth as Transformed by Human Action, Cambridge, U.S.A.: Press Syndicate of the University of Cambridge, 1990.

Vogel, D., "Israeli Environmental Policy in Comparative Perspective", Israel Affairs, 1999, pp. 246-264.

Weitz, J., In My Path – To Settle the Country, Jerusalem: Nir, 1960, (in Hebrew).

Weitz, J., Megamda Lerevaha – The History of Soil Preparation in Israel, Ramat-Gan: Masada, 1972, (in Hebrew).

Ya'ar, E. and Shavit, Z., Trends in Israeli Society, Ramat Aviv: The Open University of Israel, 2001, (in Hebrew).

Yakobovitz, M., Water in Israel, Shikmona, 1971, (in Hebrew).

Zimmerman, M. E., Heidegger's Confrontation with Modernity – Technology, Politics, Art, Indiana University Press, 1990.

Acknowledgement

The authors wish to express their appreciation and gratitude to Professor Yitzhak Reiter, Marc Schulman, and Amy Erani for their work and efforts in editing and publishing this book